12/4/96

To

with Best wishes

Sidney,

GOOD
NEIGHBORHOODS

SIDNEY BROWER

GOOD
NEIGHBORHOODS

*A Study of In-Town & Suburban
Residential Environments*

PRAEGER

**Westport, Connecticut
London**

Library of Congress Cataloging-in-Publication Data

Brower, Sidney N.
   Good neighborhoods : a study of in-town and suburban residential
environments / Sidney Brower.
      p. cm.
   Includes bibliographical references and index.
   ISBN 0–275–95181–2 (alk. paper)
   1. Neighborhood.   2. Sociology, Urban.   3. City planning.
I. Title.
HT151.B759   1996
307.3'362—dc20   95–26519

British Library Cataloguing in Publication Data is available.

Library of Congress Catalog Card Number: 95–26519
ISBN: 0–275–95181–2

First published in 1996

Praeger Publishers, 88 Post Road West, Westport, CT 06881
An imprint of Greenwood Publishing Group, Inc.

Printed in the United States of America

The paper used in this book complies with the
Permanent Paper Standard issued by the National
Information Standards Organization (Z39.48–1984).

10 9 8 7 6 5 4 3 2 1

Copyright Acknowledgments

The author gratefully acknowledges permission to quote from the following:

For permission to quote from Voltaire's "Verses on the Death of Adrienne Lecouvreur," in H. H. Brailsford, translator, *Voltaire*. Oxford, U.K.: Oxford University Press, 1947, p. 54. Reprinted by permission of Oxford University Press.

Contents

Acknowledgments

A number of people contributed to the evolution of this book without, of course, sharing responsibility for its shortcomings. Ralph Taylor helped me to design the interviews based on place descriptions, reported in Chapter 9; then he helped me understand what they all meant and reviewed my account of the results. He initiated the subsequent study of Baltimore neighborhoods described in the last part of Chapter 9, and he did the statistical analysis of the findings of that study. Most of the 95 interviews discussed in Chapter 9 were done very efficiently by Nusrat Mannan, and she and, later, John Crumm did the statistical analysis of the findings. Kristine Thompson helped with the study of housing advertisements reported in Chapter 3. Roberta Feldman, Mel Levin, Amos Rapoport, Robert Riley and Ralph Taylor suggested readings that proved to be very useful. Conferences organized by the Environmental Design Research Association and the International Association for People-Environment Studies gave me an opportunity to float ideas and elicit comments. Students in my Urban Neighborhoods class helped me to see weaknesses in an early draft. Roberta Feldman, Stanley Moss, and Mel Levin reviewed the first manuscript—a daunting task—and made thoughtful comments. Gideon Brower gave valuable editorial advice. Assembling the illustrations and obtaining the necessary permissions was a huge job, and I benefited from the persistence, enthusiasm and suggestions of Azhar Tyabji. Madis Pihlak at the University of Maryland and the editorial staff at Greenwood Press provided much assistance in the course of preparing the book for publication. I am grateful to all of these people. I am also grateful to my wife, Cynthia Brower, for the design of the book. I am most fortunate, in this as in all things, to have her help and advice.

Introduction

As a whole, the population of the United States is more comfortably housed now than ever before in history. Most of us live in houses that are more convenient, better equipped, and more suited to our own time; and most of us live outside the old city boundaries, in neighborhoods that are less dense, healthier, quieter, greener, and more widely accessible than those of yesterday. Those who create these neighborhoods—developers, public policy makers, individual householders, residents' associations and, sometimes, professional planners and designers—aim for a higher standard of living than in the past. Their plans are guided, perhaps not always consciously, by shared images of the ultimate good neighborhood. This book is about these images.

This is not to say that present-day neighborhoods are without problems. Many of them suffer from crime, noise, traffic, poor schools, and inadequate services. This book does not, however, address these problems; not because they are unimportant (indeed, they can defeat any attempt to create a good neighborhood), but because I am interested here in what neighborhoods *should* be rather than what they *should not*. Crime, noise and traffic are not deliberately introduced to make a neighborhood bad, and removing them does not necessarily make it good. A good neighborhood is one that is as good as it can be, not simply one without serious defects. This normative approach sets the direction of inquiry.

Do we already plan neighborhoods that are as good as they can be, and is it just that our good intentions are confounded by the unexpected, the unplannable? For an answer we may look at recurrent articles in the press, in magazines, and in professional journals, whose authors (as we will discover later) denounce the shortcomings of neighborhood planning. It is said that our plans lack social focus, discourage meaningful interactions among residents, promote separation among the classes, place unreasonable limits on individual freedom, do not serve the special needs of teenagers, single parents, or the elderly, and create no clear sense of place, uniqueness, or history. We need, they say, to make better neighborhood plans.

Some argue that such plans existed in the past, that time has led us astray, and that past living environments were, in many respects, better than those of today. They point especially to the small towns of the nineteenth century, each relatively self-sufficient, a walking environment, with houses disposed around a central core of community facilities and stores. The new town of Celebration is, at the time of writing, under construction in Florida. Advertised as "just like the town your grandparents grew up in," it will have its own school, hospital, golf course, and downtown with stores, post office, movie theater, and bank. It will offer a choice of estate, townhouse, cottage, and village lots and six traditional house designs (Marbella 1996). A spokesman for the developers, the Walt Disney company, owns that "Celebration is not for everyone."

There is a popular argument today that cities should be constellations of nineteenth-century-like small towns. This model has some important flaws. First, it presumes that all city people want to live as part of a small community; I will argue that some city people prefer a way of life that is substantially different. Second, it equates social organization with built form, and community with the appearance of community. I will argue that village-like forms are neither sufficient nor, in fact, necessary to support a sense of community. Third, it follows a tradition that looks for one "best" solution for all people. I will argue that different solutions are best for different people, that different ways of life call for different types of neighborhoods, that there are as many types of good neighborhoods as there are established life-styles, and that a city should provide good examples of all types. One might argue that certain life-styles are less desirable than others, but this decision properly belongs with the general public. Planners should be capable of planning good neighborhoods for all.

What are the qualities that make neighborhoods good? They are, I suggest, the qualities that support residents' preferred life-style. I will attempt to identify these qualities, focusing the discussion on three areas where, I suggest, life-style and neighborhood come together. The first is *Ambience,* by which I mean the kind of land uses, the grain of the mix, and the spatial and formal arrangement of the physical environment. These influence neighborhood activity and give the place its look and feel. The second dimension is *Engagement*—the way that residents engage and avoid engagement with one another and the extent to which they are facilitated or obstructed in this by the physical and social features of the neighborhood. It is true that the quality of residential life also depends on engagements within the household, but my interest here is the neighborhood rather than the housing unit, neighborhood planning rather than house design, the adequacy of stores rather than plumbing, the sufficiency of outdoor space rather than closet space. Clearly, I do not deal with all facets of housing. The third dimension is *Choicefulness*, by which I mean the extent to which individual residents are able to choose where, how, and with whom they will live and the range of different types of living environments from which they may choose.

This approach to neighborhoods, with its focus on life-style, does not take into account all of the factors that influence residents' housing decisions. For example, the pattern of segregated housing and services in U.S. cities effectively eliminates certain types of neighborhoods as a choice for some residents and other types of neighborhoods as a choice for others. Consider also homeowners' concerns about property values. Studies of housing choices show that people decide on the right neighborhood before they decide on the right house. Their financial investment, however, is more directly tied to the house than the neighborhood, and it is more secure in a neighborhood where nothing happens than in one where something happens that may possibly go wrong. Residents who prefer diversity, activity, and liveliness may be persuaded to choose a neighborhood that is reduced to known and predictable uses, people and relationships, a *cordon sanitaire,* not because that is where they most want to live, but because it is where they feel their investment will be protected. There are economic, social, and political forces that encourage people to settle for neighborhoods with which they will never be altogether satisfied. One may say that these forces preclude real choice, and that something more radical is needed than finetuning the present system as this book recommends.

Several additional points of clarification are necessary. First, my approach is to define neighborhoods as they are seen by residents—which is to say from the inside—and not as regional geographic, economic, or political entities. Second, I am concerned with neighborhoods that residents consider their permanent address, which means that I am not concerned with the special conditions of resorts and time-shares. Third, for reasons to be discussed later, I do not accept "city" and "suburb" as labels for distinctively different types of settings. I do not want to refer to the urbanized area in these terms. The question is, what term do I use? *Urban region* is awkward, as are *metropolitan area* and *urban area,* and they are limited: Can one refer to the medieval city as the medieval urban region, and does it really mean the same thing? My approach has been to use the word "city" to refer to the entire urbanized area, including center city, suburbs, and exurbs. I will use "center-city," "in-town," and "downtown" to refer to the older, higher-density, streetcar areas of the city, some of which may well be, or may once have been, its suburbs; and I will use "suburban" to mean the newer, lower-density, automobile-oriented areas, some of which may be, although they may not always have been, in the same jurisdiction as the center city. Sometimes I am inconsistent. For example, I use "city people" in the generally accepted sense of people who prefer in-town to suburban living. I hope I can get by without undue confusion.

There is a tendency to think of good neighborhoods as being expensive and exclusive, but this book is not only about housing for the well-to-do. I measure the goodness of a neighborhood in relation to the life-style of its residents, which means that neighborhoods that are good for one income group are not necessarily good for another. Good neighborhoods are possible at all income levels, although they may have different features; and while good high-income neighborhoods are easier to find than good low-income ones, certain types of good neighborhoods are harder to sustain in wealthy areas. The concept of a good neighborhood is relevant to all groups of the population.

I began this work in search of an explanation. I had conducted some interviews with in-town residents in Baltimore in order to understand why people who could easily have lived in suburban areas—and the "better" ones at that—had made a deliberate choice to live in the center city. The old neighborhoods had obvious problems, and they contradicted present-day principles for planning residential areas, principles that have guided the development of the suburbs. Actually, these same principles are now being used to guide the redevelopment of in-town neighborhoods, and I felt that they did not strengthen—that, in fact, they destroyed—the qualities that had made the residents choose in-town neighborhoods in the first place. Our concepts of good neighborhood planning, it seemed to me, were far too narrow. And so I began to collect ideas about good neighborhoods from as varied a set of sources as I could find. I tried to reconcile sometimes inconsistent, sometimes contradictory ideas. I worked on different hypotheses until I found one that seemed plausible, and I tested it in a series of interviews with residents. This book is the result. I have tried to present my explorations as a linear and orderly development of ideas. It would be nice to think that this is the way they really evolved.

The first two chapters lay the groundwork for the discussion.

Chapter 1 discusses the inadequacy of a city/suburb/country typology of neighborhoods and points to the need for a typology that is based on differences in residential life-style rather than geographic location.

Chapter 2 discusses the interrelationship between housing unit and neighborhood and suggests a family of definitions. Three nested definitions of neighborhood are suggested: Home settings, neighborhood settings, and compound neighborhoods.

Chapter 3 looks at how our present neighborhoods got to be the way they are. Under the headings of Ambience, Engagement, and Choicefulness, it traces changes in residents' attitudes toward housing and neighborhoods over time.

The next three chapters explore concepts of a *good* neighborhood. I start by looking at popular images of desirable places in which to live.

Chapter 4 discusses real-life neighborhoods that have been built and that are considered to be models of good design. The models are divided into three categories to illustrate different ways of dealing with Engagement.

Chapter 5 discusses concepts of the ideal neighborhood — qualities that people aim for but will never achieve. Ideal schemes are arranged to illustrate different approaches to the matter of Choicefulness.

Chapter 6 discusses mythical neighborhoods, places that exist only in the imagination, that are celebrated in literature, paintings, movies, comics, and real estate advertisements. Four types of mythical neighborhoods illustrate the dimension of Ambience.

The next four chapters develop, test, and elaborate on a typology of good neighborhoods.

Chapter 7 discusses the qualities that residents say are necessary for residential satisfaction. From these qualities and those that emerged in the earlier chapters, I derive a list of thirty qualities that are associated with good neighborhoods. These are the building blocks of a typology.

Chapter 8 considers the nature of typologies and discusses typologies based on aspects of place, activity, and the personality and culture of residents.

Chapter 9 offers a four-part typology of good neighborhoods as a working hypothesis and describes several studies whose findings support the hypothesis. Each type triggers images of real places, is associated with a distinctively different set of qualities, and is attractive to a different section of the population.

Chapter 10 discusses and elaborates on the four types.

Finally, Chapter 11 discusses the need for type-specific public policies, the goals that are appropriate to each type, and the utilization of the typology by public planners.

The reader will not fail to notice that the places I have studied and many of the places I have cited as examples are located in the city of Baltimore. That is where I live. Baltimore is typical in many respects of larger older

American cities, and my study findings, I believe, hold true for them. To what extent the findings hold true in other cities in other countries is a question that I hope readers will attempt to answer for themselves. To help them in this I have included, as an appendix, a copy of the Baltimore interview form.

GOOD
NEIGHBORHOODS

CHAPTER ONE

Urban Residential Environments

It will be such a relief to know that Motty is safe with you, Mr. Wooster. I know what the temptations of a great city are. Hitherto dear Motty has been sheltered from them. He has lived quietly with me in the country.

P. G. Wodehouse
Selected Stories by P. G. Wodehouse

Ask people where they live, and they will give you their home address or the name of their neighborhood. Most people think of themselves as living in the place where they reside, that is, the geographic area in which they have their home, whether or not they also work, shop, or recreate there. Ask people to describe a good neighborhood, and what you get if you add it up is a place with one door on Fifth Avenue, another on a New England common, and a window looking out to the mountains. People have different, quite divergent images of a good place to live.

Most Americans live (that is, have their homes) in cities of all sizes, and the percentage of people who live in cities is growing. Cities attract people because they offer unusual opportunities for employment and for personal and professional growth. This is no less true today than it was in the past, when cities were the centers of civilized life and anyone who wanted to get ahead in trade, government, society, religion, art, learning, fashion, or entertainment had to live in a city—had to be at hand, physically there. Today, merchants do not live above the store, traders do not go down to the docks to learn when the ships are in, citizens do not gather in the square to hear public proclamations, civic leaders do not haunt coffeehouses to sound out public opinion, and the social elite do not have to promenade in public places in order to be noticed. Frederick Law Olmsted noted in 1870 that the main effect of the railroad had been to educate country people in "familiarity with and dependence on the conveniences and habits of towns-people" (Olmsted 1871). Today, cars and planes make it even easier to be there without actually having to live there; and newspapers, radios, telephones, television, computers, and telecopiers make it possible to inform and be informed without having to be there. The whole country has in a sense become urbanized (Hays 1993). But with all that, the city is still the place where most central activities originate, where they are shaped, and where they come together; it is still the place where hopes, ambitions, frustrations, and efforts are concentrated, where new ideas are bred, new possibilities are tested, and changes and adventures are launched. And it is the place where most people want to live.

The size, concentration, and diversity of the city create unparalleled work and career opportunities. They also create possibilities for unexpected relationships and lively experiences and for a certain amount of disorder and chaos, which can be fascinating and liberating (Goffman 1967; Sennett 1970). The unpredictability of the city allows one, in the words of Baudelaire, to give oneself utterly "to the unexpectedly emergent, to the passing unknown" (quoted in Schorske 1966). All of this stimulates the creative mind. Some people find that the constant stimulation and challenge of the city keep them active and questioning and make them feel more alive. The feeling of being included as participant, spectator, or bystander in world-class events lends importance and immediacy to their everyday lives. The diversity of people and ideas loosens the ties of convention and creates the freedom to do extraordinary things.

Few have expressed this as well as the sociologist Robert Park, who described the city as a mosaic of little worlds that touch but do not interpenetrate. This makes it possible for individuals to pass quickly and easily from one moral milieu to another and encourages the fascinating but dangerous experiment of living at the same time in several different contiguous, but otherwise widely separated worlds. All this tends to give city life a superficial and adventurous character; it tends to complicate social relationships and to produce new and divergent individual types. It introduces, at the same time, an element of chance and adventure that adds to the stimulus of city life and gives it, for young and fresh nerves, a peculiar attractiveness. The lure of great cities is perhaps a consequence of stimulations that act directly upon the reflexes. As a type of human behavior it may be explained, like the attraction of the flame for the moth, as a sort of tropism.

The attraction of the metropolis is due in part to the fact that in the long run every individual finds somewhere among the varied manifestations of city life the sort of environment in which he expands and feels at ease; finds, in short, the moral climate in which his peculiar nature obtains the stimulations that bring his innate dispositions to full and free expression. It is, I suspect, motives of this kind which have their basis, not in interest nor even in sentiment, but in something more fundamental and primitive which draw many, if not most, of the young men and young women from the security of their homes in the country into the big, booming confusion and excitement of city life. In a small community it is the normal man, the man without eccentricity or genius, who seems most likely to succeed. The small community often tolerates eccentricity. The city, on the contrary, rewards it. (Park 1925)

Awareness of different kinds of people and the comprehensive social values it engenders is a characteristic of "city people" (Barth 1980).

But cities have a darker side, and the very qualities that draw people to cities have counterparts that make them hard to live in. Many agree with Oliver Goldsmith that the pleasures of the city come at high cost.

> Here, richly deck'd, admits the gorgeous train;
> Tumultuous grandeur crowds the blazing square,
> The rattling chariots clash, the torches glare.
> Sure scenes like these no troubles e'er annoy!
> Sure these denote one universal joy!
> Are these thy serious thoughts?—Ah, turn thine eyes
> Where the poor houseless shiv'ring female lies.
> She once, perhaps, in village plenty bless'd,
> Has wept at tales of innocence distress'd;
> Her modest looks the cottage might adorn,
> Sweet as the primrose peeps beneath the thorn;
> Now lost to all; her friends, her virtue fled,
> Near her betrayer's door she lays her head,
> And, pinch'd with cold, and shrinking from the shower,
> With heavy heart deplores that luckless hour,
> When idly first, ambitious of the town,
> She left her wheel and robes of country brown.
> (Goldsmith 1866)

People come to the city in search of change and they find that change can be unsettling; they come to find excitement and then they miss tranquility; they come because they long for novelty and they tire of superficiality; they come for diversity and they feel threatened by non-conformity; they come to be liberated from tradition and they miss old-fashioned values. People find that a stimulating and exciting place is good for work and play, but that a tranquil, stable environment is preferable for raising a family.

Americans, especially, view the city with fear and distrust, and while city living has its share of champions it has long had more than its share of detractors. Thomas Jefferson referred to cities as pestilential sores; a book published in 1841 described them as "gangrenes on the body politic;" and more bad things have been written about cities than good ones (Lees 1985). The main argument is that when people move from the country to the city they develop a warped set of values and a debased life-style. Even in the days when physical conditions in cities were far worse than they are now, the central problem of cities was seen as a moral rather than a physical one: City people looked, thought, and acted differently from country people; this was characterized by the breakdown of traditional family values, loss of innocence, depersonalization, restlessness, social disorganization, and a variety of personality disorders (Figure 1.1).

In *Their Daughter in the City* (1904), Charles Dana Gibson shows a confrontation between simple, trusting country folk and sophisticated, self-indulgent city people. From *The Gibson Girl and Her America. The Best Drawings of Charles Dana Gibson.* Edited by Edmund Vincent Gillon, Jr. New York: Dover Publications, Inc., 1969.

Figure 1.1

THEIR DAUGHTER IN THE CITY

These unfortunate conditions, it was thought, were produced by an environment that was too big and too crowded.

The multiple impressions received by the brain and the rapidity of their impressions, tend to induce shallowness of thought and instability of purpose. An increase of emotionalism and a loss of steadfastness are marked characteristics of town dwellers. (Sir Ralph Neville in 1901, quoted in Fishman 1982, p. 58)

Many eighteenth- and early nineteenth-century writers were convinced that city people are somehow unnatural, having been twisted by the environment in which they live.

> I wander thro' each charter'd street,
> near where the charter'd Thames does flow,
> And mark in every face I meet
> Marks of weakness, marks of woe.
>
> (Blake 1946. First published 1794)

This thesis attracted the attention of social scientists such as Georg Simmel[1] and Louis Wirth. In 1938, Wirth published an influential paper entitled "Urbanism as a way of life," in which he argued that when large numbers of people from different backgrounds find themselves living and working together in a limited space, they develop special ways of relating to one another. The urban way of life is a response to conditions that exist in cities, and while some country people may adopt it, it never originates in the country. It is essentially an urban phenomenon.

Wirth identified measurable qualities of urban places and measurable qualities of urban people and suggested how the former could explain the latter. He posed the issue as a researchable hypothesis: That people who live in cities are different in certain predictable ways from people who live in rural areas and small towns and that they become different as a result of specific features that are inherent in the urban setting.

As described by Wirth and his followers (such as Milgram 1970), the peculiar characteristics of city people are a litany of social ills: Compared to country people, city people are detached and superficial in their relationships with one another; they behave in ways that are hurried, brusque, and discourteous; they are selfish, disregarding the needs of others and unwilling to become involved or lend a hand; they are competitive, without sentimental or emotional ties, treating strangers as if they were objects and judging them on the basis of race, language, income, or social status rather than personal worth; they place their faith in impersonal institutions rather than in personal relations; and they are not tied by common values or common ideas about social order.

Wirth explained why it is that city people behave in these rather unpleasant ways. First, the sheer size of the urban population means that people regard one another as strangers. Second, the heterogeneity of the urban population means that there is a wide range of individual differences. Third, density causes people to infringe on one another's personal space, which intensifies the effect of numbers and differences. Together, these qualities increase the complexity of social relations and lead to a breakdown of social organization. The frequency and variety of everyday encounters place such a heavy demand on individual attention that people are forced to protect themselves by screening out much of the incoming information. As a result, city people tend to be selfish, lonely, tense, and unpredictable.

Wirth provided theoretical validation for the commonly held belief that the country is man's natural estate, that the urban way of life is an adaptation to the unnatural environment of the city. People live in cities for their opportunities and not for their living conditions; they live there because they have to, not because they want to.[2]

Research based on this premise has produced more questions than confirmations. Reiss (1970), for example, in a study of interpersonal contacts in urban and rural settings, found that urban subjects actually spent *more* time with family, close friends, and close associates. Of course, the character of both the city and the countryside has changed since Wirth's day. In those times, the countryside was essentially rural and agricultural. Country living, for many, meant a sense of separation from the outside world, dependence on natural rhythms, repeated contacts with the same people, an almost exclusive concern for local events, direct and intimate personal relationships, a leisurely pace, and a tradition of mutual help. Nowadays, however, people who live in the country have instant access to city-based news and services, travel is fast and convenient, relatively few country people live off the land, and they are all attuned to city-based institutions, information, and technology. Country people of today are less different from their city counterparts than they used to be, and the city of today is a different place than that of a hundred years ago.

When Wirth was growing up, downtown was a manufacturing center. Industries polluted the air and the streams, many roads were unpaved and unlit (Figure 1.2), sewers and water supplies were inadequate, unsanitary conditions caused the spread of disease, unsafe building practices resulted in frequent fires, and immigrant workers lived in conditions of unspeakable

In *The Streets of New York* (1898) Gibson points to the conflict between residential and non-residential uses. From *The Gibson Girl and Her America. The Best Drawings of Charles Dana Gibson.* Edited by Edmund Vincent Gillon, Jr. New York: Dover Publications Inc., 1969.

Figure 1.2

THE STREETS OF NEW YORK

squalor. Many residents lived in crowded conditions in old, often outdated housing, located in areas characterized by diverse people and buildings, a mix of activities, scattered small businesses under multiple ownerships, streets that were the primary locus of activity, and residents who mostly got around on foot or using public transportation.

For middle-income people, who could afford better, the city was an unhealthy place in which to live. H. L. Mencken said:

The Baltimore I knew as a boy was extraordinarily hot in summer, and filthy. It was full of flies and mosquitoes, all kinds of epidemics were running simultaneously. There were no sewers, and the water supply was bad. Typhoid raged all summer, smallpox all winter, malaria at all times of the year. (Mencken 1948)

Natural surroundings were believed to be healthy, not only for the body but also for the soul. Living in the city, one was divorced from the calming influences of nature.

All dangers of the town may be summed up in this: that here, withdrawn from the blessed influence of Nature, and set face to face against humanity, man loses his own nature and becomes a new and artificial creature—an unhuman cog in a social machinery that works like a fate, and cheats him of his true culture as a soul. The most unnatural fashions and habits, the strangest eccentricities of intellect, the wildest and most pernicious theories in social morals, and the most appalling and incurable barbarism, are the legitimate growth of city life. (Rev. Amory D. Mayo in 1859, quoted in Lees 1985, p. 93)

For many, the city became a socially undesirable place to live. Those who could afford to escape moved out and settled in the suburbs; and the suburbs assumed all of the virtues of the country, but suitably packaged for city people.

It is an established conclusion that the mere proximity of dwellings which characterizes all strictly urban neighborhoods, is a prolific source of morbid conditions of the body and mind, manifesting themselves chiefly in nervous feebleness or irritability and various functional derangements, relief or exemption from which can be obtained by removal to suburban districts. (Frederick Law Olmsted in his report to the Riverside Improvement Company, 1868)

The new suburban developments made an ideal of low density, of detached single-family homes set in natural surroundings, where people live with others of the same kind and where stores, offices, and institutions are excluded (Figure 1.3). Today, most people who live in metropolitan areas live in the suburbs, and many of them do not think of themselves as city people.

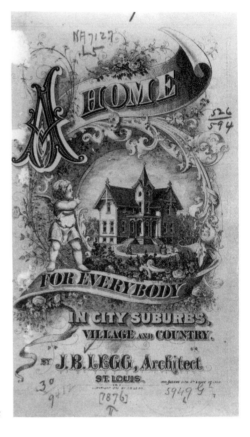

This illustration (about 1876) shows a suburban single-family house as the most desirable place in which to live. Artist Chas. Juehne. Courtesy of the Library of Congress.

Figure 1.3

As the suburbs became a major object of public attention, the focus of scholarship shifted from a comparison of city and country to a comparison of center city and suburbs and revealed differences between center-city and suburban ways of life. Scholars found, for example, that suburbanites were more involved with family, children, and community affairs; they participated more in community events, attended church more frequently, were more neighborly, more helpful, more ready to respond to strangers, and quicker to make friends.[3] These studies contended that the way of life in the suburbs is different from that in the center city; not only that, but it is better.

Many scholars dispute the validity of this premise. They argue that people of the same class, ethnicity, and family status exhibit a similar life-style whether they live in the center city or the suburbs.[4] Life-style is not a response to one's place of residence but rather an expression of the householder's guiding purpose, which may be child-rearing and homemaking (familarism), friendship and striving for belonging (quest-for-community), furthering one's career rather than family and home (careerism), or having a good time in ways that are unconnected with family or career (consumerism) (Bell 1958, 1968; Greer 1966, 1970). Or life-style may reflect the fact that one's primary interests and identification are focused on the local community (localism) or that they extend to the whole city or even the world (cosmopolitanism) (Dobriner 1958). People choose a particular physical environment because it is more supportive than others of their preferred life-style; for example, center-city environments are more supportive of careerists and cosmopolitans, while suburban environments are more supportive of familarists and localists. Guiding purposes are a response to income, education, and stage in life cycle rather than to physical setting.[5] The suburbs have a distinctive life-style because they attract certain people and exclude others (Gans 1962; Fischer 1972).

Some have also questioned Wirth's basic assumptions about the harmful effect of size, density, and diversity. They have shown, for example, that high-density living can be pleasurable (Freedman 1975); complexity can be stimulating (Geller 1960; Rapoport and Hawkes 1970); center-city dwellers need not be overloaded with acquaintances (McCauley and Taylor 1976), and can have friendships not necessarily less intimate than those of suburbanites (Franck 1980); and that center-city people, while less attentive to the needs of strangers, may be no less attentive to the needs of family and friends (Tomeh 1964). Others (Kasarda and Janowitz 1974; Sampson 1988, 1991) have shown that neither the size nor the density of a community has a significant effect on residents' social functioning; rather the crucial factor is the rate of residential mobility. The longer people live in the same place and the greater the stability of the community in which they live, irrespective of size or density, the stronger are their social ties and the greater their interest in local affairs and their sense of belonging and attachment to the community. There is also the suggestion that, while center-city environments are more chaotic than those of the suburbs, to order them would be to reduce the freedom they offer (Sennett 1970).

Still, most Americans, when asked the qualities of a good residential environment, place a high value on low-density housing, homogeneous neighbors, peace, quiet, nature and the out-of-doors, traditional values, a slow pace, and the absence of traffic congestion, which implies that most Americans would rather live in the suburbs than the center city. One could argue that this is true because suburban environments are better, that the older pattern no longer fits the expectations of a population that has become wealthier, or the standards of an age that has been liberated by the private automobile. One could argue that the older parts of the city have become outdated and that they should be rebuilt in the suburban mode; and one could support this argument by pointing to revitalized areas in many American cities where pedestrian activity at street level is displaced by the automobile, through streets are blocked to discourage traffic by outsiders, there is increasing separation of uses, and the population is becoming more homogeneous. These center-city areas are being rebuilt along suburban lines. Some planners bemoan the resulting loss of urbanity, but others say that the longing for urbanity is simply nostalgia and that those who promote center-city living do it for other people and not for themselves.

It is the apotheosis of dishonesty of fashionable architects, who sit all day at their drawing boards in County Hall designing harsh piazzas for Battersea or Bermondsey, and then at 4.51 p.m. sharp descend to the tube train, roaring out under the forgotten redevelopment areas for which they are responsible, until they come to the surface at their own cosy creeper-hung suburban cottages in Hampstead and Wimbledon. (Taylor 1973, p. 19)

Girouard points out that Daniel Burnham, a great champion of urban life, was driven by his chauffeur from his suburban retreat to his downtown office five days a week (Girouard 1985, p. 355).

There are, however, those who question the superiority of the suburbs. Some feel that "the suburbs" have not lived up to their original promise (not rural enough) or their responsibilities (for conservation of land, efficient use of public utilities, equitable housing opportunities). Some feel that the suburbs are too built up, and others that they are too spread out. Some criticize the suburbs for being too uniform, too insistent on conformity, and some criticize them as unsuited to the needs of women, children, one-parent families, the elderly, and people who work at home; they foster social isolation and contribute to family distress and civic decay.[6] Some find the suburbs boring and provincial, and some (a minority to be sure) prefer to live in the center city, or they prefer to at certain times of their lives (Hummon 1986, Michelson 1967). These people are attracted to the center city for a variety of reasons, including convenience (ability to walk to work, cultural activities, and places of entertainment and to avoid suburban gridlock), affordability, expectation of financial gain (where in-town housing prices are relatively low and thought likely to go up), and social acceptance (some of the housing is more distinctive and prestigious, and there is an opportunity to live in an interesting old house in an interesting old neighborhood). Residents of an in-town neighborhood in Baltimore told me that they rejected suburbia despite the real disadvantages of downtown living (crime and noise head the list).

I just can't stand the sameness of the suburbs. I like the idea that there are all kinds of people—all ages, all colors, all ethnic backgrounds. It makes it kind of interesting.

There's a genuine side to these people [who live downtown]. You get out in the suburbs and you get this plastic person. Their kids are all charming and, you know, you got one of them in Montrose, and this one's going into the Coast Guard, and this one's flunking out of school, but the kids are all angels, right?

Sentiments such as these put to question some of the early arguments about the dehumanizing effect of urban living. And they are not new: In 1894, a city-dweller, in a letter to *Harpers*, complained that his suburban friends were boring because they had no interest beyond each other, their house and their suburban pleasures—a stifling existence (Marsh 1990, p. 77).

The people who prefer center-city to suburban living are a special group. They are mainly middle- and upper-income people, who live alone or with a partner but without young children and are well educated. Most of them have grown up in an urban setting, just as most people who prefer to live outside the city have grown up in a suburb, small town, or rural area. Their numbers are not large in relation to the population as a whole, but their impact is significant because they are heavily concentrated in a few parts of the city.[7]

People who do not like center-city living do not necessarily, however, like the suburbs; many of them prefer rural and farm areas (Audirac, Shermyn and Smith 1990). Davis, Nelson and Dueker (1994), in their study of exurban housing around Portland, quote a respondent as saying:

We hated living in a suburban neighborhood. The houses are crammed together with little or no privacy. We were willing to give up convenient access to Portland to get out of it.

In preference to the center-city, some people choose a country estate or a small farm and accept a long commute to work in exchange for being able to live in a rural landscape. But they remain suburban in outlook, without the ties to local community and local institutions that characterize those who have grown up in the country. Other people choose to move to a small town on the urban fringe where they can be close to work, friends, and relatives.

And so we find that the idea of rural areas and small towns as good places to live is still very much alive. In a Gallup survey (1966), subjects were asked: If you could live anywhere in the United States that you wanted to, would you prefer a city, a suburban area, small town, or farm? Although only about a third of those questioned lived in rural areas or small towns, almost half said that such a place would be an ideal place in which to live. The Gallup organization conducted similar surveys in 1971 and 1972. In 1971 they found that the percentage of respondents expressing a preference for small towns and farms had risen from 49% to 56%; and in 1972, only 13% of the subjects said they wanted to live in a city. Of those who live in a city of half million or more, four out of five would prefer not to live in the city (reported in Hadden and Barton, 1977). Louis Harris and associates (1970) administered a survey aimed at defining the "quality of life" in America. Subjects were asked: If you could find just what you wanted in the way of a place to live and didn't have to worry about where you worked, would you want to live in a city, a suburb, a small town away from a city, on a farm, or where? Harris found that there was considerable dissatisfaction with the urban environment relative to the rural environment. The Commission on Population Growth and the American Future (Mazie and Rawlings 1972) conducted a survey where subjects were asked: Where would you prefer to live? On a farm, open country (not a farm), in a small town, in a small city, in a medium-size city, in a large city, in a suburb of a large city? In their responses, 53% of respondents indicated that they would prefer to live in a rural or small-town setting rather than in a more urban environment. Another 33% preferred a small- or medium-size city or suburb. Only 13% preferred large urban areas. Mazie and Rawlings also found that a major portion of the population would prefer to live in a town or a small urban setting. Zuiches and Fuguitt (1972) interviewed 906 adults in Wisconsin. Subjects were asked: If you could live in any size community you wanted, would you prefer to live in a large city of 50,000 or over, in a suburb next to a large city, in a medium-size city or town, or in a rural area? The findings showed that most people prefer to live in small-town or rural settings. Other studies showed that people in small towns are more likely to express satisfaction with public services (Mouritzen 1989), rate their neighborhoods as desirable (Dahmann 1983), feel that they influence local decisions (Finifter and Abramson 1975), walk more slowly (Walmsley and Lewis 1989), and show friendliness toward strangers (Amato 1980). In addition, small towns have less widespread use of alcohol (Peek and Lowe 1977) and lower homicide rates (Archer et al. 1978). Faith in communities of limited size and belief in the conditions of intimacy are a legacy that is passed on from one generation of Americans to another (Wood 1958, p. 18).

One might conclude that the best place to live is away from the city, in rural areas and small towns. On the other hand, however, many people who live in small towns leave them, and many who leave do not go back.

In Raleigh, and in the smaller cities and towns of America, you are forever enslaved by your kin. Other people knew or know your mother and father, sisters and brothers, and you are forever judged against that knowledge. If you are worthless and no-count, and your kin aren't, then you are a black sheep. If you try to be successful, and your father was a mundane clerk or an alcoholic or a philanderer, you are putting on airs and it is only a matter of time before the genes for mundaneness, alcoholism, or philandering take over and reduce you to the same shambles.

There is no getting away, if you stay. A few have tried to live their own lives in their hometowns, but they have not been very successful. It is much easier to start another life someplace new, and so they go from Raleigh to Charlotte, and then, some of them go to Atlanta, and, a few, to New York, and their places in Raleigh are filled by those who had to leave Cary and Garner and Knightsdale. (Powledge 1971)

Zuiches and Fuguitt (1972) found that while most people say they prefer to live in a small town or rural area, it must be within commuting distance of a large city, which means that it must be, essentially, urban. Many people who live in the suburbs actually think of themselves as living in a small town (Coleman 1978; Hummon 1990). And some argue that the American city is becoming, in effect, a collection of small towns (Elazar 1975). It seems that what people mean when they say they want to live in a small town, is that they want to live in a part of the city that has the feel of a small town.

We must conclude that no one residential environment is best for everybody. Referring back to Wirth's concept of an urban life-style, we can say that the quality that distinguishes urban from non-urban people lies in the coexistence of a great many different life-styles in close proximity to one another.[8] Some of these life-styles are best served by different types of residential environments.

What, then, are the essential qualities of each of these types of environments? Up to now I have characterized them as "center city," "suburb," "small town," and "countryside," but as urban areas have grown and changed, these words have lost their ability to define distinctively different types of places (Strauss 1960a, 1960b). The lack of distinction is evident in aerial photographs taken along city/suburb boundaries (See Figure 1.4).

The suburbs, once semi-rural bedroom communities, have become major places of employment and business. Retail centers cluster at major intersections; offices, industries, and apartment complexes create their own clusters. Some of the clusters form multi-unit complexes that rival the downtown in size and range of services, but with a very different character—buildings are scattered, separated by parking lots so that it is un-

The black horizontal line marks the boundary of Baltimore City. Similar types of neighborhoods can be seen on both sides of the line. Photo courtesy of the U.S. Department of the Interior, Geological Survey, National Aerial Photography Program.

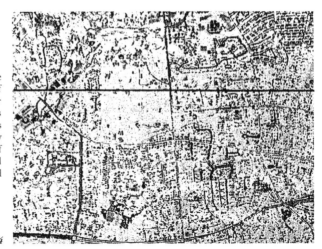

Figure 1.4

comfortable to walk from one to another, and there are few public places for coming together. The word "suburb" itself has become inadequate when describing this new environment of separate-use areas linked by highways, and names such as Technoburbs, Megacounties, and Edge Cities are being suggested (Fishman 1987; Church 1987; Garreau 1991). Sorkin refers to the ageographical city:

It's visible in clumps of skyscrapers rising from well-wired fields next to the Interstate; in huge shopping malls, anchored by their national-chain department stores, and surrounded by swarms of cars; in hermetically sealed atrium hotels cloned from coast to coast; in uniform "historic" gentrifications and festive markets; in the disaggregated sprawl of endless new suburbs without cities; and in the antenna bristle of a hundred million rooftops from Secaucus to Simi Valley, in the clouds of satellite dishes pointed at the same geosynchronous blip, all sucking Arsenio and the A-Team out of the ether. (Sorkin 1992, p. xi)

Louv (1983) calls this the anti-city, or simply "The Blob."

Vance (1977) makes a similar comment about the composition of urban areas today in noting that the collection of diverse, relatively independent places around urban centers cannot properly be called a city. He suggests that places be characterized by their distinctive life-style; and, in similar vein, Steele recommends that they be characterized by the spirit of place (Steele 1981, p. 166). What was once called a city is being called a metropolitan region (Blumenfeld 1967), an urban field (Friedmann and Miller 1965), an urban realm (Vance 1977; Sharpe and Wallock 1987), a metropolitan orbit (Blumenfeld 1986), and the American Metropolis (Calthorpe 1993).

Changes in urban settlement patterns have forced the U.S. Census to reconsider its urban and rural definitions (Lang 1986) and have forced sociologists to redefine the meaning of the word "rural." The definition of a rural area once included a place (small, unconcentrated population, relatively isolated from the influence of a large city), a range of occupations (people derive most of their livelihood from agricultural production, mining, fishing or forestry), and a set of values, beliefs, and behaviors (people who are socially conservative, slow-changing, traditional, and somewhat fatalistic; independent, honest, and God-fearing but prejudiced, ethnocentric, intolerant of nonconformity). But this definition of a rural area is no longer valid (Uzzell 1979). It has been found that values are less closely tied to occupation or current place of residence than they are to religion, income, and age; and they are less affected by present than by past place of residence (Miller and Luloff 1981).

The words *city, suburb ,* and *countryside* still evoke separate images in the public mind (Feldman 1994). But in reality these places have ceased to be monolithic areas. They may retain their distinctiveness as political jurisdictions, education systems, population groupings, and tax districts, but they do not represent mutually exclusive residential settings. One might even ask whether they are the appropriate scale at which to characterize residential areas; whether it would not be better to go with smaller units, such as the neighborhood, which, it is generally accepted, has a direct effect on the quality of residential life.[9] Neighborhood quality is not necessarily determined by regional location; similar life-styles and supportive settings can be found in center city, suburb, and countryside. A more productive approach to studying good living environments would be to study the differences between neighborhoods.

One could say that a good city should contain different types of neighborhoods, and it should contain good neighborhoods of each type. Each type should provide a distinctively different residential experience, so that different types support different ways of living. Each type will define a context within which certain neighborhood qualities are appropriate and desirable and others are not. A neighborhood typology—or family of types— is a display of alternative living environments. And because people's feelings for a place extend to other places that have the same general characteristics—so that people who enjoy living in a particular setting will, if they move, look for the same type of place in their new setting[10]—a typology can be extremely useful to planners.

The purpose of this book is to develop such a typology.

NOTES

1. For example, his essay *The metropolis and mental life*; see Simmel 1968, pp. 47–60.

2. These are the very arguments that Ebenezer Howard (1898) used in arguing for the creation of small towns which would allow each resident to live within walking distance of the countryside.

3. See, for example, Carlos 1970; Fava 1966; Fischer 1984, p. 225; Korte 1978, 1980; Korte, Ypma, and Toppen 1975; Newman and McCauley 1977; Rushton 1978; and Tomeh 1964.

4. See, for example, Berger 1966; Ktsanes and Reissman 1959-60; Ross 1965; and Tallman and Morgner 1970.

5. Brail and Chapin (1973) suggest that a resident's life-style is characterized by a spatial and temporal distribution of activities and that it is affected by the sex, responsibility for raising children, working status, and income level of the resident.

6. For a thorough indictment of the suburbs see Langdon 1995. For a summary of the arguments for and against suburbia see the paper by Hawkins and Percy (1991) and the responses and rejoinder that follow.

7. See, for example, Berry 1985, Black 1980; Baltimore City Department of Planning 1988; Clay 1980; Fischer 1982; Gale 1979, 1980, and 1984; Hunter 1975; Lansing and Mueller 1964; Lipton 1977; Livability Committee 1991; Long 1980; Patel 1980; Spain 1989; and Zelan 1968.

8. This fits with Fischer's (1975, pp. 220–221) suggestion that cities are distinguished by being the sites for many diverse and flourishing subcultures, and it is that characteristic which generates some urban-rural differences. Because of its size, the city allows for each diverse group to cohere and intensify its beliefs and values and at the same time to be influenced by the beliefs and values of other groups.

9. See, for example, Birch et al. 1973; Dahir 1947; and Solow, Ham, and Donnelly 1969.

10. See, for example, Blake, Weigl, and Perloff 1975; Campbell, Converse, and Rogers 1976; Cook 1988; Feldman 1990; Gale 1980; Hummon 1990; Krupat and Guild 1980; Lansing and Mueller 1964; Long 1980; Patel 1980; Spain 1989; and Zelan 1968.

CHAPTER TWO

Neighborhood Settings

Does the average man get enough sleep? What is enough sleep?
What is the average man? What is "does?"

Robert Benchley
My Ten Years in a Quandary, and How They Grew

Words that are the currency of everyday conversation tend to become stretched so that they embrace quite different meanings. *Neighborhood* is such a word. It is widely used, but it means many different things. Before discussing the subject of neighborhoods it is, therefore, necessary to address the subject of definitions.

There are many ways of defining neighborhood. Each definition fixes on an essential characteristic, such as the presence of local institutions, official recognition, general agreement on a name for that part of the city, an effective organization of residents, a network of social acquaintances, a cluster of like-minded people, a visually distinctive district, or a clearly bounded geographical area. According to one or another of these definitions, a neighborhood is a cluster of four or five houses, a street block, or the service area of an elementary school. Its form is derived from a particular pattern of activities or the presence of a common visual motif, or it is an area with continuous boundaries or a network of often-traveled streets. Different definitions serve different interests, so that the neighborhood may be seen as a source of place-identity, an element of urban form, or a unit of decision making.[1] A common idea running through these discrepant definitions is that of a finite, imageable, and manageable area. For this reason, planners have long found it useful to think of the neighborhood as the building block of settlements and to use it to construct models of good places to live.[2] Different models reflect the different purposes to which the concept has been put (for example, to improve efficiency or productivity, strengthen community life, or introduce new social forms, materials, or technologies). My purpose here is to come up with a definition of neighborhood that represents distinctively different kinds of residential experiences, different ways of satisfying basic residential functions.

Residential functions are activities and meanings associated with housing. They define residential use in the same way that functions associated with production define industrial use, and those connected with buying and selling define commercial use. All people, no matter who they are or where they live, need to satisfy residential functions, and at a general level all people need to satisfy the same residential functions; that is to say, there are certain universal themes. One could say, for example, that good housing everywhere should satisfy the following functions:[3]

Shelter. The housing must be available, affordable, structurally sound, and compatible with physical health and mental well-being. It must provide effective protection against inclement weather and unwanted intrusions.

Housekeeping. The cost and effort involved in housekeeping tasks must be reasonable and within the limits of the householder's resources. These tasks include preparing and storing food, providing regular care and maintenance, replacing worn and damaged parts, and disposing of waste.

Accommodation. The various spaces and facilities—their size, division, arrangement, and equipment—must be suitable for a full range of domestic activities.

Connection. There must be appropriate connections to other households and to places of employment and service. Site and occupancy conditions should create opportunities for cooperation and not promote friction among neighbors.

Meaning. The character, appearance, and conditions of use of the housing must reflect the values of the householders and foster a sense of belonging, attachment, and advocacy.

Recreation. Housing must provide householders with an opportunity to relax, rest, take time out, re-create themselves.

There is a tendency to equate the concept of housing with that of houses; to think of the dwelling as the one place to satisfy all of these residential functions. This is not so. A safe neighborhood protects the unit against unwanted intrusion and compensates for the lack of intensive security measures in the home. Neighborhood delicatessens, restaurants, and laundries cut down on housework and compensate for a lack of household help; a neighborhood day-care center increases the range of domestic activities and compensates for a shortage of play space at home. Public transportation in the neighborhood provides connection to other parts of the city and compensates for the lack of a car and garage. A distinctive neighborhood confers status on its residents and compensates for an ordinary unit, and a quiet neighborhood park makes interior rooms more restful. In these examples, the streets, parks, day-care centers, restaurants, laundries, and the like serve as extensions of the house and help it to satisfy residential functions.

These home-related facilities act in concert with the dwelling unit, the strengths of one compensating for the weaknesses of the other. Changing the capacity of the facilities may change the performance of the house, and changing the capacity of the house may increase or lighten the demands placed on the facilities. Lack of suitable facilities outside the house may be offset by adding amenities in the unit, just as inadequacies in the house may increase dependency on outside facilities. The idea of home and neighborhood as partners in a trading market is compatible with Rapoport's concept of the house settlement system (see, for example, Rapoport 1977, 1980, 1981, 1982).

Because the housing unit and its associated facilities are so closely interrelated, the burden of responsibility for satisfying residential functions can shift from one to the other, creating a range of possible options from housing heavily dependent on the unit to housing heavily dependent on outside, home-related facilities. One might think of some residents who do most of their socializing, dining, entertaining, child raising, and relaxing at home (which may call for units equipped with, for example, dens, family rooms, media rooms, and swimming pools) and other residents who satisfy these same functions in neighborhood bars, restaurants, theaters, schools, and parks. The two life-styles, clearly, have different implications for house design, which is outside our area of interest here. They also, however, have different implications for land use and neighborhood form—what I will call the *Ambience* dimension of neighborhoods.

The two kinds of housing environments—home-based and facility-based—are distinctively different in another respect: A shift in emphasis means a change not only in the way that residential functions are carried out, but also in the quality of the experience. A shift in emphasis from home to facility means a shift from private to shared spaces, with more opportunity for interaction with others and a greater chance of social (and perhaps antisocial) activities. Each situation has different social costs and appeals to a different set of people, but neither one is inherently better than the other.[4] Community, privacy, and social interaction are at the heart of what I will call the *Engagement* dimension of neighborhoods.

Of course, residents may be more ready to share facilities with some people than with others; some only want people who are known and familiar to them, others prefer people who conform to a common set of values and behaviors, while still others prefer people who are unconventional and interestingly different. Some housing environments support one situation, others another. Each has its good points and its bad. Homogeneity, conformity, and the presence of alternative living environments are characteristics of what I will call the *Choicefulness* dimension of neighborhoods.

These three dimensions of neighborhood—Ambience, Engagement and Choicefulness—will structure the discussions that follow.

Ambience refers to the nature, mix, and intensity of land uses and the form of the physical environment;

Engagement to the nature and extent of the interaction among residents and the presence of facilities and features that foster or inhibit these interactions; and

Choicefulness to opportunities for residents to choose alternative locations, lifestyles and living arrangements.

These three dimensions are not sharply bounded (for example, the mix of land uses and the social composition of the neighborhood both affect the level of interaction among residents); they are more like focal points than compartments, where the certainty of association lessens with increasing distance from the center. But despite their fuzziness, the three dimensions are useful devices for organizing the discussion of neighborhoods.

Let us return to the main line of my argument. I am suggesting that the housing unit and its related facilities, acting together, cater to residential functions. Each resident seeks a housing environment that satisfies his or her interpretation of residential functions, which in turn reflects individual and shared resources, experiences, and expectations—and preferably that does it well. Different interpretations result in different housing solutions. As housing and neighborhood have a common purpose and share common responsibilities, both should be regarded as parts of a single system. What we need is a family of definitions that starts with the housing unit and works up to the neighborhood. Here is such a family of definitions:

Housing Unit (also referred to as a "unit"). The essential housing element, which may be a house, an apartment, or a single room. I include in this definition any attendant grounds and accessory structures.

Extended Housing Unit. The combination of housing unit and home-related facilities that serves the residential needs of an individual householder. Home-related facilities (also referred to simply as "facilities") are places

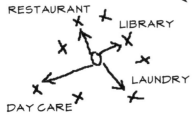

outside the housing unit, such as a park or laundromat, that extend the capacity of the unit to satisfy residential functions. A single extended housing unit may include many home-related facilities. Included as part of a home-related facility are the physical plant and associated programs and services.

It should be noted that, in this definition, facilities that do not extend the residential functions of the housing unit, even if they are nearby, convenient, suitable, and intended for that purpose, cannot properly be said to be part of a resident's extended unit; and facilities that *are* used as an extension of the unit *are* a part of the resident's extended unit even if they were never intended to be used in that way and even if they seem to be unsuitable.

The number and nature of facilities that make up an extended housing unit may vary with a householder's income, personality, and life-style, the capacity of the individual unit, and the nature and availability of convenient, suitable facilities.

Elaborations of the Extended Housing Unit

Unit-Based Extended Unit. An extended housing unit that includes few home-related facilities.

Facility-Based Extended Unit. An extended housing unit that includes many home-related facilities.

Geographically Continuous Extended Unit. An extended housing unit where the path that connects the unit and its facilities also serves residential functions (for example, as a place for interacting with neighbors or for children to play, or as a sign of social status). In these cases, the path itself is a home-related facility and part of the extended unit.[5]

Geographically Discontinuous Extended Unit. An extended housing unit where the path that connects the unit and its facilities acts only as a movement channel; it serves no residential functions. (For example, the route used by residents to drive to their regular supermarket.) The path is not a home-related facility, and the extended unit leapfrogs from one geographic area to another.

Several extended housing units that share home-related facilities may be referred to as connected housing units. The facilities that they share are connecting facilities or points of connection. An extended unit may have

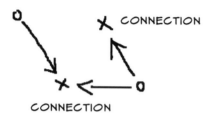

CONNECTION

CONNECTION

many points of connection; it does not have to share all of them with the same group of units—that is, a householder may share one facility with one circle of residents and another facility with a different circle of residents. Points of connection tend to be places where residents can meet one another; they provide an excuse to interact and an opportunity to develop a sense of common identity.[6]

In addition, some points of connection also provide commercial, cultural, and recreational services for outsiders—tourists, visitors, workers, and shoppers—and in this way they provide an opportunity for residents to connect with nonresidents.

The extended housing unit, as I have described it, is not contained within a clearly demarcated area. An individual's extended unit may include facilities in another neighborhood or in a nonresidential part of the city, and it may not include facilities that are next door. The extended unit says nothing, therefore, about the nature of the geographic area in which the house is located.

And yet it is clear that this geographic area affects the quality of the residential experience. Near-home facilities have an unusual chance of being used, of fostering relationships and encouraging interactions. They also have a direct effect on the housing unit, increasing or reducing its ability to satisfy the householder's need for containment, privacy, security, and control. Residents are particularly sensitive to the nuisances that they generate and to the opportunities they present for shifting activities out of the unit. Definitions of neighborhood may include different things, but they generally include, in the words of Robert Park (1925), "a collection of people occupying a more or less clearly defined area."[7] Haney and Knowles (1978), for example, define the neighborhood as:

a locality or part of the city or town where a person lives and where he feels "at home." In addition, a neighborhood can be thought of as an area that has a distinctive character or flavor to it, so that people know when they are in their neighborhood and are able to tell when they enter another neighborhood.

If the concept of the extended unit is to be useful it must be anchored in place. The obvious anchor is the housing unit itself, because each unit has a unique address. I suggest two geographic extensions of the housing unit, both firmly rooted in place. They are the *home area* and the *neighborhood area*.

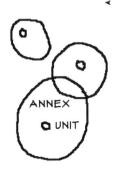

◄ *Home Area.* This coincides with a resident's idea of home. It consists of the footprint of the unit and, in addition, any area that is annexed to it. The extent of the annexed area varies with the individual resident's physical and social context[8]—it may include, for example, the yard, several adjoining houses, or the block. Because residents perceive their home areas differently, neighboring residents may have home areas of different sizes, and one home area may abut, overlap, or be circumscribed by another.

Neighborhood Area. This consists of a group of home areas that share a commonly defined residential area.[9] Often this area has a name.   ►

Home and neighborhood areas do not necessarily include all (or indeed any) of the facilities of their residents' extended units. Incorporating these connecting units leads us to a definition of neighborhood. Actually, it leads us to three definitions of neighborhood: *Home settings*, which are extensions of the home area; *neighborhood settings*, which are extensions of the neighborhood area; and *compound neighborhoods*, which are interlinked clusters of neighborhood settings. These three definitions represent three takes on a single concept; they are much like three images of an object seen through lenses of different focal lengths. A resident may live in all three simultaneously.

Home Setting. A home setting is a combination of a resident's home area and extended unit. It includes an area immediately around home, and may include connecting facilities inside and outside the area. In some situations this is the primary definition of neighborhood; residents think of their neighborhood as the area immediately around home with, perhaps, some outlying facilities.   ►

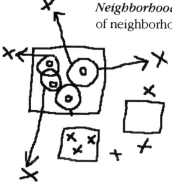

Neighborhood Setting. This is a second definition of neighborhood. It is a combination of a resident's neighborhood area and the extended units of all residents in that neighborhood area. It includes a commonly defined area and a number of connecting facilities, which may be inside the area (internal facilities) and outside it (external facilities).

Elaborations of the Neighborhood Setting

Parochial Neighborhood Settings. Neighborhood settings where all of the connecting facilities are internal.

Cosmopolitan Neighborhood Settings. Neighborhood settings where all of the connecting facilities are external.

Closed Neighborhoods. Neighborhood settings whose internal and external facilities are used only by residents of the neighborhood.

Open Neighborhoods. Neighborhood settings whose internal and external facilities are shared by residents and outsiders.

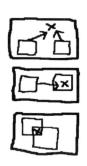

Compound Neighborhood. This is a third definition of neighborhood. It is a cluster of neighborhood settings that are connected by shared facilities. The shared facilities serve as points of connection between residents of the constituent neighborhood settings. These connections can take several different forms. For example, the external facilities of one neighborhood setting may be the internal facilities of another. Or the external facilities of one neighborhood setting may be the external facilities of another. Or the internal facilities of one neighborhood setting may be the internal facilities of another.

The elaborations of neighborhood settings (parochial and cosmopolitan, closed and open) may also be used in connection with compound neighborhoods.

The idea of nested definitions of neighborhood has been suggested by others. Russell and Ward (1982), for example, describe the environment as "a complex of immediate and distant places, psychologically arranged into a hierarchy such that each place is a part of a larger place and can be subdivided into smaller places" (p. 654). Guest and Lee (1983) refer to Greer's description of neighborhoods fitting into "local areas" and Hunter's (1979) description of a hierarchy of communities—small social blocks around home, within local neighborhoods, within larger communities within "whole regions of the city." Discussing their own study in Seattle, Guest and Lee conclude that "most Seattle residents believe themselves members of multiple, often overlapping or hierarchical communities."

The three levels of neighborhoods that I have defined are all social constructs imposed on physical space. They fit Barker's concept of behavior settings (see, for example, Barker 1978). All three look at neighborhoods as they appear from the inside—as they are experienced—rather than as they appear from the outside, the typical viewpoint of designers, geographers, and economists. The key social components are neighbors' attitudes and behaviors, and the key physical components are the places (connecting facilities) where these attitudes and behaviors are manifested. All three definitions include facilities that lie outside the geographic boundaries of a defined area. None of the definitions necessarily represents residents' shared values or images. Community organizations that advocate for the common interests of residents can be set up at all three levels of neighborhood (perhaps a block club for a home setting, a residents' association for a neighborhood setting, and an umbrella organization for a compound neighborhood), but the definitions do not require that the boundaries of a neighborhood and those of a community organization are coterminous. The service area of a community organization may be larger or smaller than a neighborhood that it represents, and a neighborhood may be represented by a number of overlapping organizations.

Neighborhoods, as I have defined them, are essentially created by residents, and they do not necessarily have official status. They have much in common with the "natural communities" of Park, Burgess, and McKenzie (1967) and with Hunter's (1975) "symbolic communities." These definitions are, however, descriptive rather than normative; they distinguish between neighborhoods and non-neighborhoods, but not between good neighborhoods and less-than-good ones.

The next task is to explore the qualities that make *good* neighborhoods.

NOTES

1. The literature on neighborhoods is extensive. A good idea of the range of meanings can be obtained from Chapin 1974; Coleman 1978; Kallus and Law-Yone 1992a, 1992b; Keller 1968; Lee 1970; Rapoport 1977, 1980, 1981, 1982; Richman and Chapin 1977; Solow, Ham, and Donnelly 1969; Stanton 1986; Warren 1978; and Watman 1980.

2. Neighborhoods (or their equivalent—sectors or wards) figure in the writings of prominent utopians and model makers, such as Howard (1945), Le Corbusier (1967), Perry (1929), and Stein (1966). For discussion, see Kallus and Law-Yone 1992a.

3. Others have suggested a different breakdown of housing functions. For example, Charlotte Perkins Gilman (*The Home: Its Work and Influence* [1903] quoted in Strasser 1982, p. 225), referring to the home and not the whole residential environment, described residential functions as "several mixed and conflicting industries," including cooking and sewing, sweeping and washing, sleeping and adult entertaining, and bringing up children. She recommended shifting child care to day nurseries. Marans (1975) listed the basic functions as providing a temporary escape from the physical stresses of the urban environment, an opportunity to experience nature, privacy, security and safety, affiliation and belonging, social recognition and status, physical exercise, and the release of tension. Richman (1979) identified housing functions as satisfying the need for shelter, security, childrearing, symbolic identification, social interaction, participation and recreation. It is also suggested that the relative priority of these functions varies by income and social class. See, for example, Birch et al. 1973 and Rainwater 1966.

4. Some societies have a less tolerant view. Posokhin (1974), for example, in discussing housing in the Soviet Union, writes: "Theoretically, there are two ways of planning housing. One is to individualize housekeeping and fit out each house or flat with air conditioners, video telephones, kitchen appliances (e.g. automatic electric stoves) and so on, for which extra area and financial outlays will be required. The other way is to socialize washing, cooking and other housekeeping chores, and to do this living space will have to be somewhat decreased. This approach to housing development is more in keeping with social needs" (p. 8).

5. The concept of the continuous extended unit is similar to Stanton's (1986) concept of the experiential network—streets that residents use frequently and experience as a part of being at home.

6. Not all home-related facilities bring residents together. Think, for example, of telephones, computers, and fax machines and services such as meals-on-wheels, trash collection, and utilities.

7. This excerpt from Park's definition of neighborhood appeared in his *Human Communities* and is quoted in Watman 1980, p. 10. For several definitions of neighborhood that do not include a defined area, see Lee 1970.

8. For example, residents' feeling of home extends over a larger area when people and traffic are not threatening. See for example, Appleyard 1981 and Brower 1988.

9. The words "sharing a commonly defined residential area" are used by Hunter 1974, pp. 113–114.

CHAPTER THREE

Past Neighborhoods

B efore entering into a discussion of the way neighborhoods ought to be, it is a good idea to look at how they got to be the way they are. In this chapter I will look at residential areas of the past, focusing on the three dimensions of Ambience, Engagement, and Choicefulness. I will review the qualities that were associated with each dimension in the past and consider whether present-day residents would find these qualities equally desirable and, if they do, what they would have to give up for them. The discussion focuses mainly on American and European cities. Information about the past is presented in the form of composite pictures that are typical of, rather than faithful to, the particulars of any one place.[1] I will highlight the best settings of the time, while recognizing that these settings were available only to those who could afford them. For information about the present—what residents look for today—I draw on a study of housing-for-rent-and-sale announcements that appeared in print in the Baltimore-Washington area over a three-month period in 1989.[2]

AMBIENCE

The nature, mix, and intensity of land uses, and the appearance and form of the physical environment.

Preindustrial cities had no clear separation of land uses. Most houses served as stores, offices, and workshops. (Purpose-built office buildings and factories did not emerge until the middle of the nineteenth century.) Artisans lived in one- or two-story houses or shacks; typically, their workshops were in the back, their products were offered for sale in the front, and the family lived upstairs. Magistrates and judges lived over the court and council chambers. Wealthy merchants and bankers incorporated stores into the street fronts of their houses, and apartments upstairs for boarders; and they lived and entertained in a suite of rooms over their business, with stables out at the back and storage in the attic.

A central location was the best place for doing business, and as people lived where they worked, it was also the most desirable place to live. At a time when the roads were unpaved and travel was slow, expensive, and uncomfortable, people wanted to live within walking distance of the markets, civic buildings, exchange, and courts. Here one could keep up with the news (which was carried by word of mouth, the town crier, and the ringing of bells), hear the latest rumors and gossip, be included in important civic and religious events, be seen in the latest fashions, and meet and mix with people of social importance. In European cities and in early settlements in America, those who could afford it lived near the center.

The general conditions of use and maintenance would be considered highly offensive today. Because the business center was considered a good place to live, it was expensive—only the most prosperous could afford it—and it was crowded. In the Cheapside retail center of London the street frontages were less than six feet wide (Boulton 1987, p. 194). The first houses in Philadelphia were sited in the center of the lot, but high land values led residents to sell off their yards for building parcels. The streets were noisy, muddy, and dirty and often so roundabout that they were hard to get through. Animal markets and tanning establishments were kept out of the center by decree, but offal and sewage were thrown into the streets, often from an overhead window; and while individual residents were expected to clean the street in front of their houses, they frequently did not, and the refuse accumulated.

During the late-eighteenth and nineteenth centuries, the problems compounded. New manufacturing plants and commercial houses concentrated in the center. Immigrants crowded the workshops, stores, wharves, and streets and jammed into nearby tenements and rooming houses, bringing increased crime and social tensions. Traffic overtaxed the roads. The noise and smell of horse-drawn traffic was replaced by the clanging of the streetcar. The smell of industrial waste in the streams and smoke in the air was added to that of thousands of privies, stables and open drains. Inadequate water supply and sewerage systems led to frequent fires and the spread of disease. In the 1830s, the Vicomte de Launay gave this description of Paris:

How one stifles in those dark, damp, narrow corridors which you are pleased to call the streets of Paris! One would think one were in an underground city, so sluggish is the air, so profound the obscurity. And the thousands of people live, bustle, throng in the liquid darkness, like reptiles in a marsh. (quoted in Lees 1985, p. 73)

In addition, the housing stock was old and uncomfortable, lacking modern conveniences such as flush toilets, hot and cold running water, gas lights, and steam heat.

Despite these deplorable conditions, Paris had a long tradition of urban living, manifested in elegant residential squares and in facilities that catered to an active, visible, and sophisticated urban society. Members of the emerging French middle class had money and considerable political influence. They could afford better housing, but they did not want to move out of the city, away from the stores, restaurants, and cabarets. At the direction of Napoleon III, Baron Haussmann undertook the task of turning the center of Paris into a desirable place to live. It was an enormous job of reconstruction. New wide boulevards with spacious sidewalks were cut through the old center. The water supply and sewer systems were improved. The university was expanded, and new schools, parks, and an opera house were introduced. Alongside the boulevards private developers erected apartment buildings with shops and restaurants on the ground floor. The boulevards thronged with people, the epitome of what we have come to regard as a sophisticated urban setting.

The liveliness of the boulevards, according to a contemporary opinion, added to their desirability as a place in which to live.

The most fortunate people in Paris are, for the moment, the tenants of the ex-rue de Rumfort. They lived in a corner cut off from the world, practically lost; no noise, no movement, no distractions; they could watch the grass grow between the paving stones; the air they breathed was charged with boredom. One bright day, without changing residence and without rise in rent, they found themselves in the middle of Paris; they went to sleep in the rue de Rumfort, they woke up on the Boulevard Malesherbes. (quoted in Olsen 1986, p. 50)

Of course, people who lived off the boulevards did not benefit from Haussmann's housing improvements, so that in 1924 Le Corbusier could still write that

the true-blue Parisian lives in damp old houses, there is no bathroom, no hot water because it is almost impossible to install it; the staircase is dark, and the kitchen almost nonexistent, and there is no electricity. He heats his flat with briquettes which grill his face and freeze his back and shed black soot over everything. (Le Corbusier 1971, p. 213)

Many poor residents who lived in squalor behind the grand boulevards dreamed of a house in the suburbs.

"How happy we shall be! We will have a little garden in the first place; Monsieur Madaleine has promised it to me. My child will play in the garden. She will chase the butterflies in the grass and I will watch her." (Hugo 1909, pp. 275–276)

A great many of them did in fact move out of the central city as a result of Haussmann's plans (it is estimated that 350,000 people were displaced), but it is unlikely that they found their dream house in the grim suburbs built to accommodate them (Wagenaar 1992).

Parisians' long-standing acceptance of apartment living and facility-dependent settings, their willingness to live in physical proximity to commercial uses, and the presence of high-density housing immediately behind the boulevards were essential to the success of Haussmann's plan. In England and the United States, however, most middle-class families would not consider apartment living—the very idea of sharing their roof with others was unthinkable. Nor would they consider mixed uses in the neighborhood. Wealthy residents even preferred to separate uses within the household, servants being relegated to quarters that were placed at some distance from the family (a network of back passages and staircases made them virtually invisible), and visitors were restricted to public rooms which were apart from the living quarters. Edith Wharton, writing about the early 1870s, tells about old Mrs. Mingott, who had

established herself (in flagrant violation of all the New York proprieties) on the ground floor of her house; so that, as you sat in her sitting-room window with her, you caught the unexpected vista of a bedroom. Her visitors were startled and fascinated by the foreignness of this arrangement, which recalled scenes in French fiction, and architectural incentives to immorality such as the simple American had never dreamed of. (Wharton 1920, p. 28)

People also became less accepting of mixed uses in the neighborhood. In London, estate subdivisions introduced covenants that ensured greater occupational uniformity. Some estates prohibited stores. In U.S. cities, middle-income residents demanded that industrial and commercial uses be prohibited from spreading into the sectors of the city in which they lived. Classification and segregation of land according to use became increasingly important ordering principles of social life (Home 1992, p. 188), and zoning became a powerful tool for prescribing and enforcing the separation of uses. Some middle-income residents moved to small towns on the urban fringe where the scale of industrial development was smaller and the associated problems were more manageable (von Hoffman 1994; Binford 1985). Or they moved out to newly developing areas in the country, where nonresidential uses were prohibited or severely restricted. The houses that they left behind became warehouses or boarding houses, or they were subdivided into small units for rent to low-income families.

People had long believed in the physical, moral, and health-giving benefits of country living. Roman, medieval, and Renaissance rulers had built villas, set in formal gardens, outside the city. English aristocrats and wealthy merchants had long kept second homes outside London. In the eighteenth century, modest shopkeepers, politicians, and poets maintained cottages along the roads that led out of town. But travel was too slow, uncomfortable, and expensive for people to be able to live in the country and commute to the city on a daily basis. The country houses were for weekend use only, or for the women and children to spend the summer months (when conditions in the city were at their worst) while the men lived and worked in the city and visited their families on weekends.

With the introduction of the steam railroad during the 1830s it became possible for wealthy households (rail travel was expensive) to live year-round in the countryside. By the middle of the nineteenth century it was quite common for London merchants and industrialists to live permanently in villas and cottages on the outskirts of town. In the United States, upper-income residents followed the same pattern. Gradually they weaned themselves of their town houses and adjusted themselves to a new way of life in the country.

Under [the landscape's] enchanting influence, the too great hustle and excitement of our commercial cities will be happily counterbalanced by the more elegant and quiet enjoyment of country life. (Andrew Jackson Downing [1815–1852], quoted in Hadden and Barton 1977, p. 40)

The beauty of the country, the pleasures of the country life, the tranquility of mind which it promises and, wherever the injustice of human laws does not disturb it, the independency which it really affords, have charms that more or less attract everybody. (Adam Smith in *The Wealth of Nations*, New York, 1937, p. 358, quoted in Schorske 1966)

According to Marsh (1990), country living in the United States had associations with rootedness to the ground, independence, and a society of property owners—ideas that had a great deal of appeal for men. But women, in the beginning, were not keen to move to the suburbs; they missed the opportunities that the center city offered for social interaction and participation in reform and religious activities.

With the streetcar, and then the electric street railway and the gasoline engine, middle-income and working-class families were able to move to the suburbs and commute to work in the center. Much of the new development consisted not of isolated houses in the countryside, but of rows of monotonous houses on look-alike streets, and commerce and industry moved out to them. By 1909, the mid-nineteenth century suburbs were being abandoned for newer ones further out (Olsen 1986, p. 162).

Wealthy residents found their arcadian settings threatened by these intrusions. One solution was to create planned communities within whose boundaries the rural beauty of the countryside would be protected—and even enhanced. A typical garden community was a planned development of detached houses, with large yards, set well back from tree-lined streets.

Probably the advantages of civilization can be found illustrated and demonstrated under no other circumstances so completely as in some suburban neighborhoods where each family abode stands fifty or a hundred feet or more apart from all others, and at some distance from the public road. And it must be remembered, also, that man's enjoyment of rural beauty has clearly increased rather than diminished with his advance in civilization. (Frederick Law Olmsted 1871)

Every attempt was made to shut out the man-made environment, to reproduce the appearance of unspoiled nature and create a quiet, soothing setting devoted entirely to domesticity. Commercial and industrial uses were excluded, and the only nonresidential uses permitted were those that added to the residential quality of the area. Sites were allocated to schools and churches, public greens, playgrounds, ball fields, resting spots, lakes and, sometimes, a sports club. Garden communities offered the kind of country living that was eminently suited to the tastes of city people—the uplifting experience of living close to nature combined with the convenience of city services and amenities. They also offered fresh air, clean water, scientific sewerage, and a high, breeze-swept, well- drained location. Waesche (1987, p. 56), in his history of Roland Park, a planned community outside Baltimore, reports on the following advertisements, which appeared in July 1892:

Are you satisfied to always breathe the city atmosphere of smells, dust and decaying filth? The house slops and all manner of refuse find their way through the open gutters, and there stagnate, filling the air with the germs of diseases. At times the odors are intolerable. They are unhealthful always.

and again,

At Roland Park there is always an air current owing to the elevation. A breeze however slight is sure to come from some direction, and the falling dew serves to change the atmosphere so that restoring sleep is possible every night. The morning is clear, fresh and invigorating, and one can face the city's heat with strength renewed.

Many stores followed their customers to the suburbs, locating at the fringes of the new communities, and leaving the old, in-town neighborhoods less well served.

Planners saw the developing suburbs as the beginning of a complete restructuring of the city, and they offered alternative visions of a good residential environment, where the activity of the city was moderated or replaced by the tranquility of the countryside. These included Howard's vision of a linked network of discrete, bounded satellite towns, each completely surrounded by countryside (Howard 1898), and Le Corbusier's vision of an undulating band of full-service high-rise apartment buildings set in continuous parkland (Le Corbusier 1971). These ideas, which incorporated a clear separation between residential, commercial, civic, and industrial uses, guided development policies, and led to the gradual evolution of an entirely new type of residential area, one from which all nonresidential uses are excluded.

Today, widespread automobile ownership has made it unnecessary for most residents to live near their place of work even if they could. And while working conditions and the nature of work have changed so that noise, pollution, and appearance are no longer a problem, many workplaces are still unwelcome in residential areas because of their increased size and traffic generation. Spatial separation of homes and workplaces is generally accepted as a tenet of good neighborhood planning; it is a feature of most ideal and prototype plans of the twentieth century, and remains a feature even of present-day plans that hark back to an earlier era (see, for example, Calthorpe 1993).

Who wouldn't prefer a wooded setting?
All other things being just about equal, wouldn't you rather be surrounded by lots of trees, shrubs and green spaces? (advertisement for *Spring Hill*, 1989)

Only in center-city neighborhoods is a mix of residential and nonresidential uses accepted—indeed, promoted as desirable.

The origins of Baltimore's renaissance—the Inner Harbor, Canton, Fells Point—are alive with markets, restaurants and nightlife all near your front door. You'll find fresh seafood, meat and produce supplied daily at the Broadway market,. You'll be surrounded by restaurants and taverns preparing a variety of cuisines to please every taste and the sound of jazz, country and classical music on almost every corner plus the historical charm of 200 year old homes and business establishments. The flourishing arts and culture of the city are close by too—you'll be minutes from the Meyerhoff Symphony Hall, home of the Baltimore Symphony Orchestra; the Mechanic, Lyric and Center Stage theaters, each offering a full season of professional performances. At Canton Square you won't just visit Baltimore's renaissance, you'll be part of it. (advertisement for *Canton Square*, 1989)

Some center-city developers, torn between the conflicting market demands for both separation and integration of uses, offer both.

Located in the midst of vibrant Adams Morgan, it is situated in a quiet residential setting.

Here you'll enjoy peaceful solitude and great natural beauty while being within minutes of everything that makes the new Baltimore the country's most talked about city.

There are some for whom the idea of separate places for home and work does not make sense, some for whom family life and employment are intimately connected. In the early days, this was particularly true of women who, when men first went out to work in factories and offices, continued to work at home. Many women had relatives living in the house who might or might not work for pay; some had paying boarders, or apprentices or servants who worked for room, board, education, and cash. Domestic servants had to work long hours with little time off, and the only private life they had was secret or marginal (Prost 1991, p. 31). Even in the early days of the nineteenth century there were

innumerable things to be dusted, scrubbed, polished, or stoned, clothes to be washed, mangled, dried, starched and ironed (a week's laundry for a small family would take two women most of a day), coals to be carried, grates to be blacked, fires to be laid, heavy meals to be prepared, and numerous children to be kept tidy, cared for and amused. Even in quite humble middle-class households much of this load was borne by one or two female servants. (Jackson 1973, p. 46)

Early in the century, many women engaged not only in housework, but also in home work—they practiced dressmaking, embroidery, laundry, or beauty treatment at home. In working-class houses it was not unusual to have a branch factory—perhaps twenty women, making lamp shades or artificial flowers, or doing china painting, beading, or embroidery (Ahrentzen 1992). Today, women home-workers are more likely to be computer consultants, programmers, systems analysts, free-lance writers, phone sales operators, public relations specialists, management consultants, and accountants. Studies suggest that working at home affects the way that they use both their home and their neighborhood—they are less inclined to entertain at home (because of the clutter of work material) and more likely to depend on the neighborhood to provide them with connections outside the family. They prefer neighborhoods where they can take work breaks—ride bicycles, spend time in parks and pathways, and use local shops, libraries, post offices, copy centers, and office supply stores (Ahrentzen 1990, 1992).

Now that electronic communications are making it easier for more people —men as well as women, self-employed as well as telecommuters[3]—to work at home, there is additional interest in neighborhoods that are not exclusively residential, that permit home-based businesses and provide services related to work, such as telecenters, copying, overnight mail, fax, and child care, as well as a grocery store, health club, and restaurant (Meyrowitz 1985; Handy and Mokhtarian 1995).

There are other groups—working mothers, teenagers, and the elderly— who find all-residential environments to be limiting, isolating, and boring and who would like to see child-care services and work opportunities in the neighborhood, as well as walk-to facilities to provide relief from the constant dependence on private automobiles. They would like local places where they can go to find companionship.

Responding to some of the dissatisfactions with housing-only areas, some recent residential developments have included commercial uses, but these uses tend to be separate, clustered, and strictly regulated.

ENGAGEMENT

The nature and extent of the interaction among residents and the presence of facilities and features that foster or inhibit these interactions.

In preindustrial cities, people did not, as they do today, expect that their residential quarters would be the private domain of the family. For one thing, the concept of the family was different from ours. Wealthy residents included a great many servants as part of their immediate family. Some of these servants were children who had been put out as apprentices to receive a practical education for life. Less wealthy families apprenticed their children to artisans in order to learn a trade. Apprentices worked at menial domestic tasks. Residents saw clients at home and gave business associates free rein there.

People spent their free time away from home. The houses were cold and draughty; they were dark by day and night (window glass and candles were expensive). They were hot in summer and cold in winter. Window screening was not introduced until the late 1880s; before that time, houses swarmed with mosquitos and bugs. The rooms were small. They did not have distinguishing names or serve special purposes—for example, no rooms were specially set aside for sleeping or entertaining or cooking (people cooked and baked in an open hearth in the living room), and it was not until the nineteenth century that large houses had separate kitchens and dining rooms. Meals were taken at folding tables. Water was drawn from a well or a fountain or bought from a water carrier and stored in a cistern and in buckets or tubs. There were no bathrooms. People bathed, often communally, in portable wooden tubs, and they heated water in pots and pans on the fire. They did not bathe often, and when they did it was for the curative value of the water rather than for cleanliness. Only the rich were clean. According to Pardailhe-Galabrun (1991, p. 136), frequent baths were thought to be bad because the water infiltrated the organs and weakened them; it "filled the head with vapours." Latrines used pails that had to be emptied, or they emptied directly into a stream or river. The general standard of sanitation would seem alarming to us today. There was, of course, no refrigeration; and housewives spent a great deal of time preserving meat and fish, which nevertheless tended to spoil and had to be highly spiced. They also spun yarn, wove cloth, and made clothes for their families; and they were responsible for health care—preparing home remedies, nursing the sick, preparing the dead for burial. In the United States, until the middle of the nineteenth century, children were educated at home. Husbands shouldered few household responsibilities until the turn of the century, when men began to spend more time at home and help raise the children (Marsh 1990).

Housewives necessarily interacted with many people in the course of the day, and they depended heavily on the presence of neighborhood services. Well into the twentieth century, housewives went shopping daily; they bought bread from the baker and sometimes took their meat and pies to be cooked in his oven; and they bought fish, eggs, and produce from peddlers who came to the door. Water carriers, knife sharpeners and, later, ice deliverymen went from house to house; and doctors made house calls.

With the house essentially a place of work, it is hardly surprising that residents chose to spend their free time elsewhere, and early cities provided many places for engagement, both within and outside the neighborhood. In preindustrial cities, people lived in facility-dependent settings. Much of public life was visible and carried on in public places. European streets and squares were the scene of constant fairs, feasts, royal visits, tournaments, weddings, funerals, and hangings. There were many inns, alehouses, and taverns, and they were central points of communication for men. There were coffee houses where merchants would gather every noon to read incoming newspapers, to discuss prices, and to arrange for cargoes and marine insurance. There were barbershops and public bath houses. Permanent leisure buildings (theaters, tennis courts, opera houses, cockpits, bullrings, racecourse buildings, and buildings in pleasure gardens) began to appear in the mid-sixteenth century, and they became popular meeting places.

With industrialization, houses started to become more comfortable and better equipped, and people started spending more time there. Piped water systems made cooking and cleaning less of a chore (although by the turn of the nineteenth century the poor still had to haul water from public hydrants, and only the rich had indoor plumbing). Water closets appeared in the last decades of the century, and the bathroom developed as a special room with sink, bath, and W. C. Wood-burning space heaters began to be used in the middle of the eighteenth century; oil burners only became common after World War I, and gas heaters a decade later. Cast-iron stoves, elaborations of the space heater, replaced the hearth for cooking, followed by gas stoves late in the nineteenth century and electric stoves in the first quarter of the twentieth. Candles and whale oil for night lighting were succeeded by kerosene in the middle of the nineteenth century. Gas lighting in the home became affordable to other than wealthy people toward the end of the century. The first homes were wired for electric light in the 1880s.[4]

Starting in the 1880s, there were sporadic attempts to ease the burdens of middle-income housekeepers by providing shared services. There were experiments with cooperative kitchens, dining clubs, cooked food deliveries, laundry service, maid service, child care, catering for special occasions, and school lunch clubs. Many of these early experiments were not long lived (Hayden 1981, p. 156). A more viable approach proved to be that of offering private services exclusively for residents of a single building or housing development. These kinds of in-house services were pioneered by the apartment house.

Apartment houses in their present form—buildings originally designed for multiple occupancy, not converted houses—were popular in Paris from the late seventeenth century. In London and the United States (where they were known as French flats) they appeared only after 1850 and became popular with upper-class residents. The early apartments were mostly rental units, and their accommodation was equal to that of a small town house, but with modern conveniences and cheaper maintenance and service costs. The buildings provided labor-saving devices such as central vacuum-cleaning systems, communal dining rooms for private parties, and laundry facilities. They also offered elevator operators, doormen and, some years later, wall safes, filtered water, and telephone switchboards. These services were intended to relieve residents living alone of the burdens of housework; but because housework was seen as a social duty, many felt that apartment living was the height of domestic irresponsibility, leading inevitably to "instability, dissipation and shallowness in human society" (Robert Kerr in 1864, quoted in Olsen 1986, p. 91). Apartments, it was thought, promoted a less stable lifestyle.

Instead of the patriarchal family life of earlier times, many English families nowadays favor variety, freedom from encumbrances, liberty of movement, social distractions. It is for this section of modern England that flats exist. (Hermann Muthesius in 1904, quoted in Olsen 1986, pp. 144–145)

Today, efforts to reduce the burden of housework are no longer considered to be irresponsible, and labor-saving devices in the home are in general use.

As home ceased being mainly a place of work, people began to spend their spare time there, and it became a place for relaxation. Today's homes, equipped with air-conditioning, radios, stereo players, television sets, video games and VCRs, are "being advertised as virtual playgrounds with every amenity for the good life" (Block 1981, p. 10). Cities have always provided places of relaxation and entertainment, but to think of one's home in these terms would, until quite recently, have been beyond the expectations of ordinary residents. Many would have considered it sinful. Neighborhoods, too, are expected to be relaxing; and parks, playgrounds, swimming pools, tennis courts, running tracks, and community centers give many of them the character of a health resort. Increasingly, these amenities are privately owned and operated.

There's a lot to do in Piney Orchard. The Community Center features indoor lap and outdoor swimming pools, exercise rooms, a wide screen television and meeting facilities. There are jogging and biking paths nearby, playing fields, tennis courts, a new ice arena, beautiful wildlife areas and a lake to enjoy and relax by. (advertisement for *Piney Orchard,* 1989)

In the 1880s, as people began spending more time at home, American social reformers began to be concerned that the effect would be to weaken the bonds of community. They saw the role of neighborhood facilities and services not only as improving housing functions, but also as a unifying and socializing force in the community. The St. Louis plan of 1907 proposed half-a-dozen small multipurpose centers scattered throughout the city, each incorporating such things as a park, school, library, police station, and bath house. The planners saw the community center as a device to stimulate the revitalization of middle-class neighborhoods, and they proposed incorporating a number of civic functions such as town forums, adult education, and recreational activities. Community centers were the spatial foci of plans for the Greenbelt towns and neighborhood units of the 1920s and 1930s (Perry 1929; Stein 1966).

But public improvements did not keep up with private expectations and gradually the private sector began to assume the responsibility for providing neighborhood amenities. In the United States, the early garden communities of Frederick Law Olmsted and his firm provided and managed their own water supplies, sewers, streets, walkways, and parks, and they provided sites for private schools and private country clubs (Moudry 1990; Waesche 1987; Fein 1972). Today, neighborhood amenities are increasingly being provided by large-scale housing developers as a part of the rental or purchase price (McKenzie 1994; Louv 1983).

Oxford apartment living. There's no residential option quite like it. Complimentary membership to the Oxford Club wins you access to an exclusive package of consumer services, community conveniences, and social activities and that's only the beginning. Oxford communities include a swimming pool and fitness center, soothing whirlpools and saunas. Even a car wash. (advertisement for Oxford housing, 1989)

A great many residents rely on condominium associations for shared facilities and services. Cooperatives had a brief period of popularity in the 1880s and then lost popularity until after World War I. The cohousing movement, which has been active in Europe for some years and is now attracting interest in the United States, includes shared facilities and services that are owned and operated by a closed group of residents. In a typical cohousing development, each household has a private residence and, in addition, shares common facilities such as kitchens and dining rooms, children's playrooms, day-care, workshops, guest rooms, and laundry facilities (McCamant, Durrett, and Hertzman 1994; Kranz and Lindén 1994; Fromm 1991).

The shift from public- to private-access facilities and from facility- to unit-dependent settings has significant implications for the quality of neighborhood life. Private-access facilities limit the field of engagement; they do not provide (indeed, they effectively reduce) opportunities for engagement outside the closed circle of their membership. One may argue that in being selective they bring together people who are similar and so likely to form a meaningful association; but, on the other hand, private-access facilities are just as likely to support independent activities and to generate no more than a fragile sense of community.

Some critics lament the absence of suitable public places that bring neighbors together.

Suburbia offers almost no facilities for accidental encounters or for collective meetings; social participation beyond the narrow range of family and friends is limited to the passive receipt of goods, information, and entertainment from impersonal and isolated sources. (Goldston 1970, p. 140)

Upon an urban landscape increasingly hostile to and devoid of informal gathering places, one may encounter people rather pathetically trying to find some spot in which to relax and enjoy each other's company. (Oldenburg 1989, p. 17)

Some critics think that a lack of engagement at the neighborhood level implies the absence of a sense of community, and that this is a loss for society as a whole.

Our lives are now centered inside the house, rather than on the neighborhood or the community. With increased use of automobiles, the life of the sidewalk and the front yard has largely disappeared, and the social intercourse that used to be the main characteristic of urban life has vanished. Residential neighborhoods have become a mass of small, private islands; with the back yard functioning as a wholesome, family-oriented, and reclusive place. (Jackson 1985, p. 280)

Interviews in ten cities across the United States suggest that many residents would agree with this as a general idea (Fried 1986). These interviews show that existing neighborhoods are felt to be deficient in offering a meaningful community life and that residents would like a greater feeling of closeness and interaction, of warmth and community.

Oldenburg (1989) argues that all neighborhoods should contain points of connection that are separate from home and work. He calls them "third places" and regards them as the core settings of informal public life. According to Oldenburg, good third places keep long hours and are open to all; they are places where anyone can feel at home, where the main purpose is socializing, the mood is playful, and the main activity is pleasurable and entertaining conversation; they are places where users are not divided by class and rank, where people come and go as they please, and where a body of regular users sets the tone and one can always count on seeing people one knows. This kind of neighborhood home-from-home, the idea behind the TV series "Cheers," evokes the image of a simpler, friendlier way of life, a past that seems both familiar and desirable (Lowenthal 1985).

Oldenburg notes the absence of third places in many of our residential areas. I suspect, however, that many residents today would not use third places as he defines them, even if they did exist in their neighborhood. Over the past three years, my students have interviewed residents in the Baltimore-Washington region, asking them about places they go to meet people. They have found that while some residents use the kinds of places that Oldenburg describes, many others do not. It is not that they do not socialize, but they do not necessarily socialize with others who live in their neighborhood or in places within the neighborhood area. They get together with people from other parts of the city, and they do it in places such as shopping malls, church halls, barber shops, markets, health food stores, and fitness centers. Many get together in one another's homes. Many prefer places that are not used by all, but that are patronized by people of similar interests and backgrounds, people of the same class, race, national origin, or sexual orientation. Some regularly go to the same place in the hope of meeting people; others make arrangements with a regular group of people to meet in different places. It seems that some residents use local hangouts as third places in Oldenburg's terms, but that many others do not depend on the neighborhood for their social relationships. Indeed, some see the neighborhood as a refuge from relationships. Feldman (1994), for example, quotes a resident discussing her suburban home:

My home is my refuge. I need to get away from everything. I like to go to these places [workplace, stores and public facilities] when I need them. When I'm home, I like to be alone or be with people one on one. It's not that I don't like other people or anything like that. I just want to be able to do anything I want and not bother anybody else, and I don't want anybody else bothering me.

The absence of local gathering places does not mean, as some have suggested (for example, Keller 1968), that the neighborhood has become an outdated concept. Residents' identification with the neighborhood remains strong and persistent even if they do not participate in community events at the neighborhood level (Guest and Lee 1983; Guest, Lee, and Staeheli 1982). It seems that some residents look for places of engagement represented by third places, while others look for something less open, less binding, less local, perhaps less intimate. The challenge is to come up with social mechanisms suited to these different ways of living.

CHOICEFULNESS

Opportunities for residents to choose alternative locations, life-styles, and living arrangements.

In preindustrial cities in the United States, where one *lived* was determined by where one worked rather than by one's social class. Merchants lived in the port area with carpenters, joiners, smiths, sailmakers, sailors, stevedores, and shipbuilders; tradesmen of all kinds lived interspersed with those who bought their goods and services; proprietors, merchants, and doctors lived with porters, laborers, carters, watchmen, and criers. There was little clustering by ethnic group. Although there were wealthy sections of the city, these sections held a social mix because the middle classes required the proximity of less affluent neighbors such as tradesmen, servants, and artisans, and they supported the activities of beggars, prostitutes, and criminals. Many houses were subdivided for letting. The rich lived on the widest and best-paved streets, the middling families on the side streets, and the poor in the mews, alleys, and courts.

Social classes were mixed even within buildings. Since early times, the homes of the wealthy had shopkeepers and artisans living along the street fronts. In apartment buildings, the poor lived in the basement and climbed the stairs to the upper floors, and the wealthy lived in between. One might find

families of all grades and classes, each in its flat in the same stair—a sweep and a caddie in the cellars, poor mechanics in the garrets, while in the intermediate stories might live a noble, a lord-of-sessions, a doctor, a city minister, a dowager countess, or a writer. Higher up over their heads lived shopkeepers, dancing-masters or clerks. (Perks 1905, p. 15)

The social mix was perpetuated in Haussmann's redevelopment in Paris where servants and lodgers were housed on the upper floors. Servants in the early apartment houses in New York also lived on the top floors. In 1859, the installation of the first elevator in a residential structure marked the beginning of the end of social mixing in buildings.

The move to segregated housing areas had been heralded in eighteenth- and early nineteenth-century England, when the attitude toward the family underwent a profound change. The family came to be seen as the primary and emotional center of its members' lives, and family life came to be focused on mutual intimacy and child-raising. This change in attitude was accompanied by a religious belief that the family was the road to salvation and that women were the moral guardians of the home and should devote themselves to the education of their children and the support of their husbands. For this purpose, they had to be protected from the crass materialism of the work world and physically separated from its temptations (Fishman 1987).

With the advent of cheap public transportation people no longer had to live where they worked, and neighborhoods began to house, in addition to those who worked there, a number of commuters—downtown clerks, businessmen, and factory workers—and a number of people worked there who lived elsewhere. Middle-class residents banded together to form improvement and protective associations, and they introduced ordinances aimed at keeping unwanted sections of the population out. In 1845, the City of Baltimore installed an iron fence around the park in Mount Vernon Place to keep the rabble out of Baltimore's finest neighborhood. Arguments in favor of comprehensive planning in the early twentieth century were really arguments for social segregation (Arnold 1979; Power 1982, 1983).

With greater freedom of residential location, similar people began to cluster; and quietly and steadily, separate social areas were formed. Upper middle-income residents were the first to seek protection from the problems of living in a mixed neighborhood. Some moved to nearby villages or small towns, others to new, exclusive suburbs designed from the outset for a single class of resident. For the first time, separate concentrations of low-paid, low-skilled, and unskilled workers were formed, and cities developed distinctively different areas based upon social rank and ethnicity. Social homogeneity came to be regarded as a desirable feature of a well-planned neighborhood.[5] People became accustomed to living in exclusive neighborhoods, and many lost the habit of living with other classes.

The combination of privacy, police, and tolerance which must exist in mixed neighborhoods came to be regarded as a burden by middle-class city dwellers. As those who have returned to the inner city have recently learned, mixed neighborhoods, to be habitable, require the restraints of locked doors, and walled yards; they require that adults discipline any children who are misbehaving in the streets and alleys of the neighborhood; they require a watchfulness against strangers and the presence of a policeman; they require a toleration of some class warfare among the children and some respect for different goals and values in the neighborhood and the neighborhood school. (Warner 1968, p. 174)

In the 1950s and 1960s, planners spoke out against residential segregation and in favor of balanced residential areas, each containing a cross-section of socioeconomic levels. Balanced residential areas, they argued, would enrich the lives of their residents, promote tolerance of social and cultural differences, provide a broadening educational influence on children, and encourage exposure to alternative ways of life. The planners suggested that heterogeneous neighborhoods could be created through land use planning, and that social interaction among the residents could be promoted through site planning. But the validity and practicality of both these ends and means were questioned, and the movement had no real effect (Gans, May 1961, August 1961).

Today, differentiated social areas are a feature of our cities. The homogeneity that is typical of so many all-residential areas makes them inhospitable to the growing number of nontraditional households, such as one-parent families, unmarried couples, gays, and single and divorced women (Wekerle 1979; Rothblatt, Garr, and Sprague 1979). The proliferation of private residential communities, known as common interest developments, is testament to the continuing popularity of socially homogeneous residential areas. These communities use restrictive covenants to screen prospective residents and establish a code of behavior, and these covenants are rigidly enforced by homeowners' associations (McKenzie 1994; Louv 1983). We have communities, even entire towns, where residency is restricted to a narrow segment of the population (FitzGerald 1981, pp. 203-245). In areas that remain mixed, advertisers are quick to emphasize the need for private measures to guarantee residents' safety; they point to uniformed doormen, electronic door entry systems, 24-hour security guards, monitored closed-circuit TV, telephone intercom systems, deadlock bolts and viewer peepholes on apartment doors, attended off-street parking, and night lighting.

SUMMARY

A study of the past teaches us that our residential environments are shaped by the practices, acceptances and expectations of our times. Admired environments of the past would not have been the way they were had travel not been so slow and inconvenient, residents not been so dependent on near-home facilities, housing choices not been so limited, houses not been so lacking in amenity and privacy, and sanitary conditions not been so primitive. These conditions—to which we would not want to return even if we could—were the context within which the old settings functioned. The challenge of the past is not simply to recreate the physical components of an earlier setting—that would produce only a semblance of the original—but rather to capture the original substance, to recreate the quality of the residential experience. This is far more difficult, because it usually means that residents would have to do without amenities that they have come to regard as necessary, but that were not available or not considered appropriate for the original settings.

The past also teaches us that the requirements for a good environment change over time. Goodness is always assessed in relation to the available alternatives. There are few absolutes. At various times in history, the kinds of neighborhoods that were considered to be good have varied considerably; neighborhoods that were considered good in the past may be quite unacceptable today. Good neighborhoods of today reflect the life-style of today's residents. That means, of course, that they will have to be adapted to suit residents of tomorrow. They should be designed to be adaptable.

NOTES

1. These descriptions draw from the work of Alpern 1975; Aries 1962; Bedarida and Sutcliff 1980; Binford 1985; Boulton 1987; Cowan 1983; Ebner 1988; Fishman 1987; Giedion 1946; Girouard 1985; Greenberg 1980; Harrison 1972; Hayden 1981, 1984; Huizinga 1955; A. Jackson 1973; K. Jackson 1985; Nasaw 1979; Olsen 1986; Pardailhe-Galabrun 1991; Saalman 1971; Scott 1969; Schuyler 1986; Sjoberg 1960; Stilgoe 1982,1988; Strasser 1982; Warner 1968; G. Wright 1981; and L. Wright 1960.

2. Altogether, 304 properties were analyzed—52 in downtown locations and 252 in the outer city and the suburbs.

3. Telecommuters are people who are not self employed, but who are able, at least some of the time, to substitute telecommunication for a commute to the office. See Handy and Mokhtarian 1995.

4. Industrialization did not always reduce the amount of time that women had to spend on housework. For example, when refined flour replaced corn meal and whole-grain flour early in the nineteenth century, it led to a taste for cakes and for yeast breads instead of quickbreads, which meant more time spent baking. When manufactured cloth became generally available and cotton replaced leather, wool, and linen, people were no longer satisfied to wear the same clothing every day, and they expected clothes to be washed more often. When the domestic washing machine was introduced, washing which had been sent out to commercial laundries was returned to the house. When the sewing machine was introduced, housewives who had relied on ready-made clothes to reduce the time-consuming task of hand sewing felt obliged to do more of the sewing at home. As material conditions improved, people enjoyed more varied diets and more complex cooking, but this made for more work in the kitchen. Women became more productive at home, but their labor was not necessarily reduced (Cowan 1983).

5. Olmsted planned Riverside (1868) for "people of taste." He did include housing for working-class residents, but he expected that under the influence of the suburban environment they would become more civilized and emulate the behavior patterns of the educated class. Ebenezer Howard (1898) described the Garden City as being for the law-abiding class. Clarence Perry (1929), described the Neighborhood Unit as intended for those who could afford it.

CHAPTER FOUR

Ideal Neighborhoods

> If a painter, then, draws an idealized picture of a man, complete
> to the last detail, is he any the worse painter because he cannot
> point to a real original?
>
> Plato
> *The Republic*

The past teaches us how neighborhoods got to be the way they are. Ideals teach us how people think they ought to be; not just how they could be better, but how they could be the very best. As the very best, ideals are uncompromising in their definition and their resolution of the problem; as the measure of all possibilities they are themselves beyond possibility. An ideal is something that resembles a real solution to something that resembles a real problem.[1] And yet, it is real in the sense that it shapes people's desires, and influences the appearance and forms of dwellings and spaces (Rapoport 1969, p. 47; Dorst 1989). An ideal exists, in Mumford's words,

in the same way that north and south exist. We can never reach the points of the compass; and so no doubt we shall never live in utopia; but without the magnetic needle we should not be able to travel intelligently at all. (Mumford 1923, p. 24)

Ideal schemes have certain common characteristics. First, an ideal is a way of imagining the future, but it takes the present as its point of departure, and it is the present that defines the possibilities. Utopian writers may have their heads in the clouds, but they have their feet firmly planted in the currents of their own time. They are concerned about the failure of their society to deal with issues of security, poverty, health, morality, and the common good; and they imagine a society where these problems have been remedied—where people have learned how to live well as part of a community, eliminate the inequities between haves and have-nots, and live a life of moral purity in accordance with natural laws, the laws of God, or the laws of human nature. The remedies are usually imaginative extrapolations of prevailing trends or counter-trends, and they build on the sentiment of their day. Changes in economic resources, technology, or social mores will expand and contract the range of what is possible and, with it, perceptions of the ideal. Ideals are rooted in time and may not travel well between one culture and another.

Second, idealism embraces new beginnings, radical change rather than fine tuning. To utopians

an ill-designed ship of state required more than the science of navigation to pull it through stormy waters: If it was in danger of perpetually foundering, it seemed high time to go back to the shipyards and inquire into the principles upon which it had been put together. (Mumford 1923, p. 31)

Utopian ideas take root in times of new possibilities, when the accepted way of life comes into question: perhaps after a war or a revolution, the discovery of new technologies or resources, or the rise of new ideologies.

Third, people are easily diverted from visions of an ideal future by practical considerations of how to get there from here. To avoid any distraction from the desirable end-state, utopias are often presented as fiction—set in the indeterminate future, on a strange island, a distant planet, a hidden valley, a lost kingdom, and reached by means of a hundred-year sleep, a chance discovery, a dream, or a shipwreck. Such fanciful devices encourage the suspension of disbelief and prepare readers for discontinuities with the present. A realistic depiction of the future enables readers to see it in the mind's eye and to experience complex interrelationships of form and use, something that is difficult to achieve with practical plans that take the form of proposals, policies, and regulations.

Utopian schemes are directed at issues that are far larger than the quality of the residential environment (in fact, it is only relatively recently that there has been serious concern about the quality of housing for people other than kings and courtiers); still, many of them do make reference to the neighborhood, and it is useful to see what they prescribe. In this chapter I will discuss residential environments that are depicted in a number of better-known utopian schemes,[2] organizing the discussion along the dimension of Choicefulness—that is, opportunities for residents to choose alternative locations, life-styles and living arrangements. At one extreme, there are schemes where the community selects the single best housing setting, and all residents live in that setting. At the other extreme, residents are essentially free to choose a housing setting as long as that setting is not determined to be destructive of the common good. Community-based schemes suggest that the role of social institutions is to check individual tendencies toward selfishness, laziness, and aggression; while individual-based schemes suggest that they are there to remove institutional barriers that obstruct the individual's natural proclivity towards industry, community, and goodwill.

COMMUNITY-BASED SCHEMES

Community-based schemes include Plato's *Republic* (about 394 B.C.), Thomas More's *Utopia* (1516), Johann Valentin Andreae's *Christianopolis* (1619), Charles Fourier's *Phalanstère* (1822), and Etienne Cabet's *Icaria* (1839). Typically in these schemes, the community owns all means of production. There is no money. Goods are exchanged in shops and markets, and food is made available to all by ration from common stores so that while people live simply, there is no poverty and no one is in want. All members are required to do a minimum amount of work, and they all work the same number of hours. As work hours are short, there is considerable leisure time, which is spent in self-improvement and conversation or prayer, not in idle recreation. In Utopia, the family is the basic unit of production, and the whole family is required to follow the father's trade. In other schemes, each individual does a wide variety of jobs and changes jobs frequently, and public duties are rotated. Unpleasant jobs command high wages; menial and degrading work is done by slaves or by an army. In some schemes, the community takes over the role of, or even replaces, the family. In some, the community controls breeding and takes responsibility for the care and education of children. In Icaria, the food that people eat, the clothes they wear, and the newspapers they read are all decided by the community, and committees decide on professional needs and education programs.

The community owns all housing and allocates it rent-free. There is no private property. Residents live in individual houses, or apartments, or (in Plato) in barracks where the men and women live separately. In some schemes the doors have no locks, and the houses are open to the public at all times. Everything is adequate but simple; nothing is luxurious. In Utopia, in order to ensure equity and to avoid personal attachments, residents move to a different house every ten years.

In most schemes the physical environment is less innovative than the social. In Utopia, for example, residents live in three-story buildings, comfortable but basic, set in rows with gardens at the back, along wide straight streets. In Christianopolis, the houses are simple but cramped, three stories high and made of stone, with a wide frontage on the street and a garden at the back. In Icaria, people live in identical houses, each with a back garden.

Neighborhood plans are a bit more interesting. In Utopia, the houses are grouped into quarters, each quarter with its own market and hospital. Groups of thirty families take their meals together (men and women at separate tables) in communal buildings presided over by elected magistrates. There are common nurseries and chapels. Bars, brothels and secret meeting places are forbidden. In Christianopolis, the houses are arranged in sectors, and each sector is zoned for a particular type of activity—farm-based, light industry (mills, bakeries, meat supplies), or heavy industry (smelting and fire-using trades). Icaria is divided into quarters, each with its own school, hospital, temple, shops, public places and monuments. The houses are arranged in blocks of fifteen along each side of the street, with a public building in the middle and one at each end. The blocks are arranged around squares, each with a public garden in the middle.

Fourier is more inventive. His social unit is the Phalanx, a closed, self-sufficient, agricultural community of 1,500 to 1,600 people, supported mainly by horticulture and arboriculture, with some accessory industries. Members all live in small apartments, four rooms or less, which are contained in a cluster of structures, connected by passages and underground tunnels, called a Phalanstery. The Phalanstery also has workshops, halls of industry, a library, a museum, scientific collections, artists' studios, banquet halls, reception salons, an observatory, and temples to the arts and to man's unity with the universe (Figure 4.1). Residents spend little time in their apart-

Residents in Fourier's Phalanstery live and work in a select, closed community. The illustration is from Victor Considérant, *Description du Phalanstère et Considérations Sociales sur L'architectonique, 2e édition, revue et corrigée*, Paris 1848.

Figure 4.1

ments, preferring to spend their time in the public rooms, workshops, fields, conservatories, hot-houses, and stables.

Even in these extreme community-based schemes, individual choice is not altogether absent. In the Phalanstery, for example, residents are permitted to do extra work and earn money on top of their basic wage, and the size of each member's apartment and allocation from the common stores are proportional to the size of the stock that a member holds in the association. In addition, the membership is selected for its diversity, representing "graduated degrees of fortune, age, character, theoretical and practical knowledge."

IN-BETWEEN SCHEMES

Utopian schemes that are essentially community-based, but that are less extreme and make more allowance for individual choice, include Le Corbusier's *Radiant City* (1929, 1967), Edward Bellamy's *Looking Backward* (1888), and Ebenezer Howard's *Garden City* (1898).

In Le Corbusier's Radiant City, the housing is reminiscent of the Phalanstery, but it is at a much larger scale, has a different social organization, and is undeniably urban. In this scheme, most residents live in apartment buildings which are raised above the ground on columns. Each apartment building is fifteen to twenty stories high, and forms an unbroken ribbon winding through a landscaped park (Figure 4.2).

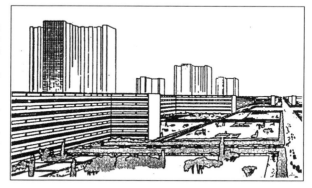

In Le Corbusier's Radiant City residents live in a residential area that includes basic residential services, and is connected by highways to distant industrial and commercial centers. This detail is from *Œuvre Complète 1910-1929.* © 1995 Artists Rights Society (ARS), New York/ SPADEM, Paris.

Figure 4.2

The park occupies all of the ground, with the exception of service roads and streetcar lanes (crossed by pedestrian underpasses), and all major roads are elevated. The park has covered walkways, swimming pools, tennis and basketball courts, and soccer fields, as well as schools, kindergartens, and nurseries. Each apartment building includes shared amenities such as food service, dining rooms, laundries, and household cleaning services, all of which are located along interior streets which take the place of traditional streets. On the roof of the building are gardens, beaches, and hydrotherapy establishments.

The apartments themselves are small and functional. Each is air-conditioned and soundproofed, with a wall of glass that is suitably screened from the sun; and each is no more than 100 meters from a bank of elevators which serves 2,700 residents and takes them down to the elevated front entrance (with parking facilities) and to the ground. The elevated roads, screened behind foliage, link the building entrances with the business center in one direction, and the industrial center in the other.

Edward Bellamy's Boston-of-Tomorrow offers residents a still wider range of housing choices. In this scheme, all work is done by an industrial army, and all people serve in the army until the age of 45; then they retire. Individuals receive annual credit allowances which can be exchanged for services and goods (including house rental), and they make their own housing choices. The houses are of different sizes and cost, the larger being more expensive. All have electricity, and the furnishings are simple and require little maintenance.

The city is divided into wards, and each ward contains public facilities to help ease the burden of housework; for example, there are public laundries, and there are public shops for making and repairing clothes. Each ward has a luxurious public dining hall, pleasure house, and social center within walking distance of all houses in the ward, along sidewalks protected from the weather. People generally eat one meal a day in the public dining hall, where each family has its own private dining room. In addition, each house is not more than ten minutes walk from a large public store—a giant distributing establishment, where everything is displayed by sample and ordered from a central warehouse. Here, one may pick up anything one needs for the home.

Ebenezer Howard's Garden City further relaxes the control of the community and increases individual choice. The Garden City consists of a cluster of towns, separated from one another and from the center city by agricultural land, all connected by roads and express trains. Each town is, in essence, a cooperative: A corporation of residents owns all of the land; it uses the rents to pay off the town's debts and taxes, and any increase in the value of the land accrues to the town. A town cannot grow to more than 30,000 people, and people live in wards of 5,000, each ward being, in a sense, a small town. Within each ward, the housing units are varied in design, some have common gardens and cooperative kitchens, and they stand on tree-lined avenues. Schools, playgrounds, and churches are located in a linear park that cuts through the ward, no more than a two-block walk from any of the houses. All houses are within five blocks of stores and a winter garden for social gathering. Just beyond the stores are the town gardens and major public buildings—town hall, concert and lecture hall, theater, library, museum, picture gallery, and hospital. In the other direction, residents are no more than five blocks from a factory district, served by a railroad line. Just beyond the factories is the zone of agricultural land, dotted with various charitable and philanthropic institutions (Figure 4.3).

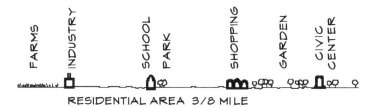

RESIDENTIAL AREA 3/8 MILE

Residents of Howard's Garden City live in a residential area centered around school, church and parks. Separate non-residential areas are located within walking distance of home.

Figure 4.3

Clarence Perry's Neighborhood Unit (1929), like Howard's ward, is a more-or-less self-contained neighborhood, a discrete social and physical entity with its own basic facilities and amenities, that serves as a building block of the city. The size of the Neighborhood Unit is determined by the number of people needed to support an elementary school (estimated at about one thousand families, or 6,000 people), located on a central common, no more than a quarter of a mile from any of the houses (Figure 4.4).

RESIDENTIAL AREA 1/2 MILE

Perry's Neighborhood Unit is a residential part of the city with its own elementary school, community center, parks and shops, all within walking distance of home. For other services, residents travel to other parts of the city.

Figure 4.4

Other institutions whose service areas coincide are also grouped around the common, which is the focus of an active community life. Small parks and recreation spaces are distributed throughout the neighborhood. Internal streets are discontinuous, designed for local traffic only. All through traffic is carried on arterial streets that form the outside boundaries of the neighborhood. Local shops are located at junctions of these arterial streets and are shared with adjacent neighborhoods.

INDIVIDUAL-BASED SCHEMES

Perry's scheme crosses the vague borderline between community-based and individual-based schemes. It shares this position with a variety of proposals for creating facility-dependent settings that would relieve individual residents of their household chores, shifting functions out of the unit and into communal facilities such as common kitchens, day-care centers, laundries, and recreation centers. A number of these proposals, in one form or another, were built into other utopian schemes, and a number of them are incorporated in present-day housing developments (see, for example, McCamant, Durrett, and Hertzman 1994; Fromm 1991). Early proposals of this kind (described in Hayden 1981, 1984) include one by John Pickering Putnam (in 1890) for a network of apartment hotels, each with a common kitchen, laundry, dining room, gentlemen's smoking room, and ladies' parlor. Edward Chambless (in 1910) proposed a continuous apartment house in the countryside with an open promenade on the roof and cooperative housekeeping centers at intervals (shades of Le Corbusier). August Bebel (in 1883) suggested central institutions for the preparation of food, large mess halls, recreation clubs, child-care centers, and kitchenless apartments. Leonard Ladd (in 1890) proposed a block of one-family row houses, with a central kitchen and a covered corridor joining the kitchen and the private dining rooms of the houses. Alice Constance Austin, in Llano del Rio (in 1916), developed a similar scheme—a cooperative colony for 10,000 people, where residents live in kitchenless row houses, each house connected to a central kitchen through a complex underground network of tunnels. Railway cars use these tunnels to bring cooked food, laundry, and other deliveries to connection points, from where small electric cars are dispatched to the basement of each house. A public delivery system handles all shopping needs, so that business traffic at the center is eliminated, resulting in a more restful, pedestrian city.

Individual-based utopian schemes extend individual choice. They emphasize opportunities for individuals to choose their living and working conditions, rather than emphasizing the efficiency of the community as a whole, or a single-minded purpose. Individual-based schemes include William Morris's *News from Nowhere* (1890), Frank Lloyd Wright's *Broadacre City* (1932), and Kevin Lynch's *Place Utopia* (1981).

In Morris's England-of-the-Future, all cities have been leveled and the land returned to woodland and meadow, dotted with villages. Each village has common kitchens and dining rooms, hostels, a guest house, outdoor markets, and paved squares with trees and fountains. The public buildings are of a splendid and exuberant style of architecture.

Outside the villages, the houses are scattered among fields, in forests, and along roads and lanes. People live alone, with house-mates or in communes. The houses have gardens and are pretty and solid, countrified in appearance, of brick or timber and plaster, reminiscent of medieval houses. Some are attached—in courts, or built in short rows with arcades over the sidewalk, some with stores downstairs and guest room upstairs. Others are detached; they include elegant villas and large country houses.

In Wright's Broadacre City, people may live in a city if they choose to do

In Wright's Broadacre City each resident lives on a large parcel of land and has a car. Separate clusters of workplaces, shops, and educational and cultural facilities are located at highway intersections. Copyright © 1995 The Frank Lloyd Wright Foundation.

Figure 4.5

so, but most choose not to. Housing is scattered over the countryside, where each family lives on at least one acre of land (Figure 4.5).

The houses are all different, each responding to the personal life of the individual and in harmony with the site. They have clean simple lines, and are sunny and open to the land. They are made of prefabricated elements, so that they can grow incrementally; and even the poorest families can evolve their own house. For those who prefer apartment living, there are eighteen-story cooperative apartment buildings, each apartment with flower-festooned balconies, each building set in a small park with its own garage, playgrounds and gardens. Other people live on small (three to ten acres) farm units and share equipment and marketing. Artists and pleasure seekers live in mobile houses.

Professionals work out of their homes. Factory workers live a short distance from their place of work, which is small in scale, beautiful, smokeless and noiseless. People buy directly from the factory, and related offices are grouped with the factories they serve. Each factory and farm is within a ten-mile radius of a large wayside market which provides a constant supply of fresh food, fed directly from farm units and private gardens.

People move rapidly over long distances by automobile and noiseless airplane. Cars travel on grade-separated, tree-lined, landscaped highways, three or six lanes wide. All desired forms of production, distribution, self-improvement, and enjoyment are located within a radius of 150 miles of home. At some highway intersections there are service centers; at others there are clusters of public buildings, and at others there are community centers. Dotted about are small garden schools (each with no more than forty students) and small hospitals (sunlit clinics in spacious gardens). Universities are monastic retreats for groups of scholars. Industrial design centers provide a link between arts and industry.

In Lynch's Place Utopia, the natural environment is respected, landscape design is artful, and public activity is visible. All land is in the hands of regional trusts, which serve as long-term managers. Each trust grants leases for the use of land. Any person or group may obtain a lease on a modest but adequate residential space on land, underground, under water, or in the air. For this they pay no rent. Leases are long-term and renewable, but they are not transferable and they revert to the trust.

A region consists of a mosaic of small, diverse territories—houses, workplaces, wastelands, and places of assembly set among trees, farms, and streams. Most people live in small communities and each community maintains its own services and productive facilities. Different communities have a different style of living. There are slow places and fast ones. In addition to small communities, there are intensive centers, accessible to everyone, that are open and active 24 hours a day and serve as foci for regional identity. Territories are distinct, but set close together within a region so that there is a degree of social mixing. If people move away, settlements may be terminated or closed.

Production, consumption, residence, education, and creation go on in one another's presence. No one need travel far to engage in any of these activities. There are schools, but work and learning are combined. Basic requirements—water, food and medicine, elementary education, transportation and communication, utility and clothing—are provided cheaply or free of charge. Other more costly goods are available for purchase. People do not set much store by material wealth.

SUMMARY

Of the Utopian schemes summarized here, some were meant to be read as social commentaries and others as practical proposals; I consider them all to be utopian because none was adopted as a blueprint for development. That is not to say that utopian schemes are without influence. Some have produced experimental communities (for example, Fourier's ideas served as a model for a number of cooperative settlements during the middle of the nineteenth century; Howard's ideas influenced the design of new towns and—much to his dismay[3]—of countless suburban developments; and Perry's ideas about residential planning are generally accepted today (Dahir 1947; Solow, Ham, and Donnelly 1969). Some foreshadowed the future even if they could not be said to have brought it about (for example, Bellamy's supermarket—but with a money economy—and Wright's decentralized city—but without the intimate scale of services—now seem quite commonplace). If some of the ideas appear old-fashioned, naive, or undesirable to us today, it is because the problems they set out to solve are not as central to us as they once were, perhaps because poverty is less extreme, work is less debilitating, and we do not fear imminent attack. In addition, some utopian political solutions have been tried and found wanting (for example, state ownership of property and the means of production have fallen out of favor); technology has created new possibilities (for example, labor-saving devices in the home have reduced the need for shared services, and widespread use of automobiles has reduced the dependency on near-home facilities); and public mores have changed in many ways (for example, women are not relegated to housework, and slavery is not acceptable).

The utopian schemes discussed here have certain common ideas about what makes a good residential area. One is an insistence on the importance of community. In physical terms it usually means groups of houses, sometimes identical, clustered around a center with shared facilities. In social terms, it usually translates into a group of people with shared values, a clear notion of the common good, and a well-established code of behavior. The notion of community also raises the issue of how to distinguish between members and nonmembers, and questions of selection, exclusion, and gatekeeping. Some utopians envision a mix of different social groups and are concerned with the composition and grain of the mix.

Neighborhood facilities are generally seen as the expression of community. Utopians do not, however, agree about what these facilities should be. Sometimes they give priority to facilities that make housekeeping easier (these might include a food shop, hardware store, laundromat), sometimes to those that serve child development (providing an elementary school, a day-care center), or that promote social interaction (providing a community center, sports club, church), or provide personal gratification (providing a beauty parlor, recreation facility, library, video store). In earlier times, convenience required that these facilities be located within walking distance of home, but nowadays there is a question as to whether it is more appropriate to provide access to the highway or hookup to electronic media. Each generation will have to come up with its own answers to these questions.

Many utopian schemes address the spatial relationship of residential and nonresidential uses. Here, too, there are different approaches. One argument is that the two uses are incompatible. A workplace is, by its very nature, active, ordered, often noisy, and public; a home place, on the other hand, should be restful, casual, quiet and private. Work can be laborious, stressful, threatening, and unpleasant, while domestic life should be relaxing, satisfying, entertaining, and make you feel good. Work is an activity that you *have to* do even if you would rather not, while home activity is something that you *want to* do even if you do not have to. This approach, which is embraced by many of the schemes described here, argues for a clear spatial separation between place of work and place of residence, allowing each to develop its own distinctive character. A different approach argues for the integration of home and workplace. Utopians who take the second approach propose a change in the nature of work—reducing its scale, tailoring it to the individual, making it more creative and fulfilling, something that one does for satisfaction rather than just for money, less like work and more like an avocation—so that it is compatible with home life, making workplaces suitable uses within neighborhood areas, even within housing units.

Another common concern of utopian writers is that land be treated as a community resource rather than a medium of exchange. Utopians have consistently taken the view that planning, design, and regulation of the physical environment should recognize the interests of future as well as present users. Proposals include eliminating private property, handing over all land use decisions to the state or to a master architect, or setting up a public land trust to exercise continuing public stewardship of land, manage growth, retain open land for collective use, and encourage technological and design innovations leading to more sustainable communities.

As to the question of whether it is better to live in man-made or natural surroundings, most utopian writers come down firmly on the latter side. This is a view that the suburbs, from their earliest days, have promoted with much success (see, for example, Fishman 1987; Stilgoe 1988). Arguments in favor of natural surroundings note the quality of the air, lower population density, and the need to get back to essentials and to satisfy man's biological urges. Natural surroundings are felt to be good for physical, mental, and moral health. Contemporary plans draw on Howard's ideas for building houses in the countryside, Le Corbusier's ideas for building country-like settings in the city, and Wright's ideas for scattered housing in rural surroundings.

Ideal schemes are a useful source of ideas about a good place to live, but they do have their limitations. First, they go beyond basic needs, and so they only apply in situations that look beyond what is necessary to what is desirable; residents who are concerned with basic issues of survival will gladly settle for less. Second, the link between the quality of one's residential setting and the quality of one's life leaves considerable room for slippage; essential human relationships are not necessarily affected by the design of one's residential setting, so that belief in the healing quality of good design is largely an act of faith. And third, ideal schemes tend to become separated from the conditions that generated them and acquire a life of their own; they must constantly be reassessed in relation to changing circumstances of time and place.

For planners, the practical limitation of ideal schemes is also their greatest value: They describe places not necessarily as they are, but as they "want to be."

NOTES

1. There is not general agreement on this or any other definition of the ideal. For a discussion of some of the arguments, see Levitas 1990.

2. For these descriptions, I have consulted the following original sources: Bellamy 1968; Franklin 1901; Howard 1945; Le Corbusier 1967, 1971; Lynch 1981, pp. 293-317; More 1986; Morris 1969; Perry 1929; Plato 1955; and Wright 1932, 1958. There are also many good secondary sources of information about utopias; I have used Fishman 1982, 1987; Hayden 1976, 1981, 1984; Mumford 1923, 1961; and Tod and Wheeler 1978. The scale of neighborhood varies considerably between one scheme and another. Plato's ideal city is divided into twelve sections of about 2,500 people each (Mumford 1961). Moore's cities have about 1,500 people in residential groupings of about 400. Christianopolis is the size of four city blocks, with 400 people. Fourier's Phalanx consists of 1,500 to 1,600 people divided into 16 tribes and 32 choirs. Howard's Garden City contains 5,000 people in each of six wards. In Le Corbusier's Radiant City, 2,700 people share a bank of elevators. Perry's neighborhood unit houses about 6,000 and Broadacre City between 4,000 and 5,000 (Nelson 1995).

3. See the essay by Howard (in Purdom 1985) in which he complains that the idea of garden cities as a way of checking the growth of the city has become confused with the idea of garden suburbs as a way of extending the city.

The Medieval Street (see page 62) is seen here in
Rijkswehr, France. It is a complex, intimately scaled
residential setting. Photograph by the author.

Figure 5.1

CHAPTER FIVE

Models of Neighborhoods

I n this chapter I will look at environments that designers today regard as prototypes of good neighborhood design. Like ideals, these are highly desirable environments, but unlike ideals they are real and not imaginary; they are places that have been built and lived in. My descriptions of these environments draw upon personal observations, photographs, drawings, and the writings of others.[1] My selection of places is somewhat eclectic—the places are of different sizes, different times, and different cultures —but each represents a particular design theme, a set of design principles that characterizes a family of places; and it is the family of places, more than the place itself, that is the model.

I will discuss three models, organized around the concept of Engagement. In the first model, which I call the *Marketplace*, residents have an opportunity to engage with many, diverse people. In the second model, the *Club,* residents have an opportunity to engage with people who are within their own circle. And in the third model, the *Refuge*, residents are protected from engagements with people other than guests. Despite their differences, all three are models of good neighborhoods.

MARKETPLACE MODELS

Marketplace models are neighborhoods that are active and lively, with many shared facilities. These facilities cater to large and diverse populations, residents as well as nonresidents. Residents tend to spend a great deal of time away from home. Models in this category include the *Medieval Street* and the *Boulevard.*

The Medieval Street

European examples of this model include the medieval quarter in Barcelona and the Shambles in York. Examples can also be found in cities in North Africa, and in the Middle and Far East. Contemporary applications may be found in Ralph Erskine's plan for *Ekerö Kommun* outside Stockholm, Sweden, and Gordon Cullen's drawings (see, for example, Cullen 1961, p. 17).

The Medieval Street is a mixed-use neighborhood with an extremely fine-grain blend of uses and combination of public and private buildings (see Figure 5.1). Traditionally, the street level of the houses is reserved for commerce and services. Each use is small in scale, is in separate ownership, and has clear architectural articulation. A street may contain a concentration of certain activities, but it includes a wide range of uses within a short distance of home. Uses are revealed through open-air displays, show windows, and architectural expression.

Kinesthetic experience is one of the main attractions of the model. The street-space is strongly defined, with few freestanding buildings, and has the feeling of being carved out of a solid building mass. The streets meander, offering a succession of vistas interrupted by sudden unexpected views; road widths vary, building lines are staggered, and facades have projections and overhangs. As a result, the street makes a dramatic visual response to every movement of the observer, and it creates the impression of liveliness and surprise. These qualities are especially striking to newcomers and tourists.

Population density is high, and housing units are small; this creates a facility-dependent setting, one where many residential functions—such as playing, sitting and talking, eating and drinking—spill out into the street space. The diversity of the population is exposed to view, and this adds to the vitality of the setting. Floor heights are low, which allows easy communication between the street level and the upper floors. Traces of the residents—such as glimpses of the interior rooms, washing hanging out, and plants in window boxes—are visible from the street. Street life is intensified in squares or plazas, which tend to be widenings of street junctions and are preferred locations for important public buildings. The whole setting has a quality of transparency—one is aware of what is going on around one.

The general transparency increases the need for devices that will provide residents with a measure of privacy. These include back gardens and courtyards, screens and lattices that can be closed, and living rooms raised above the level of the street so that passersby cannot see in.

The crowded streets can be noisy and unsanitary, and so measures are taken to reduce nuisances and increase security and the level of amenity for residents. In some of the better-known examples the streets have been converted to pedestrian malls. Covered porches increase the comfort and convenience of street life, and overhanging floors provide shelter from sun and rain. Bay windows make it possible for residents to exercise surveillance up and down the street.

With the rise in housing standards, few will say that the medieval street in its original form is an exemplary living environment for today. Many of those who champion it trumpet the quality of the visual experience, and, indeed, most well-known examples attract more sightseers than residents. Other scholars, however, point to qualities of the medieval street that recommend it as a model for our time—not just as a picturesque stage set, but as a good place in which to live (see, for example, Rapoport 1990).

The Boulevard

Well-known examples of the Boulevard include the Avenue des Champs Elysées in Paris, Pall Mall in London, and the Ringstrasse in Vienna. They range from monumental to domestic (Figure 5.2).

Contemporary examples include Kalinin Prospekt in Moscow, Boulevard Victory of Socialism in Bucharest (Cavalcanti 1992) and, on a much more modest scale, streets in Letchworth in England and Seaside in Florida

Camille Pissarro's *The Boulevard Montmartre* (detail, 1897) shows a formal, bustling, lively place in which to live. From the book: *Paintings in the Hermitage* © 1990 by Colin Eisler. Reprinted with permission from Stewart, Tabori and Chang, Publishers, New York.

Figure 5.2

The Boulevard is an important connector that links popular destination points inside and outside the neighborhood. Considerably more space than is necessary is given for this purpose, an extravagance that makes the Boulevard a distinctive feature of the city. Its importance is sometimes accentuated by means of gateways, strong focal buildings, and impressive architecture. It functions as a public promenade. Sidewalks are wide and tree-shaded. Curb-cuts are kept to a minimum so as not to interrupt the continuity of the walkway. Many well-known examples have stores lining the sidewalk, which generate intense pedestrian activity and make the boulevard a good place to see and meet people. There are also, however, tranquil, all-residential examples.

The Boulevard is a clearly bounded, continuous space, whose form is revealed at first glance and affirmed from all viewpoints. Its edges are defined by buildings or tree-lines or both. Individual elements of the setting conform to an overall design which establishes standards for, for example, the treatment of building facades, planting, signage and street furniture. An environment organized at this scale reflects on the resolve and authority of those associated with it. The combination of distinctiveness, centrality, recreational character, amenity, and abundant light for the abutting buildings tends to make the Boulevard a desirable and fashionable address.

The Boulevard serves as a point of connection; it is a promenade that encourages social activity and brings people together. Olmsted envisioned such a place in his plan for Riverside.

The promenade is an open-air gathering for the purpose of easy, friendly unceremonious greetings, for the enjoyment of change of scene, of cheerful and exhilarating sights and sounds, and of various good cheer, to which the people of a town, of all classes, harmoniously resort on equal terms, as to a common property. (Olmsted 1868, in Schuyler and Censer 1992)

The Boulevard serves as a recreational facility, a place for pleasure, exercise, and social interaction. Sometimes there are park strips along the curb, at times in the median. Recreational and cultural facilities and meeting places located along the Boulevard—such as skating ponds, boating lakes, and restaurants—create opportunities for chance meetings. Seating, lighting, fountains, playgrounds, and small parks attract residents and visitors.

CLUB MODELS

Club models are exclusive neighborhoods that use selection and screening procedures to separate those who "belong" there from those who do not. Shared facilities, open only to members and their guests, create opportunities for residents to meet one another and develop a sense of community. Models in this category include the *Green Square*, the *Garden Suburb*, the *Radburn Ideal*, the *Gated Community*, and the *Monastic Colony*.

The Green Square

The seventeenth-century squares of London, such as Bloomsbury and Bedford Squares, were created by great landowners as speculative residential developments. Eighteenth-century examples include the squares, circuses, and crescents of Bath and Edinburgh New Town. Louisburg Square in Boston is a nineteenth century example of the model. Most Green Squares in the United States, however, incorporated something of the New England Green, which meant that in addition to being residential squares they also served as places for meetings and markets, and the surrounding buildings included churches and civic buildings. Examples from the eighteenth century include the squares in Savannah, Georgia; examples from the nineteenth century include Mount Vernon Place and Union Square in Baltimore. A contemporary example is the Green in Kentlands, Maryland.

In this model, the buildings—which may be detached or attached—face a central park and wall it off, creating a cool and quiet oasis (Figure 5.3).

The Green Square (the example shown here is Louisburg Square in Boston) is a quiet residential setting in the heart of the city. It offers abutting residents a shared prospect, front yard, and identity. Courtesy Landslides Aerial Photography, Boston.

Figure 5.3

The park has grass and trees; it is a place for watching, walking, and sitting, not for active games or sports. It may be rectangular, round, or irregular in shape, formal or informal in layout, and it may contain statuary, fountains, and benches.

The park is bounded by streets, which give access to houses that turn their best faces toward the park. Traffic on the bounding streets is neither heavy nor fast and so does not weaken the relationship between houses and park. The square connects with the city grid at the corners or in the centers of the block.

A variation on the model has the green park as an entrance court or quadrangle inside the block. The housing units are still entered from the court, with access to the court through openings in the surrounding building walls.

Individual buildings lining the square are seen together rather than sequentially, and with a common foreground; this creates the impression of a single street facade rather than a collection of individual houses. To ensure that the street facade is visually coherent, individual buildings may be required to conform to an overall plan. The plan may require complete uniformity, or it may establish standards for building lines, materials and setbacks.

The park serves as a collective front yard for residents who live around it. It is a place to relax, and to see familiar people. Sometimes the park is reserved for the use of residents only; it is fenced and gated, owned and run by an association of homeowners.

With the square as a common point of reference and the housing a visual unit, residents tend to think of themselves as a social unit. This perception is reinforced by their shared interest, sometimes their shared responsibility, for the use and appearance of the square. As internal agreement is easier in groups of like-minded people, procedures (sometimes overt, sometimes unstated) are instituted to attract residents who are compatible and to screen out those who are not.

The Garden Suburb

This model dates back to the English ideal of combining the advantages of country living with the conveniences of the city. An early example is Park Village, in London's Regent's Park. The model also includes the classic tree-lined "Elm Street" of many American small towns. The developed model, described by Frederick Law Olmsted as one of "leisure, contemplativeness and happy tranquility," is found in suburban environments designed by Olmsted and the Olmsted firm in the late nineteenth century; it is exemplified in the plans for Riverside, near Chicago, and Roland Park, in Baltimore.

The Garden Suburb is a residential area, separate from the commercial parts of the city, with which it is connected by good roads, and sometimes by public transportation. The arrangement and character of the develop-

In the Garden Suburb the house is set in country-like surroundings, with a front yard at the entrance side and a private yard at the back. The photograph was taken in Roland Park, Baltimore, by the author.

Figure 5.4

ment serve the needs of family life rather than commerce (Figure 5.4).

The model is characterized by streets that are scaled to pedestrian traffic, lined with substantial, varied, freestanding houses, set well back from the road, with grassy front yards sheltered by large trees. There are extensive public parks, with meadows and woods where families can enjoy picnicking and strolling; and there are spaces for active sports and spaces for large public gatherings. All of these public spaces are clearly distinguished from the yards around the houses, which allow each householder to have a private outdoor space. The community includes basic housing-related facilities such as schools, churches, libraries, and essential retail services. These are essentially local facilities, for the convenience of residents. They provide a common point of contact, and they help to build a sense of community. Some models include a private country club.

In some communities, the buildings are subject to restrictive covenants, intended to ensure compatibility of uses and design quality and to preserve and maintain the country-like quality of the setting. The covenants also effectively screen out people who cannot afford to satisfy them. They ensure that Garden Suburbs are exclusive, middle-class communities—even though some may have been originally intended for a range of classes and income groups. Typically, the covenants are administered by a residents' association, which also manages the common spaces and provides local supplementary services.

The Radburn Idea

This model came together in 1928 with the design of Radburn, New Jersey. It was developed by Clarence Stein and Henry Wright (Stein 1951), building on Ebenezer Howard's idea of the Garden City (as interpreted by Raymond Unwin) and Clarence Perry's idea of the Neighborhood Unit. Other examples of the model include the Greenbelt towns of the New Deal, the new town of Columbia in Maryland, and a great many suburban developments. A separate branch of the model follows the work of Le Corbusier and is exemplified by large-scale projects such as Bijlmermeer, outside Amsterdam in the Netherlands.

The heart of the model is the superblock—a large block that contains a central park or green, reserved for pedestrians and cyclists, surrounded by residential units in individual, cooperative, or condominium ownership. Access roads are kept to the outside of the block, and automobile entry to the units is obtained directly off these roads or via a series of cul-de-sac service roads. Cars are parked in shared lots. The houses have a street side facing the service road and a garden side facing the park (see Figure 5.5).

In the Radburn Idea pedestrians enter the house from a pathway that connects with public open spaces and, through underpasses, to schools and the town center. This picture is of Greenbelt, MD in the 1940s. Courtesy of the Greenbelt Museum.

Figure 5.5

In order to reduce automobile traffic within the neighborhood, the streets are separated by function: There are highways for long-distance travel, main roads for traffic between neighborhoods, collector roads that feed the superblock, and service roads that provide direct access to the houses. Pedestrian footpaths are separated from automobile traffic. They form a continuous network that connects the garden side of each house with the park and crosses under the bounding roads to connect adjoining superblocks.

The superblocks are part of an overall community plan that focuses on family life and the safety of children.[2] Facilities such as an elementary school, library, and recreation and community center are located along the pedestrian pathway. Basic shopping facilities with accessory parking are located on a main road or at the edges of the neighborhood. Places of employment are located outside the neighborhood, in other neighborhoods, or in non-residential areas.

The plan also provides for community governance. Usually there is an association of residents which is responsible for the maintenance of the common space and, sometimes, for providing supplemental municipal services such as day care and recreation for residents. There is a concern for the overall appearance of the community, and the plan provides for covenants and controls on all properties; these are administered by the community association. The activities of the association are supported by dues paid by all residents.

The plan anticipates a population of compatible people, usually one that has a high percentage of middle-income families with a high school or college education and with young children.

Gated Communities

This model has become increasingly popular in recent years. There are several variations.

Serviced Apartment Houses. The rental or maintenance fees for each apartment unit pay for shared in-house services, such as a doorman, swimming pool, lounge, and day-care center. A well-known contemporary example is Le Corbusier's *Unité d'Habitation* in Marseilles. In the United States, the model can be traced back to the residential hotels and apartment buildings of the turn of the century. Its present popularity came with the condominium movement, beginning in the late 1960s.

Common Interest Developments. A formal association of single-family houses, where mandatory membership fees are used to provide members with a range of residential services, such as security forces, nursing homes, and recreation centers; these may replace neighborhood services typically provided by public agencies. In the United States, the model dates back to the communitarian movement of the last half of the nineteenth century. It became popular again in the 1960s, with condominium movement.

Cohousing. A group of units with shared facilities, where residents live a communal life-style, sharing the burdens of cooking, housework, and child care and providing companionship and a sense of community. The model harks back to the communes of the 1960s, and before that to the dining clubs and cooperative housing movement of the late nineteenth and early twentieth centuries. Cohousing communities in Europe, in their present form, date back to the 1970s (see; the first cohousing community in the United States was completed in 1991.

In all three variations, the neighborhood is a complete housing package that includes the unit and a range of shared facilities and services that are owned and operated by residents (Figure 5.6).

Cohousing developments are comparable to family compounds. Residents own and share the common facilities, and they cooperate in many home-related activities. The picture is of a community in Beder, Denmark. Photo courtesy of the Cohousing Company.

Figure 5.6

In some cases these facilities and services supplement those of local government; they may include day-care centers, hobby rooms, repair shops, storage facilities, laundries, and guest accommodations. In other cases they substitute for public services, providing, for example, private streets, security officers, shops, offices, and recreation facilities and programs, making the neighborhood largely self-sufficient.

These services are supported through the rental or sale of the units and a mandated annual fee. Typically, they are managed by a residents' association. Membership in the association is not voluntary, and in some models the members are expected to participate in community decisions and chores.

As residential functions are transferred out of the individual units and into one or more community buildings, the units may give up space typically assigned to these functions and be reduced in size; for example, the units may be kitchenless, and the community building may contain a common kitchen and dining room. Residents are able to spend less time caring for the house.

There is often an attempt to have the neighborhood read as a unit, one that expresses and reinforces the social cohesion of the residents. The result is often a uniformity of appearance, clearly defined entrances, and clear display of the neighborhood name. Within the neighborhood, the community buildings are given special prominence, and great care is taken of the outdoor spaces, pedestrian paths, and places where people gather.

Concern for security and tranquility is often behind the popular appeal of this model. Residents see privatization as a way of gaining control over their residential environment. They see the neighborhood as a cocoon that surrounds them and protects them from the larger problems of society, and so measures are taken to make sure that the problems are kept out. Gatekeepers, doormen, or concierges are used to screen outsiders. There is a serious effort to avoid internal conflict by ensuring that residents conform to common norms. Prospective members may be carefully screened for compatibility—typically, they must submit to an interview—or there may be a set of rules, backed by lease or restrictive covenants, that effectively dictate what residents may and may not do. These may say, for example, where and what they may plant, what building materials and colors they may select, how much their house has to cost, what services they must provide to the community, and what constitutes offensive conduct (McKenzie 1994).

Monastic Colonies

This model has its roots in remote religious settlements, such as those on Mount Athos in Greece and at Mount Sinai in Egypt. A contemporary example is the Israeli kibbutz. In the United States, the model refers back to early religious and communitarian settlements such as Armana in Iowa and Brook Farms in Massachusetts; recent examples include Frank Lloyd Wright's Taliesin East in Wisconsin and Taliesin West in Arizona, and Paolo Soleri's Arcosanti in Arizona (Figure 5.7).

In a Monastic Colony, as here in Arcosanti, in Arizona, a select group of residents live together, away from other people. They work and play where they live, in a setting designed to express a collective purpose. Courtesy of the Cosanti Foundation.

Figure 5.7

Few well-known examples were built inside the city, but some of them are now surrounded by development, and there is no reason why the model cannot be located within the now-expanded metropolitan region.

In this model, residents are a tightly knit group, bound by common purposes, activities, and beliefs that go well beyond the desire to share a good residential environment. Usually, they choose to separate themselves and create a society that reflects their own special rules and values. Often they are followers of a charismatic leader.

Residents know one another and engage with one another in work and play. In most models, residents are required to participate in the work of the community, and there is a fine integration of residential, community, and work areas. Some colonies grow their own food; most are not, however, self-sufficient, and they depend on services from outside. The community's unity of purpose tends to be mirrored in the unity of its architectural expression. All parts of the development conform to an overall design. Central functions—which may be housed in studios, dining rooms, prayer halls, drafting rooms, or gardens—are focal and dominant elements. Symbols of the community are incorporated as decorative features. In order to maintain its isolation, the colony seeks to control all of the area within view and protect it from development. The sense of isolation is enhanced if this area is inhospitable to settlement—for example, a desert, lake, ravine, or craggy mountainside. In order to be accepted as a resident of the colony, one may have to demonstrate special qualifications, submit to a trial period and, sometimes, undergo initiation rites. Everyday activities may become ritualized, and so further accentuate the distinction between residents and outsiders. Special accommodations are provided for visitors, and there may be rules governing visitation rights.

REFUGE MODELS

In Refuge models, the housing unit is not part of any neighborhood. The unit is, in essence, a neighborhood in itself, so that all neighborhood residents are members of a single household and all adjoining residents and shared facilities are outside the neighborhood area. As a result, there is little or no special sense of community with the neighbors. Models in this category include the *Country Place* and the *Enclosure.*

The Country Place

Examples of the Country Place include the weekend houses around ancient Rome, the sixteenth-century villas of Palladio, Jefferson's Monticello, the summer homes of the nineteenth century, and the picturesque cottages of Andrew Jackson Downing. Contemporary examples include many of the icons of domestic architecture—Frank Lloyd Wright's Fallingwater was built in a remote country property, Le Corbusier's Villa Savoye in a meadow, Richard Neutra's Kaufman House in the Colorado desert. All of these places were once outside the city, but today, with the expansion of the metropolitan region, many of them are well within the metropolitan area. Country Places are possible within the city.

The model is best located in areas that are secluded, off the beaten track and away from prying eyes. The landscape provides both a backdrop and a view when seen from inside the house. It is designed for pleasure rather than profit, with gardens, lakes, and walks rather than fields, retention basins, and access roads (Figure 5.8).

A Country Place stands alone. It is its own neighborhood. The photograph of Drayton Hall, a pre-revolutionary plantation house outside of Charleston, SC, is by the author.

Figure 5.8

Because the house is seen alone and not in the company of others, it lends itself to an expression of the individuality of the resident and the special qualities of the site. As a result, house and landscape design are often idiosyncratic and whimsical.

Being isolated means that even the nearest facility is some distance away, and so there must be some convenient means of transportation. To cut down on travel, the house is often more-than-usually self-sufficient, with its own recreation and entertainment facilities, vegetable gardens, and guest quarters. It may make extensive use of the grounds for these functions. The only engagements encouraged are those among members of the household, and between them and their guests. Public areas such as living rooms and outdoor living spaces such as terraces and lawns, are the central spaces for these engagements.

Adjoining houses are outside the neighborhood area and residents are only dimly aware of their presence, there are no facilities that bring adjoining residents together, and external facilities also cater to residents of other neighborhoods. As a result, residents are no more likely to engage with their neighbors than with people who live further away, and they may not feel any differently about facilities that are close to home than about those that are not.

The Enclosure

This model consists of houses built around their own, secluded inner courts, completely walled off from the streets outside. Examples include the peristyle houses of Rome and Greece, the courtyard houses of Marrakesh in Morocco, the walled hut-groups of the Southern Sotho in South Africa, the garden-and-pavilion compounds of Suzhou in China, and the aristocratic town houses of sixteenth- and seventeenth-century Paris that face onto enclosed gardens. A contemporary example is the house that Philip Johnson built in Cambridge, Massachusetts (Figure 5.9).

An *Enclosure* includes exterior views, light, and air as part of the unit itself and so reduces residents' dependence on the neighborhood. The house, by Philip Johnson, is in Cambridge, MA. Copyright © 1942 Philip Johnson. Reprinted by permission.

Figure 5.9

In this model, the unit consists of a building or a complex of separate or linked buildings that face into enclosed courtyards or walled gardens. All open spaces that are necessary for light, air, and view are, therefore, interior and private. Windows that face outward onto public or neighboring spaces tend to be screened with shutters or grilles. As with the Country Place, the only facilities for engagement are for members of the household, and they are part of the house—primarily the living rooms (sometimes a special pavilion) and landscaped courtyards. Typically, the individual unit is not seen as a separate object in space, but as part of the street facade, and nothing of the interior is visible from the outside. Often there is a strong architectural expression of the entrance door or gateway.

There are many courtyard houses that do not function as Refuges; but those that do serve both as home and neighborhood area. The unit is the immediate neighborhood, and within it, residents' engagements are limited to members of their household and invited guests. All external facilities lie outside this neighborhood—in nonresidential areas or in Marketplace or Club neighborhoods (which may or may not be part of a compound neighborhood)—and this is where residents see their neighbors.

Enclosures make it possible for residents who live in densely settled areas to maintain a high level of privacy and a sense of separation from their larger setting. People who choose enclosures see these features as highly desirable; they may also want to maintain a high level of security and control over their home environment. For some, it is desirable in order to observe ritual seclusion.

SUMMARY

When we look for common themes in the three categories of models, we find widespread agreement that a good neighborhood gives priority to domestic needs and that it provides both privacy and community. Privacy means that the unit is closed off from its neighbors, and this is accomplished through various techniques, which include spacing the units far apart, inserting screening devices between them, and designing all rooms to face onto an interior court or garden.

Community means that residents interact with one another and are involved in community affairs. This usually means that the neighborhood provides special places that bring people together—members of a family or of a larger community—in situations that encourage interaction. Interactions are more likely in pedestrian environments. They are more likely to be friendly if the activities are in the spirit of play, and so there is an emphasis on leisure facilities such as pleasure gardens, promenades, restaurants, parks, and cultural centers.

These communal facilities tend to be located close to the geographical center of the neighborhood. Designers' preference for the center is hardly surprising, because a central focus is a basic and powerful ordering device. The neighborhood center represents, however, not only a spatial but also a social focus; it is the symbolic center of the neighborhood. The design of the center celebrates community; it is pleasurable and spiritually uplifting. This is desirable because good design has both educational and social value; it teaches taste and refinement, and it has a civilizing influence, reducing the likelihood of conflict.

The grand fact, in short, that [the residents] are christians, loving one another, and not Pagans, fearing one another, should be everywhere manifest in the complete-ness, and choiceness, and beauty of the means they possess of coming together, of being together, and especially of recreating and enjoying them together on common ground, and under common shades. (Olmsted 1868, in Schuyler and Censer 1992)

The models also have significant differences. Some assume that one can-not count on the power of design to civilize the "Pagans;" there are people in society who simply do not get along and are better kept apart. Good designs protect the neighborhood from larger problems outside; they bring the *right* people together, which generally means that they attract certain people and keep others out. Techniques include targeting the units to a particular economic group and creating private neighborhoods with restricted membership.

Another difference among the models is their attitude toward change. Some favor a setting in which there is constant change—one with a wide range of land uses, that is stimulating and attracts visitors, where one can see and meet new people. Other models favor a setting that is comforting and familiar; a setting where one is known, is sure to meet people one knows, and is protected from outsiders.

NOTES

1. The following were particularly useful sources of information. For the *Medieval Street*: Cullen 1961; de Wolfe 1966; Hillier and Hanson 1984; Kostof 1991; Olsen 1986, Rapoport 1990, Rubenstein 1992, and Sitte 1889. For the *Boulevard*: Girouard 1985; Kostof 1991; Olsen, 1986; Rasmussen 1973; and Rubenstein 1992. For the *Green Square*: French 1978; Giedion 1946; Rasmussen 1973; Webb 1990; and Zucker 1959. For the *Garden Suburb*: Fishman 1987; Moudry 1990; Olmsted 1868 (Report to the Riverside Improvement Company), 1871. For the *Radburn Idea*: Birch 1980; Dahir 1947; Howard 1898; Perry 1929; Solow et al. 1969; and Stein 1966. For *Gated Communities*: Alpern 1975; Fromm 1991; Hancock 1980; McCamant, Durrett, and Hertzman 1994; and McKenzie 1994. For *Monastic Colonies*: FitzGerald 1981; Forsyth and Weitzmann (no date); and Hayden 1976. For the *Country Place*: Fishman 1982, 1987. For the *Enclosure*: Blaser 1979; Dennis 1988; Macintosh 1973; Walton 1956; and Schwerdtfeger, 1982.

2. Laurence Gerckens, in his 1995 series of lectures on American city planning, pointed out that the completion of the pedestrian pathways in Radburn coincided with the shift in policing from foot- to automobile-patrols. This did not allow the paths to be policed and residents felt that they were unsafe.

CHAPTER SIX

Mythical Neighborhoods

M ythical neighborhoods are places that people imagine, perhaps hear or read about, or see in pictures or the movies. They are general impressions rather than specifications of good places to live, impressions that are popular, persistent and recurring, and they arouse deep, commonly felt emotions. Some of these myths evoke images of the city, others of the country; all of them influence what residents see and what they look for in urban neighborhoods.

In this chapter I will present four popular myths through images taken from literature, poems, paintings, cartoons, newspaper articles, and films. Each myth incorporates a particular set of land uses and physical forms, and so a particular Ambience. I call these myths *Paree*, the *Hamlet, Arcadia* and *Suburbia*.

THE MYTH OF PAREE

This is a vision of the Big City at its very best and most exciting. It is the Montmartre of Gertrude Stein and Picasso. The setting is lively, impressive, and inspiring. The people who live here are knowledgeable, sophisticated, and in the vanguard of what is new. They know interesting and important people, and do interesting and important things.

> The Boulevards are blazing. Half closing the eye it seems as if one saw on the right and left two rows of flaming furnaces. The shops cast floods of brilliant light across the street, and encircle the crowd in a golden dust. The kiosks, which extend in two interminable rows, lighted from within, with their many coloured panes, resembling enormous Chinese lanterns placed on the ground, or the little transparent theatres of the marionettes,

Gustave Caillebotte's painting *Jeune Homme à sa Fenêtre* (1875) shows the city center as an elegant and interesting place in which to live. Private collection, Paris.

Figure 6.1

In the 1931 film *The Easiest Way*, a dramatic view of downtown is used to suggest that this stylish apartment has a good address. Copyright © by Universal City Studios, Inc. Courtesy of MCA Publishing Rights, a Division of MCA Inc.

Figure 6.2

give to the street the fantastic and childlike aspect of an Oriental fete. The numberless reflections of the glasses, the thousand luminous points shining through the branches of the trees, the inscriptions in gas gleaming on the theatre fronts, the rapid motion of the innumerable carriage lights, that seem like myriads of fireflies set in motion by the wind, the purple lamps of the omnibuses, the great flaming halls opening into the street, the shops which resemble caves of incandescent gold and silver, the hundred thousand illuminated windows, the trees that seem to be lighted, all these theatrical splendours, half-concealed by the verdure, which now and then allows one to see the distant illuminations, and presents the spectacle in successive scenes—all this broken light, refracted, variegated, and mobile, falling in showers, gathered in torrents, and scattered in stars and diamonds, produces the first time an impression of which no idea can possibly be given.

Eduardo de Amicis 1882, in Girouard 1985, p. 296.

Here was my city, immense, overpowering, flooded with energy and light; there below lay the river and the harbor, catching the last flakes of gold on their waters, with the black tugs, free from their barges, plodding dockward, the ferry-boats lumbering from pier to pier, the tramp steamers slowly crawling toward the sea, while the rumbling elevated trains and trolley cars just below me on the bridge moved in a restless tide. And there was I, breasting the March wind, drinking in the city and the sky, both vast, yet both contained in me, challenging me, beckoning me, demanding of me something that it would take more than a lifetime to give, but raising all my energies by its own vivid promise, to a higher pitch. In that sudden revelation of power and beauty all the confusions of adolescence dropped from me, and I trod the narrow, resilient boards of the footway with a new confidence that came not from my isolated self alone but from the collective energies I had confronted and risen to.

Lewis Mumford 1982, p. 130.

Four or five o'clock. Grey-pink, iridescent air like the enamel inside a shell. We inhaled Paris with open nostrils, cutting across it on foot, diagonally from north toward the Seine. The moist flowers, the vegetables, the coffee, the damp pavement, the mingling odors of night and day. Where the wide sidewalks changed into a market place, we took pleasure in submerging ourselves in the human stream, its color, movement, gestures and glances. We lost count of the streets, we forgot about our own existence. The promise was infinite, it was the promise of life.

Czeslaw Milosz 1931, in Mansfield 1990, p. 27.

Rival of Athens, London, blest indeed,
That with thy tyrants had the wit to chase
The prejudices civil factions breed,
Men speak their thoughts and worth can win its place.
In London, who has talent, he is great.

Voltaire, in Voltaire, *1947, p. 54. Translated by H. H.*
Brailsford. By Permission of Oxford University Press.

From my own second-floor living room in Notting Hill I can look several hundred yards in four different directions down four different sets of streets. I can watch fifty different neighborhood cats, rubbing against the legs of passers-by, stalking birds, and nosing hopefully among the garbage cans. I can watch the first wave of school children hurrying past, with or without their mothers, alternating with smart young girls off to television studios or estate agents' offices, and the second wave of senior citizens, out for their laboured morning constitutionals. I can see, at various times, lovers, roller-skaters, policemen, the local busybody, the local lavatory attendant, who exercises dogs for a moderate fee, and the local cripple, progressing slowly past in his electric chair, waving to people on the pavement. Twice a year a religious procession goes past, once a year the steel bands and dancers of the Notting Hill carnival. I am within two to ten minutes walk of a street market, at least six churches and chapels, four cinemas, four good restaurants and many bad ones, and at least twenty pubs. I am twenty-five minutes from Piccadilly Circus. The area has its disadvantages, but it does me well enough.

Mark Girouard 1985, p. 382.

I not only was totally in love with Manhattan from the earliest memory, I loved every single movie that was set in New York, every movie that began high above the New York skyline and moved in. To me, people who lived in Manhattan would go from the Copa to the Latin Quarter; they'd hear jazz downtown, they'd go up to Harlem, they'd sit at Lindy's until four in the morning. Then they'd come back home and go up in their elevators to their apartments, and their apartments were not like my apartment in Brooklyn, where six million people lived together and it was small. They'd go to these apartments that were often duplexes. It was astonishing. It was also so seductive that I've never recovered from it.

Woody Allen, in Lax 1991, p. 21.

No dramatist could prosper in a village, and I can think of few novelists who, lacking an acquaintance with cities, wrote anything but pious nonsense. The peace of the country is the peace of a deserted battlefield, its silence the silence of an empty room. The excitement of a city is its sense of infinite possibility, of its ceaselessly becoming something else.

Lewis Lapham 1976.

Impressionism might not have developed into a full-fledged movement if Claude Monet, Auguste Renoir, Alfred Sisley and Frederic Bazille had not met in 1862 in the Paris cafes and restaurants. The history of modern art is largely the history of chance encounters that developed into irreversible historic trends. Humankind has progressively discovered its intellectual and emotional wealth through the unpredictable encounters and confrontations made possible by life in the city.

Rene Dubos, in Piel and Segerberg 1990, p. 320.

The public will have an opportunity from 11 a.m. to 3 p.m. Saturday to recapture some of this Baltimore history, when the Bolton Hill Neighborhood Association and Historic Mount Royal Terrace present "Secret Gardens Revealed," a tour of 10 homes and gardens in Reservoir Hill.

Judy Estes, who began restoring her 101-year-old Reservoir Street house in 1973, and found pre-World War I graffiti under some wallpaper, said tickets for the tour will cost $5, and can be bought Saturday at 713 Reservoir Street.

"It's very rewarding to me to live in a house with a history," said this member of the current crop of the hill's pioneers.

The Sun, *May 8, 1995, p. 2B.*

Gradually our placid country life lost its appeal as we realized that our kids were paying heavily for our rural idyll. Admitting that our sons had little to do and nowhere to go (the local hangout is a traffic island in the center of town) made me confront the fact that I had never stopped missing the buzz of city life. By April we had decided to move to the city.

Meanwhile, I tell this story to people who ask why we moved and don't believe me, no matter what I say. I tell them how happy it makes me to lose myself in the reassuringly anonymous and various crowds of strangers going off to work. I tell them that no matter how I loved our quiet country road, it finally offered little to compare with the thrill of long brisk walks along the busy streets of Manhattan. Living in the country required an active inner life and the energy to make things happen; here in the city that world thrums around us with an energizing momentum independent of our inner resources.

Francine Prose 1996.

THE MYTH OF THE HAMLET

In the Hamlet, people are tied to one another by a strong sense of community. It is Mayberry and Grover's Corners. It is small in scale, familiar, and distinctive. The people are friendly, without guile or pretension, and ready to offer a helping hand in time of need.

This poster suggests a place that has all one needs for a full residential life, but remains manageable in size: A small-town place. From the National Center on Child Abuse and Neglect, Washington, DC.

Figure 6.3

The Neighborhood. That's what residents call Little Italy. "I've lived here for 69 years," screen painter Frank Cipollini says proudly. "All my life. I was born here on the second floor. I still sleep in the same bed in the same bedroom that I did when I was a child."

"You got everything you need in the neighborhood," says Mary, Frank's wife of 44 years. "It's all at your fingertips. If you never wanted to leave you wouldn't have to."

The young professionals work downtown or in Fells Point and find the relative security and convenience of Little Italy a winning combination. They are regarded with some degree of suspicion by the old timers. "We know just about everybody except the young people," reports Frank. "I mean, we say hi to them, but they're not like the *paesans.*"

This is a neighborhood where family is treasured above all else, and the neighborhood becomes a sort of family, too.

"There's this little old lady who lives across the street," says Mary. "Every once in a while, she leans out her window and hollers, 'Mary, I want a cup of coffee.'"

"And Mary makes her a cup of coffee and brings it over there," says Frank.

"If the lady next door, she's 90 years old, wants her air conditioning turned on and she can't do it, Frank will go over there and do it," says Mary. "If the lady up the street don't feel good and is stuck in bed, you bang on her door and ask, `I'm going to the store. Do you need something?'"

"We look out for each other here in Little Italy," says Frank. "That's the way it's always been and it's the way it always will be."

Weiss 1994.

The couple stumbled on a house in need of repair in Beaumont Avenue. As they stood on the front lawn, a neighbor from across the street walked over and introduced himself. "Right there, I said this is where I want to live," Mrs. White recalled yesterday. "I want to live where people care about people."

The Sun *September 21, 1991, p. B1.*

"Hampden is like one big family," sums up Kathy Turner. And she should know. Mrs. Turner grew up in Hampden and is part of four generations of Turners who live within walking distance of each other. Many residents echoed her assessment of the neighborhood.

"You can walk down the street and you'll always know somebody," says Viola Herd. The 35-year old waitress grew up in Hampden and moved back five years ago with her husband, Willam, 42. "The best thing about it is the feeling of a small-town community," [Mr. Smith] says. But the neighborhood's friendly familiarity doesn't always extend to outsiders, so newcomers should plan to stay a while if they want to feel accepted in the community, according to Mr. Wheatley.

The self-contained nature of the neighborhood is by design, since it was a bustling textile mill town before it was officially incorporated into Baltimore in 1888.

Tanya Jones 1994.

This May, my husband and I retired to the city after 25 years of living in Baltimore County. I was born in a row house, love them and am glad to be back. True, there is no central air, but here is a cleaner, a movie theater, food stores, video stores, banks and friendly neighbors close at hand. With my children grown, I am back where I want to be.

Letter to The Sun, *September 29, 1992, p. 8A.*

There were two drug stores crammed with delights like ice cream sodas. But they weren't within my economic reach. I could only look at them, as I did—furtively—the girlie magazines. The druggist, Dr. Garner, was given to calling my mother. "Henry's down here looking at those books again; what shall I do?"

"Send him right home...and watch him across that busy street; he's sure to be killed."

So right there in my neighborhood there seemed to be everything—a hint of life's possibilities mixed in with all kinds of people. And it was within walking distance. It was small—just my size—and they even knew my name.

That's what a neighborhood does, it seems to me. It takes the world—or at least a slice of the world—the more complete and varied the better, and makes it just our size—where our lives, with our neighbors, can be rich and meaningful and significant—where they know our names.

Anton Nelessen 1994, p. xi.

I consider myself enormously fortunate to have grown up in a house that my parents owned, which had a yard and a vegetable garden, and was located in a village. Life in a village offered many advantages. I experienced what it was like to be able to walk to school, church, the park, the post office, Hazsacker's woods, a viable downtown, and my summer and after-school jobs. I was part of a neighborhood and a community. Most of the people in the village knew my parents and knew my name. I experienced tree-lined streets and the joy of riding my bicycle. I could pedal across the village in about 15 minutes. The village was surrounded by farms and woods and a canal and river on one side. The village was important in the biography of my past; it was a small community.

Interview quoted in Langdon 1995, p. 195.

Illustration by Frederic Dorr Steele, reprinted from "Committee of One," *The Elks Magazine*, July 1932.

Figure 6.4

Imagine. It is five o'clock in the evening, and Anne is glad the work day is over. As she pulls into her driveway, she begins to unwind at last. Some neighborhood kids dart through the trees, playing a mysterious game at the edge of the gravel parking lot. Her daughter yells, "Hi Mom!" as she runs by with three other children. Instead of frantically trying to put together a nutritious dinner, Anne can relax now, spend some time with her children, and then eat with her family in the common house. Walking through the common house on her way home, she stops to chat with the evening's cooks, two of her neighbors who are busy preparing dinner—broiled chicken with mushroom sauce—in the kitchen. Several children are setting the tables. Outside on the patio, some neighbors share a pot of tea in the later afternoon sun. Anne waves hello, and continues down the lane to her own house, catching glimpses into the kitchens of the houses she passes. Here a child is seated, doing homework at the kitchen table; next door, John reads his ritual after-work newspaper. After dropping her things off at home, Anne walks through the birch trees behind the houses to the child-care center where she picks up her four-year-old son, Peter. She will have some time to read Peter a story before dinner, she thinks to herself.

McCamant, Durrett, and Hertzman 1994, pp. 11–12.

More than 40 years ago, E. B. White etched a city of small, self-sufficient villages in his tautly descriptive essay "Here is New York." "Each area is a city within a city within a city. Thus no matter where you live in New York, you will find within a block or two a grocery store, a barbershop, a newsstand and shoeshine shack, an ice-coal-and-wood cellar, a dry cleaner, a laundry, a delicatessen, a flower shop, an undertaker's parlor, a movie house, a radio-repair shop, a stationer, a haberdasher, a tailor, a drug store, a liquor store, a shoe-repair shop."

Some of these establishments, like the coal places, have disappeared.

Others, like shoe repair shops, are often hard to find. Chain stores have homogenized some consumer choices. Named neighborhoods, like Turtle Bay, Bloomingdale, Yorkville, have been absorbed into their surroundings while TriBeCa and SoHo have emerged. In the meantime, neighborhood institutions that Mr. White never knew have come to define the tiny communities—nail salons, pizza parlors, video renters, Korean all-night grocery-stores-cum-florists-cum-delicatessens, and addiction treatment centers

Michael Kaufman 1994.

It is difficult to overestimate the vigor and persuasiveness of the belief that local communities should maintain their own identity and manage their own affairs. Small communities apparently experienced the sense of self-identity, the compactness, the self-sufficiency necessary to produce interdependence and equality and the sharing of common values and objectives. Small towns deserved their autonomy because they were the natural home of democracy. In this way, the image became a legacy, and like all legacies, was accepted as something precious and therefore useful for each generation.

Wood 1958, pp. 20, 27, 28.

THE MYTH OF ARCADIA

Arcadia is a hideaway, a refuge, a place of perfect peace. It is Shangri-La, the house of the Seven Dwarfs. To live here is to be removed from the outside world and protected from its problems. It is a place to be alone with one's thoughts, inspired by the beauty of the physical surroundings.

The morning sunshine descended like an amber shower-bath on Blandings Castle, lighting up with a heartening glow its ivied walls, its rolling parks, its gardens, outhouses, and messuages, and such of its inhabitants as chanced at the moment to be taking the air. It fell on green lawns and wide terraces, on noble trees and bright flower-beds.

P. G. Wodehouse 1980, p. 9.

And he thought of what it would be like to have one day a horse of one's own. He would call it Rider, and mount it at morning when the grass was wet, and from the horse's back, look out over great, sun-filled fields, his own. Behind him stood his house, great and rambling and very new, and in the kitchen his wife, a beautiful woman, made breakfast, and the smoke rose out of the chimney, melting into the morning air.

James Baldwin 1970.

A View of the Mountain Pass Called the Notch of the White Mountains—Crawford Notch by Thomas Cole (1839) shows arcadia as a place where one can live as part of the natural order of things, get away, and be a self-reliant individualist. Courtesy the National Gallery of Art, Washington, DC, Andrew W. Mellon Fund.

Figure 6.5

Walt Disney's Cottage of the Seven Dwarfs, from the movie *Snow White and the Seven Dwarfs,* is an isolated, romantic house in a clearing of the woods. It is the essential arcadian setting. © The Walt Disney Company.

Figure 6.6

One also finds arcadia in man-made surroundings. Architect Pierre Koenig's 1958 Case Study house in Los Angeles is clearly in an urban setting, but the city appears as a backdrop, a distant abstraction of lights and patterns. Photo by Julius Shulman, Los Angeles.

Figure 6.7

Mr. Blandings, his wife by his side, stood looking out through the amethyst window lights at an arc of beauty that made them both cry out. The land rushed downward to the river a mile away; then it rose again, layer after layer, plane after plane of hills and higher hills lighter beyond them. The air was luminous, and there were twenty shades of browns and greens in the ploughed and wooded and folded earth.

"On a clear day you can see the Catskills," said the real-estate man.

Eric Hodgins 1947, p. 12.

To live in such a place as this, to die in such a place, if ever death could conquer the everlasting joy of such a life! What daring dream had made my heart beat so violently a moment ago when Mastro Vincenzo had told me he was getting old and tired, and that his son wanted him to sell his house? What wild thoughts had flashed through my boisterous brain when he had said that the chapel belonged to nobody? Why not to me? Why should I not buy Mastro Vicenzo's house, and join the chapel and house with garlands of vines and avenues of cypresses and columns supporting white loggias, peopled with marble statues of gods and bronzes of emperors and...I closed my eyes, lest the beautiful vision should vanish, and gradually realities faded away into the twilight of dreamland.

Axel Munthe 1950, p. 10.

Rounding a bend in the river, they came in sight of a handsome, dignified old house of mellowed red brick, with well-kept lawns reaching down to the water's edge.

"There's Toad Hall," said the Rat, "and that creek on the left, where the notice-board says, 'Private. No landing allowed,' leads to his boathouse, where we'll leave the boat. The stables are over there to the right. That's the banqueting hall you're looking at now—very old that is. Toad is rather rich, you know, and this is really one of the nicest houses in these parts."

Kenneth Grahame 1933, pp. 25–26.

"If you could live any way you wanted," Sarah had once told him, "I suppose you'd end up on a desert island with no other human beings."

"Why! That's not true at all," he'd said, "I'd have you, and Ethan and my sisters and brothers..."

"But no people. I mean, people there just by chance, people you didn't know."

"Well, no, I guess not," he'd said, "Would you?"

Anne Tyler 1985, p. 47.

Sometimes, in a summer morning, having taken my accustomed bath, I sat in my sunny doorway from sunrise till noon, rapt in a revery, amidst the pines and hickories and sumachs, in undisturbed solitude and stillness, while the birds sang around or flitted noiselessly through the house, until by the sun falling in at my west window, or the noise of some travellers' wagon on the distant highway, I was reminded of the lapse of time.

Henry David Thoreau 1968, p. 139. (Original publication 1854)

Le Corbusier, from *Œuvre Complète 1938-1946.* © 1995 Artists Rights Society (ARS), New York/ SPADEM, Paris.

Figure 6.8

THE MYTH OF SUBURBIA

Suburbia is an automobile-oriented place consisting almost entirely of newer, single-family homes, and with a name such as Happy Acres, Rolling Ridge or Forest Glen. It has all of the comforts and conveniences of modern life, and is devoted to the welfare and protection of family life.

[Shady Hill is] a *banlieue* and open to criticism by city planners, adventurers, and lyric poets, but if you work in the city and have children to raise, I can't think of a better place. My neighbors are rich, it is true, but riches in this case mean leisure, and they use their time wisely. They travel around the world, listen to good music, and given a choice of paper books at an airport, will pick Thucydides, and sometimes Aquinas. Urged to build bomb shelters, they plant trees and roses, and their gardens are splendid and bright.

John Cheever 1978, p. 258.

Charlesbridge appeared to us as a kind of Paradise. The wind blew all day from the southwest, and all day in the grove across the way the orioles sang to their nestlings. We were living in the country with the conveniences and luxuries of the city about us. The neighborhood was in all things a frontier between city and country.

William Dean Howells 1880, p. 12–14.

Middle-sized gracefully fretted wooded houses built in the late nineties and early nineteen hundreds, with small front and side and more spacious back yards, and trees in the yards, and porches. These were softwooded trees, poplars, tulip trees, cottonwoods. There were fences around one or two of the houses, but mainly the yards ran into each other with only now and then a low hedge that wasn't doing very well. There were few good friends among the grown people, and they were not poor enough for the other sort of intimate acquaintance, but everyone nodded and spoke, and even might talk short times, trivially, and at the two extremes of the general or the particular, and ordinarily nextdoor neighbors talked quite a bit when they happened to run into each other, and never paid calls.

James Agee 1967, p. 3.

The myth of Suburbia differs from the other three in that it tends to mock rather than praise the place. Suburbia is depicted as being without traditions. It is known for its cookie-cutter houses, tract developments, car pools, PTA meetings, cookouts, lawn mowers, picture windows, station wagons and Tupperware parties. Its residents live in idyllic surroundings, but they are alienated, disillusioned, trapped and confined, victims of empty materialism, their relationships marked by pettiness, hypocrisy, and superficial values (Riley 1981).

Above me on the hill were my home and the homes of my friends, all lighted and smelling of fragrant wood smoke like the temples in a sacred grove, dedicated to monogamy, feckless childhood, and domestic bliss but so like a dream that I felt the lack of viscera with much more than poignance —the absence of that inner dynamism we respond to in some European landscapes. In short, I was disappointed. I sensed some disappointing greenness of spirit in the scene although I knew in my bones, no less, how like yesterday it was that my father left the Old World to found a new.

John Cheever 1978, p. 433.

"Are you sure this is it?" asked my husband.
"I'm sure," I said tiredly. "This is the eighth house from the corner, and the builder always staggers his styles so that they won't all look alike. I counted them. There were the Williamsburg, the Richmond, the Shenandoah, and the Pee Wee, a Williamsburg, a Richmond, a Shenandoah, and this is our Pee Wee."

Erma Bombeck 1972, p. 9.

She stood looking out her picture window and for the first time became completely aware of the picture windows across the street. For a horrid moment she stood there, staring. Then she ran to her door and tore it open, looking up and down the block. And everywhere she looked, she saw houses exactly like her own, row on row of them, the same, the same, the same.

John Keats 1952, p. 50.

Brenda Starr. Artists Fradon and Schmick. Reprinted by permission: Tribune Media Services, Chicago.

Figure 6.9

I am a fugitive from the suburbs of all large cities. God preserve me from women who dress like *toreros* to go to the supermarket, and from cowhide dispatch cases, and from flannels and gabardines. Preserve me from word games and adulterers, from basset hounds and swimming pools and frozen canapes and Bloody Marys and smugness and syringa bushes and P.T.A. meetings.

John Cheever 1978, p. 289.

For every morning the neighborhood emptied, and all vital activity, it seemed, set forth for parts unknown. The men left in a rush. And inside all the forgotten houses in all the abandoned neighborhoods, the day of silence and waiting had begun.

Annie Dillard 1987, p. 15.

What is there to do with her free time in Rolling Knolls?
    She can take her children out to play. Only this, and nothing more.
    And where will she take them?
    Why—to the front lawn, of course. There is no other place. There is no school- or churchyard, no community center. Mary has no car. The shopping center is two miles away; the bust stop one mile away. Mary will therefore take her children out to play on the tiny lawn just like everyone else.

John Keats 1952, p. 138.

Suburbia is often shown in aerial photographs in order to emphasize the uniform house designs and ubiquitous street patterns. Photo courtesy of the Library of Congress.

Figure 6.10

In *The Little House,* a popular children's book by Viginia Lee Burton, a house sees its surroundings destroyed by suburban development. The story ends happily—the house is moved out into the countryside. Copyright 1942 by Virginia Lee Demetrios, renewed 1969 by George Demetrios, reprinted by permission of Houghton Mifflin Company. All rights reserved.

Figure 6.11

There is little doubt that Suburbia refers to the type of neighborhood that is most characteristic of the suburbs, which is where most people in the United States have chosen to live. Why is the myth so often so unflattering? The explanation, I believe, is that Suburbia is an evolving myth, in the process of being born out of the older myths of the Hamlet and Arcadia, with which it is still entangled. Seen as a Hamlet it looks too superficial and lacking a sense of community, and seen as Arcadia it looks overly conforming and lacking privacy. I believe that in time Suburbia will evolve as its own myth, neither No-Hamlet nor No-Arcadia, one that represents what it is and not what it is not.

The four neighborhood myths bring out the different and sometimes contradictory qualities that we look for in a good place to live, Each myth represents a particular set of qualities carried it to its logical conclusion. Paree is the last word in glamour and self-importance, the Hamlet in simplicity and community, Arcadia in tranquility and privacy, and Suburbia in comfort and convenience. All of these things are important, but in varying degrees to different people. By giving shape to our ultimate desires, the myths help us to decide on the compromises that we will make when choosing a place in which to live.

CHAPTER SEVEN

Satisfactory Neighborhoods

I n this chapter I will discuss the qualities that residents themselves associate with good places to live. With this information and information from the earlier chapters I will derive a list of the qualities that are
most commonly associated with good neighborhoods. In a later chapter, I
will use these qualities to build a typology.

Residential satisfaction studies—systematic surveys that ask residents what
qualities they associate with a good housing environment—are a surpris-
ingly recent form of enquiry; few studies date back before the 1960s. Most
of these studies use a random sample of residents, although some use special population groups, such as residents of central areas, the suburbs, middle-
income neighborhoods, or public housing projects. The typical procedure
is to prepare a list of potentially desirable qualities (such as "a friendly
place," "convenient public transportation," and "lots of things to see and
do"). Sometimes the items on the list are elicited from the residents, but
more often they are provided by the researchers. Usually the residents are
asked to rate these qualities according to whether they like them or are
bothered by them in the place where they presently live, but sometimes
they are asked to rate them in relation to "an ideal place to live" and sometimes in relation to what they themselves look for in choosing a place to
live.

Respondents are given a rating scale. The scale may be one of importance ("How important is it for a neighborhood to have each of the following qualities?") or the questions may be phrased in terms of satisfaction
("How satisfied are you with your present neighborhood?") or liking ("What
things do you especially like about living in this neighborhood?"). Some
studies ask residents to rate the area as a place to live, others ask them the

reasons why they chose to move to this kind of neighborhood (usually center-city or suburban) or about their intentions to move to another place. In some studies it is their neighborhood that residents are asked to rate; in other studies, residents are asked to rate their housing or residential area, their existing environment, block, community, or town. In several studies residents are asked to respond to photographs of neighborhood scenes. Shlay and Digregorio (1985) ask residents to respond to vignettes made up out of randomly assembled elements. We assume that all of these questions tap the same vein of responses, but we cannot be sure.

There are other reasons why the findings of residential satisfaction studies should be interpreted with care. In the first place, people tend not to extend themselves beyond what they feel is reasonable; they are bounded by their expectations and by the range of options that are (or are considered to be) currently available to them. In this way, for example, large yards and lots of greenery are given more importance by people who live in the suburbs (where they are likely to have them) than by people who live in the center city (where they are not). Amenities that are taken for granted tend to be overlooked, while those that are at risk take on exaggerated importance. For example, residents in unsafe neighborhoods are more likely to mention safety as being important. In familiar settings, residents who have adapted to sources of dissatisfaction and stress tend to downplay their negative value (Fried 1986; Campbell, Converse, and Rogers 1976; Brower 1988). A respondent in my own research provides an extreme example: Although she expressed the need for elaborate safety precautions (she minded her own business, and stayed close to home so that at the hint of trouble she could whip inside and shut the door), she did not find any problems with her neighborhood. Others might have problems, but she did not; she had learned how to cope. When asked to rate an unfamiliar setting, residents sometimes base their assessments on a stereotype. For example, residents who know in-town neighborhoods with poor schools think of poor schools as an inherent feature of in-town neighborhoods.

Another problem with residents' evaluations is that different subsets of residents tend to use different standards. For example, residents who are younger, married, and female heads of families, and families with many children, consistently record less satisfaction with any given housing setting, and their satisfaction ratings are more strongly tied to perceptions of crime, run-down properties, and the friendliness and similarity of neighbors (Galster and Hesser 1981).

Perhaps the main weakness of these studies is that they tend to regard residential satisfaction as the measure of a good environment, whereas it is more likely the measure of a good fit between the individual and the environment, so that different individuals may find satisfaction in different environments (Pervin 1968). It is important to disentangle what the responses reveal about the settings from what they reveal about the respondents themselves.

A review of the qualities that residents associate with satisfaction reveals a great many inconsistencies. Many of the qualities form bipolar pairs, where a higher rating on one means greater satisfaction for some respondents but not for others. For example, some people think that a good neighborhood must include a full complement of community facilities, others that it is perfectly acceptable to rely on facilities outside the neighborhood; some think that it must include different types of people, others that all residents must be of the same class, income, race or ethnic background; some think that neighbors must have strong social ties with one another, others ask only that they be civil and considerate; some think that a good neighborhood must cater primarily to families with young children, others favor nontraditional households; some think that it must be tranquil and quiet, others enjoy activity and liveliness; some think that it must be devoted more-or-less exclusively to housing, while others require the inclusion of other uses. These apparent contradictions spring from different images of a good place to live, images of different types of good neighborhoods.

The following findings of residential satisfaction studies are taken from 36 studies that were done over about as many years. I started with the early studies and added later ones as I came across them, and when I found that I was no longer finding new information I ended the search.[1] I will describe the findings as they apply to each of the three dimensions of neighborhood—Ambience, Engagement and Choicefulness. Based on these findings and those of previous chapters, I will then derive a list of qualities that are strongly associated with good neighborhoods—although clearly not all of these qualities are associated with any one place.

Let us first see what we can learn about qualities of use and form—what I have called the Ambience dimension of neighborhoods.

AMBIENCE

When asked what qualities are necessary for a satisfactory neighborhood, residents mention good maintenance more frequently than any other single quality. They refer to the general physical condition of the housing and the outdoor spaces, which is associated with the apparent expense and age of the buildings, and the absence of disorder, deterioration and obsolescence. They speak of the neighborhood as being well cared for, clean, tidy, neat, well kept up, with no dilapidated structures. Lansing and Marans (1969) found that maintenance is the most important single determinant of how well people like their neighborhood. Good maintenance is associated with good appearance, and with safety—a well-looked-after neighborhood looks safer.[2]

Tranquility emerges as another important quality in most studies; it is associated with greenery, low density, lack of crowding, and social homogeneity. Peterson (1967) found that harmony with nature is a preferred quality, and Hinshaw and Allott (1972) found a preference for suburban and rural locations. On the other hand, some studies, particularly those in center-city neighborhoods, indicate a preference for the built environment. Berry (1985) found that one of the top attractions for new in-town residents who move downtown is the excitement of center-city living. Intense activity is associated with urbanity, high density, and diversity. It is also associated with man-made rather than natural features—buildings that are interesting, historic, and well designed. Gale (1979), for example, found that the architectural and/or historical character of the houses and neighborhood consistently show the highest ratings; and Berry found that new in-town residents rank the style and historic character of the neighborhood and the house as one of the main reasons why they moved there. Studies of downtown residents suggest that they are willing to trade residential tranquility for the convenience of being able to walk to work and not having to depend on the automobile. Hunter (1975) and Berry (1985) found that proximity to work is among the first three reasons for moving into a downtown area; the Baltimore City Department of Planning (1988) found that it is the most popular feature of living downtown; and the Livability Committee (1991) identified it as one of the favorite things about downtown. Baltimore.

Tranquility and activity, although opposite qualities, are both associated with good looks. Both tend to be associated with walking environments, places where there is convenient, adequate public transportation.

QUALITIES ASSOCIATED WITH AMBIENCE

1. A place that is clean and well maintained.
   People want to live in a place that is clean and tidy, where buildings and spaces are well maintained. Such places look more attractive and safer. There is general agreement on this quality; nobody thinks that a neighborhood is better if it is dirty or poorly maintained. This is the most frequently mentioned quality in satisfaction studies. It is implicit in all models, myths and ideals.

2. A place that is quiet and relaxing.
   A good neighborhood is a place that is peaceful, that offers a break from

the hurry and anxiety of the work place. It is a place where one can unwind. This shows up frequently in satisfaction studies. It is a basic quality of the Arcadian myth and of Refuge models.

3. A place that is entirely residential.

It is good to live in an area that is dedicated solely to the needs of home
and family life; where there is no need for compromise in order to satisfy competing uses. This is cited in many satisfaction studies. It is a basic quality of the models and ideal schemes that guided the development
of the suburbs. Its value is questioned by those who find the results to
be lacking in interest and identity.

4. A place that has a definite center.

There should be a central place that serves as a geographic focus, where
everyone goes, and with which residents identify as a community. This
is a quality of the Paree and Hamlet myths. It is a basic form of spatial
organization, popular with designers.

5. A place that is right in the center of activity.

It is desirable to live in a place where you will be an on-the-spot participant in the latest events, activities, and fashions. This quality is characteristic of Marketplace models and the Paree myth. It is a very undesirable
quality in the Arcadia myth and in Refuge models.

6. A place where neighboring homes are close to one another.

One needs a certain density in order to achieve an active and lively environment and to support effective public transportation. This is associated with a desire for an active environment. It is a quality that is
present in many models, and is much promoted by public planners as a
way of achieving efficiency and creating a good place for walking.

7. A place that is full of surprises.

It is good to live in a place that is constantly changing; one that is never
altogether predictable, never gets boring. This is a quality whose aesthetic value is much favored by urban designers. It is an essential element of the Paree myth. It is, however, not desirable in most Club models and in the Hamlet myth.

8. Living here, one can manage without a car.

It is convenient to be able to walk to most places one wants to go and
not to be dependent on the automobile. Walking environments are also
healthier and more pleasant. This is a quality of in-town neighborhoods
that is frequently cited in satisfaction studies. It is associated with Marketplace models and myths of Paree and the Hamlet and is a feature of
some (but not all) Utopian schemes. Walking neighborhoods of the past
are cited as models for new development.

9. A place with convenient public transportation..

> Living in a place with public transportation increases the range of one's activities without having to use a car. This is frequently mentioned in satisfaction studies. It is an essential quality of Marketplace models and the Paree myth and is sometimes a feature of Club models and the Hamlet myth.

Returning to the satisfaction studies, let us now see what they tell us about social relations in the neighborhood—what I have called the Engagement dimension.

ENGAGEMENT

People will not engage with one another in a climate of fear, and safety emerges as the most important single quality in a number of studies. For example, Cook (1988) found that neighborhood safety contributes most to satisfaction in both center-city and suburban locations. Safety means a feeling of security without fear from harm. Threats to safety include traffic, vandalism, and social abuse; also mentioned were robbery, fighting, gambling, theft, and assault. People associate safety with lower densities, and with residential stability. Safe neighborhoods are also associated with good looks (beauty and upkeep) and with the presence of friendly neighbors.

Friendliness is mentioned in a number of studies as important for neighborhood satisfaction. Munson (1956) noted that six of the ten most important features of a good neighborhood are concerned with the attributes of the neighbors, and Troy (1973) noted that half of overall satisfaction is explained by satisfaction with the social environment. People want neighbors to speak and be friendly, but they do not necessarily want them to be close friends. Lansing and Marans (1969) found that the best neighborhood is one where people are friendly, but not intimate; and Lamanna (1964) noted that while friendship is important, it is more important to avoid interference and surveillance. He pointed out that the statements "A town where people attend to their own business" and "A town where you can be by yourself and not have to worry about what other people think" received higher scores than "A friendly town that has the kind of people with whom you can stop and chat a while on the street or visit often." It seems that most residents enjoy close, if not necessarily intimate, friendships with their neighbors. Some residents like having friends and family nearby. Friendship is also related to presence of places and activities—such as schools, shops, churches, clubs and community associations—that bring residents together and foster a sense of community. Sampson (1988, 1991) found that people are more likely to be satisfied with their neighborhood if they have friends and acquaintances there; which, in turn, is more likely in neighborhoods with a stable residential population. Sampson also found that residents are more satisfied in neighborhoods where, they feel, "people mostly help one another."

Shared places and activities were mentioned in more studies than any other single attribute. But while residents agree that neighborhood amenities are desirable, they do not agree about *which* amenities: Some want amenities that serve household needs (a shopping center, grocery, drug store, house of worship, place for outdoor recreation), others those that cater to the needs of children (schools, and opportunities to use the outdoors), and still others those that satisfy the individual's need for self-fulfillment and career advancement (workplace, cultural and entertainment facilities). Cook (1988) found that residents of the suburbs and the center-city look for different kinds of amenities. There are also different views as to where these amenities should be located: Some want them on a public transportation line or on a highway; others want them within easy walking distance of home. In-town residents are particularly insistent on shared places near home. They are also more concerned about easy access to cultural facilities.

Not all residents look for friendly neighbors and convenient meeting places. There are some who prefer to go their own way, not get involved with their neighbors, not be tied down by local social obligations. The advantages of friendship include companionship and support, but the disadvantages include loss of independence and less freedom of action. In one study (Krupat and Guild 1980), "city people," when compared to "small-town people," were characterized as often lonely and keeping to themselves, but also as having a greater choice of friends and life-styles and being more interesting. Friendship is often associated with social homogeneity, and independence with social diversity.

Based on these findings and the sources discussed in the previous chapters, we can identify a number of qualities associated with good social relations among neighbors. Once again, not all of these qualities apply in any one neighborhood.

QUALITIES ASSOCIATED WITH ENGAGEMENT

10. A place where residents feel safe and secure.

    One wants to live in a place where residents feel that their person and property are not threatened. This is a generally agreed-upon quality; nobody prefers an unsafe neighborhood. This was the most frequently mentioned quality in a number of satisfaction studies. It is a feature of early utopian schemes and is taken for granted in all models and myths.

The following seven qualities (11–17) suggest engagement with many diverse people.

11. A place with world-class restaurants, stores, and cultural facilities.
    People enjoy living in a place where there is always somewhere to go, where there is something interesting and desirable to see and do. This is an essential quality of Marketplace models and the Paree myth. It is often cited as a reason for choosing to live downtown, and its absence is cited as a reason for dissatisfaction with existing downtown areas. It is considered quite undesirable in many suburban neighborhoods.

12. A place where there are many tourists.
    The presence of tourists means that there are always new people, that there are places to go that are unique and unusual, and that these places are economically viable. This is an essential quality of Marketplace models and the Paree myth. It is cited by residents who find satisfaction in a lively and diverse environment. It is not compatible with Refuge models or the Arcadia myth.

13. A place that suits the needs of newcomers.
    No one wants to live in a place where one can easily get lost, and where one is unwelcome. Designers stress the need for a clear organization of the physical environment. This quality is also characteristic of the Paree myth and of many Club models.

14. A place to meet new people.
    Many people, not only newcomers, want to live in a place where it is easy to make new friends and acquaintances and perhaps to meet a mate. This is a basic quality of the Paree myth. It is a quality that is particularly attractive to young people and newcomers.

15. One can have an active social life close to home.
    Having friends and acquaintances living nearby makes it easier to get together informally and on the spur of the moment. This is a quality that is credited with attracting people to in-town neighborhoods. It is a feature of the Hamlet myth and is often cited in advertisements for Club models.

16. A wide selection of goods and services close to home.
    It is convenient to be able to find what one needs without traveling outside the neighborhood. This appears as an important quality in many satisfaction studies. It is a feature of Marketplace models, the Paree and Hamlet myths, and many utopian schemes. It is not part of the myth of Suburbia.

17. Living here you do not have to spend as much time caring for the house.

> People like being relieved of the chores of housekeeping. In the past, there have been many schemes for relieving the drudgery of housework. This quality is reflected in many utopian schemes and underlies many Club models. It is cited by people who move into apartments and condominiums. It is particularly attractive to singles and to families in which both parents work.

The next seven qualities (18–24) suggest a more intimate form of engagement, largely with people who are compatible, known, and familiar.

18. A place where neighbors are outgoing and friendly.

> It is reassuring to live in a place where residents feel accepted and where they develop a strong sense of belonging. This is cited with great frequency in satisfaction studies. It is an important feature of the Hamlet myth. Oddly enough, it is cited both by people who prefer country life to city life and by those who prefer in-town neighborhoods to suburban ones.

19. A place to put down roots and settle.

> It is good to live in a place that is stable, and one can make a long-term commitment to living there. This shows up in satisfaction studies. It is related to confidence in the future and willingness to invest. It is a feature of the Hamlet myth.

20. A place where most people know one another.

> Many people enjoy living in a place where they are known and where they do not have to deal with strangers. This is a feature of the Hamlet myth and of Club models.

21. A place where one will always meet people one knows.

> One feels more at home in a neighborhood that has its own facilities and where these facilities develop a local flavor. This is related to the idea that local institutions bring residents together to promote friendship and a sense of community. It is a feature of the Hamlet myth and of many Club models.

22. A place where people take care of one another.

> It is good to live in a place where neighbors are kind and thoughtful and can be depended upon for help in case of need. This is a feature of most utopias and of the Hamlet myth.

23. A place where relationships are long-lasting and personal.

> Many people like to live among people whom they know well and

whose friendship will withstand the test of time. This shows a preference for settled, stable neighborhoods where there is little change. It is a feature of the Hamlet myth.

24. A place where residents are involved in community affairs.
One feels more in control in a neighborhood where residents take an interest in the common good and are prepared to work together to solve common problems. The importance of a strong community is stressed in most utopian schemes and cited in many satisfaction studies. It is a basic feature of many Club models.

The next two qualities represent a somewhat different viewpoint—a wish *not* to engage with one's neighbors.

25. A place where there is no pressure to socialize or join anything.
Some people prefer living in a place where they are free to participate or not as they want and where certain people do not try to impose their values on others. This is cited in some satisfaction studies. It is a feature of the Paree myth and Refuge models. It is one of the reasons given for preferring life in a big city to that in a small town.

26. A place where residents are private and go their own ways.
Some people choose to remain anonymous. They prefer living in a place where the neighbors mind their own business, where they can have privacy without isolation. This is cited in some satisfaction studies. It is a feature of Refuge models and the Arcadian myth, and sometimes a feature of the Paree myth. It is considered undesirable in the Hamlet myth.

CHOICEFULNESS

Let us see what satisfaction studies tell us about the quality of Choicefulness.

Residents agree that a neighborhood should have a good reputation; about this there is no dispute. Respondents refer to a nice neighborhood, the right part of town, a place you can feel proud of, a place where the people you want to emulate—"the right kind of people"—want to live.[3] Good reputation also means an area where investors have confidence that property values will hold steady and preferably will appreciate.

A prime consideration is the diversity of people who live in the neighborhood, and on this issue respondents have strongly differing opinions. Many prefer to live among people of their own kind—people of their own class, race, income, values, and background. Campbell, Converse, and Rogers (1976), and Galster and Hesser (1981) found that an important characteristic of a good neighborhood is having it composed entirely of one's own race, and Dobriner (1963) commented that the quality "better for children," which appears in a number of studies, implies ethnic and religious homogeneity. Lamanna commented that references to "the right kind of people" implies relatively homogeneous individuals and groups who do not pose a threat to one another's social status. Sampson (1991) found that heterogeneity reduces neighborhood satisfaction. Galster and Hesser concluded that higher satisfaction is related to racial homogeneity. Homogeneity is also associated with higher property values. Shlay (1985), however, found that people are ready to overcome their aversion to diversity if a diverse neighborhood has the types of units and the amenities they want.

Residents of in-town neighborhoods, on the other hand, tend to prefer diversity. They say that they enjoy living with people who are different from themselves in life-style, activities, ethnic and religious background, and culture. Berry (1985) found that in-town residents are attracted by the promise of an integrated neighborhood. Hunter (1975) found that they consciously reject suburbia and express a positive assertion of the values of "urban living." The Baltimore City Department of Planning (1988) found that the diversity of people and life-styles is an attractive feature for people who live downtown. A separate study (Brower 1988), found that the variety of people, places, and buildings is one of the most important qualities of a downtown neighborhood as a place in which to live. Finally, the Livability Committee (1991) found that one of the favorite things of residents of downtown Baltimore was the diversity of life-styles, cultures, and people in a relatively small area.

Based on these and previously discussed findings, we can identify a number of neighborhood qualities that score high on the Choicefulness dimension. Once again, not all of these qualities apply in any one neighborhood.

QUALITIES ASSOCIATED WITH CHOICEFULNESS

27. A place that has a reputation as a desirable place to live.
     There is general agreement on this quality. No one prefers a place that has a bad reputation. It is good to live in a place where the people you respect live, and where property values appreciate. This quality is frequently mentioned in satisfaction studies.

28. A place where all residents have a similar life-style.
     It is common to want to live among people who have the same values and customs as oneself; they are more predictable and more considerate of one's interests, and they are better role models for one's children. This is a feature of most utopian schemes and Club models. It is frequently cited in satisfaction studies. In-town residents, however, say that

it makes for conformity and that it is this that made them move from the suburbs.

29. A place that is protected from the larger problems of society.
Some like to live in an area where they are not exposed to people who may threaten their values and way of life. This is cited in many satisfaction studies. It is important in Club models, where it supports the provision of private services. It also supports geographic separation, characteristic of many Club and Refuge models.

30. A place to raise children.
Parents prefer a place where their children need not be confined and where they will have friends, the schools are good, and the neighbors are suitable role models. This shows up frequently in satisfaction studies, especially in the responses of residents who live in suburban areas. It is a feature of many utopian schemes.

The following quality presents an alternative viewpoint.

31. A wide diversity of people live here.
It is interesting to live among people with different customs and viewpoints. In such an environment there is less pressure to conform to a norm, and you are free to be whoever you want to be. This is desired by people who choose to live in in-town neighborhoods. It is a feature of Marketplace models and the Paree myth. It is not part of the myth of Suburbia.

Finally, there are different views about the level of sophistication that is desirable in a neighbor.

32. A place one can find sophisticated neighbors.
Some residents like to live among people who are educated, interesting, and not bound by tradition. This is one of the qualities that attracts young, ambitious people to cities, and it is a feature of the Paree myth.

33. A place where neighbors are genuine and down-to-earth.
Some like to live with people who are open and honest, who are easy to befriend, and are not fooled by pretensions and superficial impressions. This reflects a desire to return to the simple life, where people do not try to dissemble and things are the way they seem. It is a basic feature of the Hamlet and Arcadian myths.

SUMMARY

These 33 qualities are important attributes of good neighborhoods. As we see, they represent quite different, often conflicting views about a good place to live. Studies suggest that these views are tied to a resident's social class, early residential experiences, range of options, race, gender, stage in the life cycle, and marital and employment status. For example, Coleman et al. (1978) found that upper-class residents prefer a neighborhood that is in the right part of town, has people with similar incomes, tastes, and interests, is removed from the center city, is private, has good schools, and looks good. Middle-class residents, he found, have a different set of priorities: They prefer a neighborhood that is outside the city, is quiet and peaceful, has good schools, houses friendly people with similar values and interests, includes convenient shopping and churches, and provides good transportation. Working-class residents have still other priorities: They prefer a neighborhood that is clean and safe, where residents are of the same racial group, there are no welfare families and no absentee landlords, and the houses are well kept up. Coleman notes that only among upper-status residents is there any sizeable interest in living "almost downtown." St. John and Clark (1984) found that lower-class residents attach more importance to activities that take place within the neighborhood, and Fried (1986) found that the higher the social class, the less the dependence on the neighborhood for leisure and recreation. Fried found that lower-class residents place a higher value on closeness to work, public transportation, church, friends and relatives, and parks and playgrounds, and also on ethnic homogeneity and mutual help among neighbors. Middle- and upper-class residents, on the other hand, put more emphasis on the use of the car, easy access to the outdoors and the country, and a sense of urbanity.

Residents' criteria for a good neighborhood are also influenced by the size and nature of the community in which they live or in which they grew up (Campbell et al. 1976; Hummon 1990; Cook 1988; Krupat and Guild 1980; and Blake, Weigl, and Perloff 1975). Hummon found that people who prefer small towns enjoy peace, quiet, nature, slow pace of life, care, and traditional values. People who prefer cities, on the other hand, enjoy a diversity of people and activities, liberality, and enhancement of personal freedom; or else they enjoy cities for their community, human contact, and organizations. People who prefer the suburbs see them as quieter, smaller, more natural and safer than the city, and yet with more amenities and cultural life than a small town. Hummon also found that people are rather vague in their characterization of the suburbs—in fact, suburbanites often think of themselves as living in a small town.

Michelson (1980) found that people's feeling of satisfaction is influenced by their ability to make future housing choices. He found that most apartment dwellers view their housing as transitional, and that they are quite satisfied to live there as long as they feel that they are able to move should they want to. Apartment-dwellers who feel locked in are extremely dissatisfied. Berry (1985) found that many residents see downtown neighborhoods as places where young, middle-class adults, while renting, can meet and marry before settling down to raise families in the suburbs.

There is also a suggestion that gender influences people's concept of a good neighborhood. Shlay and Digregorio (1985) found that men and women have similar responses to some characteristics (no more than 30 minutes travel time to work, close social network within the immediate environment, and at least half of the area population of their own race), but that they have different responses to others. Men attach importance to income, racial composition, proximity to work—that is, status and travel— but little importance to amenities that affect daily life in the area. Women's responses differ according to their work and marital status. Housewives attach importance to neighborhood status, but they also value facilities and playmates for their children, and a low-density environment with good public transportation. Single women attach importance to diversity in family composition (but not racial composition), convenient public transportation, and institutional facilities. Employed women attach importance to access to work. Shlay and Digregorio conclude that different people look for different types of neighborhoods: Men prefer a middle-class suburb, housewives a citified suburb, single women a city neighborhood, and employed women a center-city neighborhood or inlying suburb.

The next problem is to define different types of neighborhoods and, for each, the qualities that make it good. This means arranging the qualities of good neighborhoods into discrete categories, so that each category represents a distinct type of setting and contains the features of good settings of that type. In the next chapter I will consider the prime variables that distinguish one type from another.

NOTES

1. My review included the following:

Munson (1956) interviewed 288 residents in Indianapolis, Indiana.

Wilson (1962) surveyed 385 people from Durham and Greensboro, North Carolina.

Dobriner (1963) cited four studies of people who moved from urban to suburban areas. See Dobriner for references to: Dewey (1948), who surveyed twelve thousand families in Milwaukee County, Wisconsin; Anderson (1953) who surveyed residents of the fringe area around

Ithaca, New York; Martin (1953) who surveyed the rural-urban fringe around Eugene-Spring-field, Oregon; and Bell (1963), who surveyed two Chicago suburbs.

Lamanna (1964) surveyed 211 adult residents of Greensboro, North Carolina.

Peterson (1967) interviewed 140 test subjects using 23 color photographs of residential neighborhoods.

Lansing and Marans (1969) surveyed 396 adult residents living in private dwellings in the Detroit region.

Hinshaw and Allott (1972) interviewed 204 undergraduate students at Hunter College of the City University of New York.

Troy (1973) interviewed residents (number not reported) in the suburbs of Melbourne, Australia.

Blake, Weigl, and Perloff (1975) conducted a mail survey of 4,600 adults in Indiana.

Hunter (1975) observed and interviewed residents of 154 blocks and households in an inner-city neighborhood in Rochester, New York.

Carp, Zawadski, and Shokrkon (1976) tapped data from several sources, including four studies of poor, elderly residents in San Antonio, Texas, and a study of 183 residents of a low-income area in Berkeley, California.

Campbell, Converse, and Rogers (1976) drew from a national study of people's sense of well-being in which 2,164 persons were interviewed.

Coleman (1978) interviewed 900 people in three metropolitan areas in the United States and also drew on findings from earlier surveys that involved 1,000 people in three metropolitan areas.

Gale (1979) surveyed new residents in central areas in six major cities.

Krupat and Guild (1980) surveyed 154 Boston College students.

Michelson (1980) surveyed 751 families in the vicinity of metropolitan Toronto, who were in the process of choosing housing. Respondents were interviewed immediately before moving into the new housing and again two months after moving, a year after that, and three years later.

Miller, Tsemberis, Malia, and Grega (1980) surveyed 556 residents in four middle- and up-per-middle-income neighborhoods of New York City.

Galster and Hesser (1981) surveyed 767 households in Wooster, Ohio.

Fried (1982, 1986) surveyed 2,622 respondents from 42 municipalities in ten metropolitan areas across the country.

Weidemann and Anderson (1982) surveyed 245 adults in a multifamily public housing site in Decatur, Illinois.

Nasar (1983) interviewed 96 people from six neighborhood groups in the area of Harrisburg, Pennsylvania, using slides of 60 residential street scenes. Respondents were asked to judge each scene using bipolar adjective scales.

St. John and Clark (1984) used data obtained from a survey of 450 adults in Oklahoma City, Oklahoma.

Berry (1985) reviewed a number of U.S. studies of revitalization in neighborhoods close to downtown.

Shlay and Digregorio (1985) and Shlay (1985) interviewed 177 residents in and around Syracuse, New York, using a factorial survey technique in which housing characteristics were randomly assigned to short vignettes.

Varady (1986) used longitudinal survey data collected by the federal Department of Housing and Urban Development in connection with the Urban Homesteading Demonstration program. The survey included 1,754 families in 40 neighborhoods in 23 cities.

Hummon (1986, 1990) interviewed 77 adults in four communities—one urban, two suburban, and one small-town—in Northern California.

Baltimore City Department of Planning (1988) surveyed 1,759 people who work in the downtown area.

Cook (1988) surveyed 449 single-parent women in the Minneapolis-St. Paul region of Minnesota; of these, 217 lived in suburban and 232 in urban areas.

Brower (1988) interviewed 50 residents in two in-town neighborhoods in Baltimore, Maryland, using ten photographs of each of the two neighborhoods. Respondents were asked to rate the scenes on twelve bipolar scales and then rate the importance of each scale in relation to a place to live.

The Livability Committee (1991), a subcommittee of Baltimore's Mayor's Task Force, was charged with developing recommendations for improving living conditions downtown. The members of the committee were asked to respond to the question, "As residents, what is your favorite thing about living downtown?"

Sampson (1991) analyzed survey data from a 1984 national sample of over 11,000 residents in over 500 localities in Great Britain.

2. See also Hunter's (1978) reference to good maintenance as a symbol of a more civil and therefore safer community.

3. The same idea was expressed in the *Los Angeles Times*, March 19, 1972, quoted in Downs and Stea 1977, p. 18:

What labels a place "socially desirable" is not totally explainable: views, gates, protection, high real estate values, clean air, schools, proximity to ocean/hills, chic shops—these can all play a part. On the other hand, areas with none of these to offer attract top Los Angeles leaders. Maybe Beautiful People buy where other Beautiful People buy, or buy where they think they buy.

CHAPTER EIGHT

Neighborhood Typologies

N eighborhoods are many-faceted environments, and it is possible to categorize them in many different ways, which means that many different typologies are possible. In order to create a typology that satisfies the particular purposes discussed previously, we need to establish some organizing criteria. The following criteria are derived from the discussions in the early chapters.

Each type must be considered by a significant number of residents to be the most desirable place to live.

No one type must be inherently better or worse than any other and no type must combine either the advantages of all or the disadvantages of none.

Different types must provide different satisfactions to suit different groups of people and people at different stages of the life cycle.

Each type must bear a clear resemblance to places in the real world.

Each type must be stable over time, and examples must have been around (perhaps in different forms) over a long period of time.

Each type must have clear implications for design practice, so that changes in type will be accompanied by changes in the overall form and appearance of the place.

It must be equally possible (if not equally likely) for all types to be found in all parts of the metropolitan area.

In order to be useful for policy-making the typology must be parsimonious—it must have no more elements than are necessary.

The next step is to identify the prime variable that will distinguish one type from another. I have argued that each type should serve a particular residential life-style, which suggests life-style as the variable. But is life-style a variable in itself, or is it simply a response to a particular landscape or pattern of activities or to the particular personality of the residents? In this chapter, I will examine typologies based on each of these variables and see which comes closest to satisfying the ordering criteria.

PLACE-BASED TYPOLOGIES

Place-based typologies are favored by people who believe that we are essentially an expression of the places in which we live; that a particular landscape will, over time, turn residents into "a special breed of men and women with common psychological and physical characteristics" (Jackson 1980, p. 11). Lawrence Durrell, for example, argues that landscape has the equivalent of a magnetic field which acts upon the personality of its inhabitants, so that a distinctive national landscape produces a distinctive national temperament.

I believe you could exterminate the French at a blow and resettle the country with Tartars, and within two generations discover, to your astonishment, that the national characteristics were back at norm—the restless metaphysical curiosity, the tenderness for good living and the passionate individualism: even though their noses were now flat. (Durrell 1969, p. 157)

This suggests a typology where the main variables are the physical characteristics of the place.

Conzen (1968), for example, offers a place-based typology of cities based on the historical periods during which British and European towns evidenced a distinctively different arrangement of streets, lots, and buildings. The elements are:

Early Modern Times (c. 900–1500)
The Earlier Phase of the Industrial Revolution (c. 1850–1900)
The "Garden City" Period and the Period Between the World Wars (c. 1900–1940)
The Post-War Period

Coleman (1978) suggests a typology of the sub-areas within contemporary cities. Once again, the elements refer to the formal and locational characteristics of places and not necessarily to the activity or behavior of users.

The Old Central City represents areas that are almost downtown, that contain older renewed houses, major cultural institutions, and counter-culture neighborhoods.

Older Suburbs are areas that are in the city but with a touch of the country. They are on bus lines and have a convenient location and a settled feel. Some of these areas are like pleasant small towns.

New Subdivisions are areas that have a feeling of the country, but at the same time are not far from the city. They feature the latest ideas in lot arrangement, access design, and in-home luxury. These areas include small towns, farms, woods, virgin land, country clubs, and highway commerce, all about to be swallowed up in the expansion of the metropolis.

Rural Areas are areas characterized by gardens, farms, woods, streams, hunting, fishing, and camping. They reflect a yearning for non-metropolitan existence, a longing to get away from the rat-race.

Both of these typologies recognize differences in the density, age, and pattern of development—important neighborhood distinctions. They do not, however, recognize variations of use and activity within physically similar places, variations that have an important effect on the quality of the residential experience.

ACTIVITY-BASED TYPOLOGIES

Activity-based typologies take the opposite approach. They assume that the essential quality of a setting depends on the actions and interactions of the people who use it. A single type may manifest itself in different physical locations and forms. A common typology of this sort, one that is the basis of most land use regulation, classifies land according to the way it is or may legally be used. Chapin and Kaiser (1974), for example, suggest eight basic land use categories:[1]

Residence
Retail business
Transportation, utilities, and communications
Industry and related uses
Wholesale and related uses
Public buildings and open spaces
Institutional buildings and areas
Vacant and nonurban uses

This typology assumes that there is a one-for-one relationship between a particular kind of use and the places that accommodate it and that places where activities typically happen can serve as proxies for the activities themselves.[2] The result is that the use-categories end up as place-categories, so that attempts to distinguish between different residential uses, for example, result in distinctions based on physical features such as building type, size, height, density, and coverage. This activity-based approach is a thinly veiled place-based typology.

There are, however, typologies that are really concerned with activity. Warren and Warren's (1977) six-part typology of neighborhoods, for example, is based on patterns of social organization.

Integral Neighborhood is an active neighborhood, where people know one another. They interact informally and participate in organizations that deal with issues both at the local level and at the level of the larger society.

Parochial Neighborhood is a self-contained world, often with a strong ethnic identity or homogeneous character, insulated from the larger community by local institutions that screen out foreign influences and values. It is more traditional or conventional than society as a whole.

Diffuse Neighborhood is a neighborhood where residents have little interaction with one another, but they achieve a degree of consensus simply because they have so many things in common. Their friends are outside the neighborhood.

Stepping-stone Neighborhood is an active neighborhood with a large turnover of people. Residents do not identify with the neighborhood, but they participate in local affairs because they want to get ahead in their careers.

Transitory Neighborhood is a neighborhood with considerable population turnover and little collective action or organization. There is little cohesion among residents; they often break up into little clusters of people, and often the old timers and newcomers are separated.

Anomic Neighborhood is a neighborhood where people simply go their own ways. The neighborhood is not a focal point of community, and it lacks the capacity to mobilize for common actions from within. This makes it particularly vulnerable to outside influences.

The problem with this particular typology is that it does not recognize distinctions based on the place itself. In addition, some of the types are clearly unstable over time, there are clear implications that some types are more desirable than others, and the types are driven by group dynamics that have only marginal implications for design practice.

Moore (1972) provides an example of an activity-based typology that does give recognition to the effect of place. His types are based on changes in use pattern over time.

Type 1 Neighborhoods are characterized by high mobility and significant neighborhood change. They include neighborhoods where low-income residents displace higher income ones (invasion and succession), where high-income residents displace low-income ones (gentrification), and where the sudden intrusion of undesirable land uses causes old-time residents to move out. Neighborhoods of this type are a temporary phenomenon and not easy to predict.

Type 2 Neighborhoods are characterized by high mobility and little neighborhood change. These are neighborhoods where the housing is not adaptable and caters to a specific sub-group of residents. Examples include neighborhoods of small houses that are suitable only for starter families, those that cater to a transient population of young singles, and those that serve as a reception area for new immigrants and in-migrants.

Type 3 Neighborhoods are characterized by low mobility and significant neighborhood change. These are neighborhoods with flexible housing and high ownership rates, where the older residents remain in place as their children move out, and as the residents age the housing deteriorates and gradually filters down to a lower socioeconomic group.

Type 4 Neighborhoods are characterized by low mobility and little neighborhood change. Examples include many tightly knit ethnic neighborhoods, communities with strong social networks, and settled affluent communities, where similar environments cannot be found elsewhere in the city and people would rather build anew within the neighborhood than move out.

Moore's typology has some of the same limitations, from our point of view, as that of Warren and Warren, but it does incorporate features of the physical environment—in particular, the adequacy, flexibility, and desirability of the housing structures.

A shortcoming of both place-based and activity-based typologies is that they fail to recognize that people do not all interpret places and activities in the same way; neighborhoods of the same place- or activity-type may have quite different meanings for different people. The way of dealing with this is to interpret physical and social attributes as they are revealed through residents' eyes rather than by objective measurement. Such an approach is characteristic of personality-based and culture-based typologies.

PERSONALITY-BASED TYPOLOGIES

Personality-based typologies assume that meanings can be traced to the personality of the individual observer. This argument is made by Hamerton (1885), who argues that people who belong to different personality types look for different qualities in a setting.

Each of us is constituted with a special idiosyncrasy related in some mysterious way to a certain class of natural scenery; and when we find ourselves in a scene answering to our idiosyncrasy, the mind feels itself at home there and rapidly attaches itself by affection. (Hamerton 1885, p. 27)

And again:

One very intelligent and cultivated person looks upon mountain scenery with an indifference that would certainly pass into dislike if he were compelled to live in the midst of it; while another lives in a perpetual state of lively interest in a mountainous country, and feels dull only in the plains. The effect of the sea upon some minds is extremely depressing; others find it to be a tonic and a stimulant. (Hamerton 1885, preface)

The idea that certain people have a special affinity for particular natural settings is easily extended to man-made settings. Douglas (1925), for example, theorizes that suburban locations are preferred by people with certain personality traits—those with an "aesthetic affinity" for open living; they are "a chosen people separated from their fellow city-men by the strength of a particular group of inner attributes." Geller (1960) refers to certain personalities as having an affinity for complex sensory inputs, and Proshansky (1978) suggests that one's affinity for complex sensory inputs depends on whether one has learned how to deal with them. Center-city residents, for example, develop an unusual ability to shift from one setting to another, to make choices among a wide range of settings, and to practice strategic interaction techniques.

The notion that particular individuals have a special affinity for particular types of landscapes has been extended to apply to entire racial or ethnic groups. The German National Socialists, for example, believed that people of the German race would only feel really at home in a particular kind of landscape (Wolschke-Bulmahn and Groening 1992; Wolschke-Bulmahn 1992). They attempted to guard the German landscape against alien plants and went so far as to set up a landscape planning board to

remodel Polish landscapes into German landscapes so that after the expulsion of the Polish people and the reshaping of the landscape, German settlers could feel at home. (Wolschke-Bulmahn 1992)

The idea of a link between personality and race has been revived in recent times with an attempt to distinguish between white ice people—hyperrational, cold, and exploitative—and dark sun people—warm, emotional, and communal (Berreby 1996). There is, however, no scientific evidence to support a link between personality and race. Nor can we show a link between personality and place, and the associated line of reasoning—that members of certain groups are wired in accordance with their personal or racial identity and that preference for certain settings is determined by an invariant trait—contradicts the idea of individual choice, which is a key concept in democratic societies. A more acceptable idea is that individuals' preferences are shaped by habits, beliefs, and understandings that they share with other members of their culture. This is the approach of culture-based typologies.

CULTURE-BASED TYPOLOGIES

Culture-based typologies focus on the meanings that attach to a place and make it understood to all members of society as the kind of place where certain uses, attitudes, and activities are expected and appropriate (Meinig 1979).

We do not know much about the elements that forge a common culture. Some suggest that the constricting sounds in language interrupt the flow of blood to certain parts of the brain, and that the frequency of these sounds helps to explain the difference between, for example, the German and the French national temperament; others point to the effect of climate, suggesting that people who suffer long winters are more gloomy and than people who enjoy a lot of sunlight; yet others say that common culture is forged by a shared history that forces people to solve the same problems over and over again (Berreby 1996). While there is no scientific evidence to back up any of these theories, general agreement about the meaning of everyday activities seems to go along with agreement about the proper location, appearance, and use of the spaces used for these activities. Lawrence (1987), for example, in a study of dwelling types, shows that cultural groups differ in the ways that they interpret domestic functions and organize domestic space. He suggests a typology of dwellings built around the way people classify common household chores and rituals as either clean or dirty, front or back, day or night, and public or private. Clean/dirty classification affects the separation of places used for cooking, eating, laundry, and bathing; front/back classification affects the location, appearance and use of places for receiving and entertaining; day/night classification affects the separation of sleeping and living quarters; and public/private classification affects the treatment and use of outdoor spaces immediately around the dwelling. Such a typology gives equal weight to place, activity, and meaning.

Meinig (1979) gives an example of a culture-based typology at the neighborhood scale.

The New England Village. A white wooden church with its slender steeple, facing onto a large village green lined with elms and maples, and surrounded by large, elegant clapboard houses. The scene symbolizes an intimate, family-centered, God fearing, morally conscious, industrious, thrifty, democratic community.

Main Street of Middle America. A nineteenth-century street lined with three- or four-story red brick business blocks, with storefronts below and professional offices and meeting rooms of various fraternal orders above. Nearby are the bank, the courthouse, various churches, and a residential area with big houses on treeshaded lots. Main Street symbolizes the seat of a business culture of property-minded, law-abiding citizens devoted to "free enterprise" and "social morality," a community of sober, sensible, practical people.

California Suburbia. Low, wide-spreading single-story houses on broad lots, faced by open, green lawns. A two-car garage opens onto a driveway, connecting to a broad curving street and then to great freeways that lead to recreation areas, shopping plazas, and drive-in facilities. The house with its swimming pool, patio, and backyard barbeque symbolizes the relaxed enjoyment of each day in casual, indoor-outdoor living, with an accent upon individual gratification, physical health, and pleasant exercise.

Meinig notes that his typology does not include the kind of place in which most Americans live today, a place that consists of

diverse parts, including old densely urbanized areas, suburbs of various ages and character, engulfed towns, roadside strips, shopping plazas at beltway interchanges, a wide variety of discrete residential tracts, former hamlets, towns, farms, and all manner of individual shacks, cottages, mobile homes, houses and estates scattered over the countryside.

Meinig's types are counterparts of those defined in the chapter on popular myths; and in both a suburban type is conspicuously absent. The inclusion of place, activity, and meaning amounts to a focus on life-style.

Another example of a culture-based typology is offered by Weiss (1988). Weiss's typology builds on the observation that people with similar incomes, occupations, home values and levels of education tend to buy the same products, read the same newspapers, books, and magazines, and vote for the same political party. They also tend to cluster together in residential areas with the same locational features, housing styles, street scenes, and racial, ethnic, and life-cycle characteristics. This clustering is of particular interest to advertisers, politicians, and recruiters who, using census, voting, and sales data, are able to pinpoint the location of different clusters and so identify different target groups. Weiss describes forty of these residential clusters, thirty-three of them in and around cities (the rest are in remote small towns and rural areas). Here, somewhat edited, are his descriptions of four of them.

Urban Gold Coast. Upscale highrise neighborhood in a big city, Urban Gold Coast tops many demographic lists: most densely populated, most employed, most white-collar, most renters, most childless, and most New York based. Urban Gold Coast residents have the lowest incidence of auto ownership in the nation; they get around by taxi and rental car. And they usually eat out for lunch and dinner.

Young Influentials. Young Influentials is home to the nation's young, upwardly mobile singles and dual-career couples. Their neighborhoods are filled with expensive condos, recently built townhouses, and midrise apartments. Young Influentials don't care about good schools, because they don't have children. They want a mall with a sushi bar, gourmet cookie shop, travel agency, and psychotherapy center.

Furs and Station Wagons. Furs and Station Wagons is typified by new money, parents in their 40s and 50s, and sprawling houses filled with teenage children. Their newly built subdivisions may include shuttered colonials, all-glass contemporary structures, or luxury townhouses, but all share hefty price tags. And they usually feature amenities such as tennis courts, swimming pools, bike paths, and rich soil to nurture elaborate gardens. In Furs and Station Wagons, a country-club membership is a fact of life. You have to drive half an hour to get anywhere.

Blue-Chip Blues. Blue-Chip Blues is a blue-collar version of the American Dream: the majority of adults have a high-school education, earn between $25,000 and $50,000 annually, and own comfortable middle-class homes. Boasting one of the highest concentrations of married couples with children, Blue-Chip Blues is the kind of neighborhood with fast-food restaurants attached to every shopping center, baseball diamonds in the parks and motorboats in the driveways.

Weiss's residential clusters are, clearly, a model for our typology of good neighborhoods. They have the advantage of being measurable and having demonstrable practical value. There are, however, two important drawbacks. The first is that forty categories are too many to be useful for design policy —although the number may be reduced by combining groups of clusters to create fewer overarching types. The other drawback is more basic: Clusters are not stable. Weiss predicts that each decennial census shows the disappearance of some cluster-types and the emergence of others. Types that are defined by trends and fashions are important for purposes of marketing, but they are too ephemeral to serve as the basis for urban design policy.

This review has not produced a typology that serves our purposes exactly, but it does demonstrate the feasibility of using life-style differences as a major variable. With this reassurance, I am now in a position to formulate a typology of good neighborhoods.

NOTES

1. More detailed breakdowns include over 700 sub-categories of land use.

2. Judicial opinions confirm that it is legitimate to regulate the physical qualities of a place in order to get at activities associated with, for example, safety and security, traffic, noise, and a favorable environment in which to rear children. (These particular activities were named in the 1927 landmark case *Euclid vs. Ambler Realty Company*, which upheld the legality of zoning.)

CHAPTER NINE

A New Typology

I n the early chapters, I discussed the need for a typology of good neighborhoods. Then I identified qualities that recur in different formulations of a good neighborhood and found that they contradict one another; they belong, I suggested, to different types of good neighborhoods. In Chapter 8, I developed criteria for a neighborhood typology. Many of the criteria describe residents' perceptions, which means that only residents can test the validity of a typology. In this chapter I will present a typology that, I think, meets the criteria and provides a logical explanation for the contradictory qualities associated with good neighborhoods. I will describe the method used to test this typology and the results of the test.

Taking into account and trying to reconcile the many different, often conflicting qualities associated with good neighborhoods, I formulated a working hypothesis. I said that there are four distinctively different types of neighborhoods:

TYPE 1. A part of the city that is lively and busy, with lots to see and do. It has a mix of many different people and uses, and it attracts visitors from other parts of the city and beyond.

TYPE 2. A part of the city that has the feeling of a small town, with its own institutions and meeting places. People who live here know one another and are able to recognize those who do not live here.

TYPE 3. A separate residential part of the city, a place for family and home life. Residents go to other parts of the city for work, shopping, and entertainment.

TYPE 4. A part of the city where one feels removed from other people and their activities. People who live here tend to be independent and go their separate ways.

These terse statements will be referred to as *place descriptions*.

In order to show that these place descriptions meet my requirements for a typology, I must show that each description is associated with a different set of qualities, that it triggers images of places that people have experienced, suits different groups of people, is considered by some to be the best place to live, and is manifested in various regions of the city.

A test of the place descriptions was conducted in the following way. A study team met with two professional planners on the staff of the Baltimore City Department of Planning who were thoroughly familiar with the urban area and asked them to nominate neighborhoods that, in their opinion, match each of the four place descriptions. In this way we hoped to include respondents with a range of different residential experiences. The first two neighborhoods that were nominated by both planners in response to each descriptor were selected as study sites, and in each a random sample of twelve residents was interviewed. This meant, in all, ninety-six respondents in eight neighborhoods. Seven of the study sites were in Baltimore City, and one was in Baltimore County. The interview schedule is shown in Appendix 2. A screening procedure was used to reduce distortions that might result from differences in the respondents' age, familiarity with the setting, and level of education: Respondents had to be at least eighteen years old, to have lived in that part of the city for at least two years, and to have completed at least ten years of schooling. Respondents were interviewed in their homes. In all, ninety-five usable interviews were obtained. The respondents were found to be a reasonable cross-section of the general population.

We prepared thirty cue cards, each containing one of the qualities listed in Chapter 7.[1] Respondents were given the four place descriptions and the stack of thirty cards. They were asked to think of an ideal place that matched each place description. (This was to prompt them to think of a typical rather than a specific place.) Then they were asked to go through the cards and pick out the qualities that, ideally, "belong in" such a place and to rate the importance of each of these qualities on a three-point scale. If each place description were found to be associated with a different set of qualities, then we would say that each description represents a different type.

The mean ratings for each quality in relation to each place description are shown in Table 9.1. For each quality, we noted which place description received the highest mean rating (that is, the one for which this quality was most important), and we conducted paired-samples T-tests to see whether these ratings were significantly different across the place descriptions (that is, whether the quality set this description off from the others).

The results show that in the case of twenty qualities, the rating of the highest-rated place description is significantly higher than that of any other

Table 9.1

Rating for Each Quality across the Four Place Descriptions
(Quality numbers refer to the descriptions in Chapter 7)

	Quality	Desc. 1	Desc. 2	Desc. 3	Desc. 4
2	Quiet	0.19	1.99	2.32	1.46
3	Entirely residential	0.06	0.75	1.87	0.86
4	Has a center	1.21	1.20	0.21	0.12
5	Center of activity	2.05	0.33	0.08	0.26
6	Homes close together	0.97	1.12	1.00	0.41
7	Full of surprises	1.51	0.23	0.08	0.27
8	Need no car	2.06	0.98	0.34	0.58
9	Public transportation	2.41	1.15	0.80	0.79
11	World-class facilities	2.20	0.24	0.01	0.42
12	Many tourists	1.55	0.11	0.06	0.25
13	Suits newcomers	1.13	0.85	0.57	0.35
14	Meet new people	1.78	0.67	0.21	0.23
15	Active social life	1.94	1.28	0.57	0.43
16	Selection of goods	2.17	1.17	0.47	0.67
17	Easy care of home	1.11	0.22	0.23	0.79
18	Neighbors friendly	0.85	2.15	1.60	0.16
19	Put down roots	0.14	1.94	2.09	0.59
20	Know one another	0.31	2.01	1.39	0.23
21	Meet people one knows	0.66	1.80	1.06	0.16
22	Neighbors care	0.41	2.13	1.24	0.16
23	Long-lasting relations	0.14	2.00	1.32	0.25
24	Involved in community	0.75	1.96	1.64	0.25
25	No pressure to join	0.74	0.73	0.92	1.87
26	Residents private	0.61	0.36	0.73	2.15
28	Residents similar	0.41	1.03	1.29	0.67
29	Protected from society	0.20	1.19	1.35	1.08
30	Place for children	0.29	2.19	2.57	0.56
31	Residents diverse	2.14	0.75	0.71	0.98
32	Residents sophisticated	1.03	0.47	0.66	0.73
33	Residents genuine	0.32	1.68	1.06	0.40

These are average ratings over 95 respondents. They were obtained in this way: Say 30 respondents gave a particular quality a 3-rating (90 points), 40 gave it a 2-rating (80 points), 20 gave it a 1-rating (20 points), and 5 gave it an 0-rating (0 points), then the total number of points for this quality is 90+80+20+0=190, and as there are 95 raters the average rating is 2.0. The highest rating possible is 3.0.

description, which means that these twenty qualities are strongly associated with a single place description (see Table 9.2 for the significance of each pair comparison). In the case of the other ten qualities, the difference between the highest rating and one or more of the other ratings is not significant, which means that these qualities are associated with more than one place description.

Table 9.2

Paired Samples T-Tests of Ratings for Each Place Description
(Table only shows ratings over 1.00)

QUALITIES RATED HIGHEST FOR PLACE DESCRIPTION 1

Quality		Ratings	Comparative Ratings		
			1/2	1/3	1/4
9	Public transportation	2.41	* * *	* * *	* * *
11	World-class facilities	2.20	* * *	* * *	* * *
16	Selection of goods	2.17	* * *	* * *	* * *
31	Residents diverse	2.14	* * *	* * *	* * *
8	Need no car	2.06	* * *	* * *	* * *
5	Center of activity	2.05	* * *	* * *	* * *
15	Active social life	1.94	* * *	* * *	* * *
14	Meet new people	1.78	* * *	* * *	* * *
12	Many tourists	1.55	* * *	* * *	* * *
7	Full of surprises	1.51	* * *	* * *	* * *
4	Has a center	1.21	x	* * *	* * *
13	Suits newcomers	1.13	x	* *	* * *
17	Easy care of home	1.11	* * *	* * *	x
32	Residents sophisticated	1.03	* * *	* *	x

QUALITIES RATED HIGHEST FOR PLACE DESCRIPTION 2

Quality		Ratings	Comparative Ratings		
			2/1	2/3	2/4
18	Neighbors friendly	2.15	* * *	* *	* * *
22	Neighbors care	2.13	* * *	* * *	* * *
20	Know one another	2.01	* * *	* * *	* * *
23	Long-lasting relations	2.00	* * *	* * *	* * *
21	Meet people one knows	1.80	* * *	* * *	* * *
33	Residents genuine	1.68	* * *	* * *	* * *
24	Involved in community	1.96	* * *	x	* * *
6	Homes close together	1.12	x	x	* * *

Table 9.2 *continued*

QUALITIES RATED HIGHEST FOR PLACE DESCRIPTION 3

Quality		Ratings	Comparative Ratings		
			3/1	3/2	3/4
30	Place for children	2.57	* * *	* *	* * *
3	Entirely residential	1.87	* * *	* * *	* * *
2	Quiet	2.32	* * *	x	* * *
19	Put down roots	2.09	* * *	x	* * *
24	Involved in community	1.64	* * *	x	* * *
29	Protected from society	1.35	* * *	x	x
28	Residents similar	1.29	* * *	x	* * *

QUALITIES RATED HIGHEST FOR PLACE DESCRIPTION 4

Quality		Ratings	Comparative Ratings		
			4/1	4/2	4/3
26	Residents private	2.15	* * *	* * *	* * *
25	No pressure to join	1.87	* * *	* * *	* * *
29	Protected from society	1.08	* * *	x	x

* * * *p=<.001*   * * *p=<.010*   *x   not signifivcant*

QUALITIES RATED HIGHEST FOR PLACE DESCRIPTION 1
(The numbers in parenthesis refer back to Chapter 7.)

Convenient public transportation (Quality 9)
World-class restaurants, stores, and culture (Quality 11)
A wide selection of goods and services (Quality 16)
A wide diversity of people (Quality 31)
One can manage without a car (Quality 8)
Right in the center of activity (Quality 5)
One can have an active social life close to home (Quality 15)
A place to meet new people (Quality 14)
There are many tourists (Quality 12)
A place that is always full of surprises (Quality 7)

QUALITIES RATED HIGHEST FOR PLACE DESCRIPTION 2

Neighbors are outgoing and friendly (Quality 18)
People take care of one another (Quality 22)
Most people know one another (Quality 20)
Relationships are long-lasting and personal (Quality 23)
One will always meet people one knows (Quality 21)
Neighbors are genuine and down-to-earth (Quality 33)

QUALITIES RATED HIGHEST FOR PLACE DESCRIPTION 3

A place to raise children (Quality 30)
Entirely residential (Quality 3)

QUALITIES RATED HIGHEST FOR PLACE DESCRIPTION 4

Residents are private and go their own ways (Quality 26)
There is no pressure to socialize or join anything (Quality 25)

Knowing the component qualities of each type, we can now replace the numerical labels used in the interviews with more descriptive ones. Place description 1 is a cosmopolitan, active, lively type of neighborhood, and we will call it a *Center*; place description 2 is a settled, familiar, friendly type of neighborhood we will call a *Small-town*; place description 3 is an exclusive, homogeneous, family-directed type of neighborhood we will call a *Residential Partnership*; and place description 4, the type of place where one can find respite from people and pressures, we will call a *Retreat*.

The findings support the hypothesis that the place descriptions represent distinct types. The lines separating the types are, however, not as sharply drawn as I had hypothesized—there is some overlap.

QUALITIES OF CENTERS AND SMALL-TOWNS

A place that has a definite center (Quality 4)
Suits the needs of newcomers (Quality 13)
Neighboring homes are close to one another (Quality 6)

QUALITIES OF SMALL-TOWNS AND RESIDENTIAL PARTNERSHIPS

Protected from the larger problems of society (Quality 29)
A place to put down roots and settle (Quality 19)
Residents are involved in community affairs (Quality 24)
Neighboring homes are close to one another (Quality 6)
Quiet and relaxing (Quality 2)
All residents have a similar life-style (Quality 28)

QUALITIES OF RESIDENTIAL PARTNERSHIPS AND RETREATS

Protected from the larger problems of society (Quality 29)

QUALITIES OF RETREATS AND CENTERS

You can spend less time caring for the house (Quality 17)
A place where one can find sophisticated neighbors (Quality 32)

Centers and Small-towns both cater to diverse populations, Small-towns and Residential Partnerships are both exclusive, Centers and Retreats both cater to unconventional life-styles, and all types other than Centers are somewhat protected from the larger problems of society. The greatest overlap is found between Small-towns and Residential Partnerships.

Respondents were now asked whether the place descriptions have counterparts in places that they have experienced. They were asked the following questions.

Please tell me the name of a place that, in your opinion, fits each of these descriptions. Think, if you can, of places in and around the city.

Which of these four descriptions, in your opinion, comes closest to describing this part of the city where you live now?

Think of the places you have lived in, including places you have lived in the past. Have you ever lived in a place like Place [1, 2, 3, 4]?[2]

Most respondents had no trouble nominating a place to match each of the place descriptions (100% of respondents were able to nominate a Center, 98% a Small-town, 97% a Residential Partnership, and 93% a Retreat). In all, respondents gave 34 different examples of Centers, 50 each of Small-towns and Residential Partnerships, and 53 of Retreats. One-third of the respondents characterized their present neighborhood as a Center, another third as a Small-town, and just over a quarter said that they lived in a Residential Partnership. More than 60% said that they have, at some time, lived in any one of these three types, and all have lived in more than one (see Table 9.3).

Table 9.3

Respondents Who Have Lived in Each Type of Place

Quality	Center	Small-town	Partnership	Retreat
Live there now	34%	34%	27%	5%
Have ever lived there	62%	73%	86%	39%

It is fair to assume, then, that all three of these types are to be found within the area that was sampled, which is essentially within Baltimore City. Very few respondents (5%) classified their present neighborhood as a Retreat, but almost 40% said that they had at some time lived in a Retreat-type place.

It seems that the place descriptions do indeed trigger images of places that people have experienced.

The next question is whether each place description is associated with a particular segment of the population. Respondents were asked:

What kind of people do you think would most want to live in Place [1,2,3,4]?

Residents described the client group for each place as follows:

Centers. Centers are most attractive to yuppies, newly marrieds, kids just out of home or school, adults in their 20s and 30s. (Young, single people were mentioned five times more often in relation to the Center than to any other place.) Center people are thought of as sophisticated, outgoing, friendly, cultured, interesting, progressive people, with many interests, and they represent a wide mix of ages, types, cultures, races and incomes. They include newcomers, tourists, foreigners, and people who want a change, do not want to settle down, are carefree, and have few family ties. Centers attract people who are working, ambitious, professionals, and upwardly mobile. This is the only place for people who like excitement, adventure, are curious, lead active lives, and enjoy stimulation. It is the place that is least attractive to elderly people, people with young children, and people who like privacy and seclusion.

Small-towns. Small-towns attract people who want to settle down, are stable, homebodies, established, have a secure job, prefer routine to surprises, and like to live in a cohesive neighborhood where they know everyone; they are thought of as straightlaced, with a traditional view of home life, who prefer to live among their own kind. Many of them grew up in this type of place. They include married people with families, elderly people and retirees, single people, and families just starting out. Small-town places are least attractive to people who have no family ties.

Residential Partnerships. Residential Partnerships attract many of the same people as Small-towns, but with somewhat higher incomes, and they are even more attractive to married people with families. This is the place that is most attractive to people raised in the suburbs, who do not like the city, and who have their own transportation.

Retreats. While few respondents wanted to live in a Retreat, most had no trouble describing the people who did. Retreats are the most attractive of all places for people who enjoy privacy and quiet, being alone, staying to themselves, and not socializing with their neighbors. Retreat-type people are thought of as independent, involved with their own activities, and self-sufficient; they do not care about community, and they want to call their own shots. Retreats attract some of the same people as Centers, Small-towns and Residential Partnerships, but they also attract people who are antisocial, lonely, and out of the mainstream. Retreat-type places are least attractive to people who have lived in a big city.

There is a degree of correspondence between the characteristics of the people who are said to be attracted to each type of place and those of the respondents who already live there. Respondents who said they live in a Center were likely to be younger, unmarried, and renters; those in a Small-town were likely to be married; and those in a Residential Partnership were likely to be older. Too few respondents said they live in a Retreat to allow for separate analysis.

These findings support the hypothesis that the four place descriptions evoke places that appeal to different tastes and attract different segments of the population. Center-type places draw from one pool of people, and Small-towns and Residential Partnerships from another; Retreats draw from both pools. The Center is the easiest to characterize in terms of its resident population and the Retreat is the most difficult. It is easy to characterize residents of Small-towns and Residential Partnerships, but less easy to distinguish one population from the other.

The next question is: Does each descriptor refer to a setting that is considered, by some, to be the best place to live? The respondents were asked:

Imagine for a moment that you are moving from your present home, and that you are able to choose from all four types of places to live. Which type of place would be your first choice as a place for you to live now? Which would be your second, third, and fourth choices?

The findings show that about half (48%) of all the respondents would like to live in a Small-town, and the other half are about evenly divided between a Center (27%) and a Residential Partnership (22%). Only three in a hundred say they would like to live in a Retreat. The Center is the first choice of 59% of the people who presently live there; the comparable figures are 91% for Small-towns and 42% for Residential Partnerships. Respondents who live in a Small-town, as well as those who would like to live there (whether they do or not), tend to give a Center as their second choice, and vice versa; those who live in a Residential Partnership and those who would like to live there tend to give a Small-town as their second choice. Retreats are everyone's last choice of a place to live (see Table 9.4).

Comparing respondents' preferences with their present place of residence, we see that those who lived in Small-towns and Residential Partnerships were most likely to be retired and to prefer Small-towns. Respondents who lived in Centers and Retreats were most likely to be young and to prefer Centers. Men were most likely to live in Centers but prefer Residential Partnerships, while women were most likely to live in Residential Partnerships, but least likely to want to live there.[3] Overall, Small-town was the most widely valued type of place, and more people would like to live in Small-towns than actually live there (48% to 34%). More people want to live in Centers than in Residential Partnerships, but fewer people want to live in both than actually live there (Centers: 26% to 34%; Residential Partnerships: 22% to 27%).

Table 9.4

Choices of Place to Live by Current Place of Residence (Percentages)

BY PEOPLE WHO LIVE IN A CENTER (n=32)

Quality	Center	Small-town	Partnership	Retreat
First Choice	59	13	28	0
Second Choice	19	56	19	6
Third Choice	13	28	34	25
Fourth Choice	9	3	22	66

BY PEOPLE WHO LIVE IN A SMALL-TOWN (n=32)

Quality	Center	Small-town	Partnership	Retreat
First Choice	0	91	36	0
Second Choice	44	9	38	9
Third Choice	34	0	44	22
Fourth Choice	22	0	16	62

BY PEOPLE WHO LIVE IN A RESIDENTIAL PARTNERSHIP (n=26)

Quality	Center	Small-town	Partnership	Retreat
First Choice	15	39	42	4
Second Choice	19	31	27	23
Third Choice	46	23	27	4
Fourth Choice	19	8	4	69

BY PEOPLE WHO LIVE IN A RETREAT (n=5)

Quality	Center	Small-town	Partnership	Retreat
First Choice	40	60	0	0
Second Choice	20	20	40	20
Third Choice	20	20	40	20
Fourth Choice	20	0	20	60

The fact that so few people live and want to live in a Retreat calls for an explanation. One possibility is that we were not successful in including Retreat-type neighborhoods in the sample; another is that residents think of the housing unit and not the neighborhood as the proper place for a Retreat; a third is that the idea of removing oneself from community life is considered to be socially undesirable, and residents do not want to seem to support it. The explanation that at first glance seems the most obvious— that the Retreat is not a valid setting type—is, I suggest, counter-intuitive. The material discussed in previous chapters strongly suggests the presence of Retreat-type places, and besides, residents responded to the Retreat place description with images that have a distinctive character and value.

Overall, the findings show that respondents discriminate among the four place descriptions and, further, that they attach a different value to each of them.

The next question is whether each of the types is tied to a particular geographic location and whether there is general agreement about the way that a particular area should be classified. Neighborhood settings are, after all, districts that are imagined by residents, that mirror social relationships, and that evolve naturally and spontaneously in the course of domestic life. As a result, outsiders and residents are likely to pick up on different features, and two residents living in the same neighborhood may see it in quite different ways. Without objective determinants of type, is there sufficient agreement between insiders and outsiders to permit a general classification?

To answer this question, I compared the way that the eight interview neighborhoods were classified by the city planners who made the original nominations and by the residents who live there (see Table 9.5).

Table 9.5

Comparison of Classification by Planners and Residents

PLANNERS		RESIDENTS (By number of residents)			
		Center	Small-town	Partnership	Retreat
Center	Federal Hill	10	1	1	0
	Fells Point	8	2	1	0
Small-town	Dickeyville	10	2	0	0
	Hampden	2	8	1	1
Partnership	Lauraville	1	5	6	0
	Howard Park	1	1	8	2
Retreat	Apartments	10	0	1	1
	Oella	5	6	1	0

In the two neighborhoods that planners nominated as Centers, most residents (73% and 83%) agreed with this classification. The same is true in the two neighborhoods that the planners nominated as Small-town places (67% and 83%). The Residential Partnership category shows less agreement: In one of the neighborhoods that the planners nominated as a Residential Partnership, 66% of the residents agreed with the classification, but in the other one only 50% agree, and 42% classify it as a Small-town. In each of the neighborhoods nominated as Retreats only one resident agreed with the planners; in one, over 80% classify it as a Center, while in the other residents are more or less evenly divided between a Residential Partnership and a Small-town (50% to 42%).

These findings suggest that outsiders are able to recognize Center and Small-town places, that they tend to confuse Residential Partnerships with Small-towns, and that they have trouble recognizing Retreats. (They tend to think of apartments and semi-rural areas as Retreats.)

Next, I looked at the places that residents gave as examples of each type; I wanted to see what these places had in common.

The Center had 95 nominations; of these, 35 respondents mentioned downtown Baltimore, 25 mentioned inner-city neighborhoods by name, and 6 mentioned other large cities (such as London, San Francisco, Vancouver). Centers are, then, seen as "downtown-type" places. The Small-town had 93 nominations; the places mentioned included self-governing small towns outside the metropolitan area (such as Mt. Airy, Hagerstown, St. Michaels), small towns in fiction (Mayberry, Cabot's Cove), and urban neighborhoods characterized by diverse land uses and usually including a commercial center (such as Howard Park, Parkville, Catonsville). The Residential Partnership had 92 nominations; the single most frequently mentioned place (18 mentions) was "the suburbs," and places mentioned by name included neighborhoods in various parts of the urban area that were primarily residential and were without a distinct center. Partnerships are, then, seen as "suburban-type" places. Retreat had 88 nominations, which included 26 mentions of a big city (such as New York City, London), and 14 of the suburbs. Also mentioned were a range of urban neighborhoods and small towns. It seems that Retreat refers to the widest range of places, some of which may also qualify as Centers, Residential Partnerships and Small-towns.

These findings suggest that examples of Small-towns, Residential Partnerships, and Retreats can each be found in different parts of the urban area, while Centers are associated with downtown and the inner city. They also show that while attributes of the physical and social landscape are neither necessary nor sufficient as a basis for classification, nevertheless the form, appearance, and social structure of an area are effective indications of type. Places that received many nominations as prototypical examples provide a clue to these characteristics.

Center. Fells Point received twelve nominations as an example of a Center. It is an historic waterfront neighborhood within walking distance of downtown Baltimore, to which it is connected by bus and water taxi. It is a dense, row-house area with a diverse residential population; and it has a public market, a square, churches, stores, theaters, galleries, inns, bars, and restaurants that attract tourists as well as visitors from other parts of the city. Important characteristics include a mobile population, an active, lively streetscape, relatively high density, a diversity of people and places, and the presence of facilities catering mainly to visitors and tourists (Figure 9.1).

Fells Point was cited as an example of a Center. Photograph by the author.

Figure 9.1

Small-town. Ellicott City received seven nominations as an example of a Small-town type of place. It is the seat of Howard County; a sprawling, low-density, residential community with a picturesque, historic main street whose antiques stores and restaurants attract visitors from around the metropolitan area. Important characteristics include a stable population, small size, the presence of a clear center of activity, and a range of stores and institutions that serve primarily local residents (Figure 9.2).

Ellicott City was cited as an example of a Small-town. Photograph by the author.

Figure 9.2

Residential Partnership. Roland Park received 10 nominations as an example of a Residential Partnership. It is a residential community developed between 1890 and 1920. All houses are bound by restrictive covenants, and the community has a reputation for being exclusive. The site is hilly and wooded, and the layout and architecture are varied and picturesque. Within the area are a country club and a small planned shopping center.[4] Important characteristics include low density, a tranquil environment, residential character, and the presence of local churches, schools, and upscale commercial uses located on the fringes of the community (Figure 9.3).

Roland Park was cited as an example of a Residential Partnership. Photograph by the author.

Figure 9.3

Retreat. An apartment complex was mentioned eight times as an example of a Retreat (Figure 9.4). Oddly enough, only two of the twelve apartment dwellers in the sample said that they lived in a Retreat, and only one nominated her own building. This is probably because most apartment dwellers in the sample thought of the downtown area rather than the apartment

Downtown apartment buildings were cited as examples of a Retreat. Photograph by the author.

Figure 9.4

.lding as their neighborhood, and because some buildings provide communal facilities such as a health club, concierge service, and community rooms for residents. It is reasonable to assume, then, that respondents who nominated an apartment complex as a Retreat were thinking about the kind of place where there is little or no opportunity for social interaction. Important characteristics include the absence of any signs of community and of places that bring people together.

These findings suggest that key physical elements signal the existence of each type and facilitate identification. This is, of course, only an initial identification, and before using it as the basis for policy it must be confirmed by local attitudes and practices.

In summary, the study findings show that each place description evokes familiar images, is associated with distinctively different experiences, and serves different kinds of people, and so it is reasonable to say that the findings support the validity of the typology. The findings also identify the special qualities that are the norm for each type. When respondents were asked to relate the four types to places they have experienced—where they live, have lived, and would like to live—some types appeared to be more relevant than others; but some looseness of fit is to be expected when comparing ideal types with real-world places, and the degree of slack is not enough to invalidate the typology.

Two further questions must be raised. The first is whether respondents in the Baltimore study, in assigning qualities to each of the types, drew from real-world experience. It is conceivable that their image of Type 1 places, for example, was speculative or fantastical and that the qualities they assigned to it would be unlikely or inappropriate in real places of that type. To test this I assembled the quality ratings for Type 1 into two subsets—one for respondents who actually lived in Type 1 places (by their own reporting) and a second for those who did not. Then I compared the ratings for each quality in the two subsets. I did the same with the quality ratings for Types 2, 3, and 4. I found little significant difference between the subset pairs, and so it is reasonable to assume that the quality ratings for each type were compatible with real-world experiences.[5]

The second question is whether residents in responding to questions about "the place where you live" all interpreted the word "place" to mean the same thing. If two people each select a different place as a point of reference, then their responses may reflect differences between places rather than differences in the way the same place is characterized. An exploratory study suggests that residents do, in fact, use different reference points in response to questions about their neighborhood. In this study, conducted in a gated garden-apartment development in suburban Washington, DC,[6] 25 randomly selected residents were asked questions about their apartment, their apartment complex, and the "part of the city where you live now." Then, they were asked which of these three locales they considered to be their neighborhood. Ten respondents identified the complex as their neighborhood, and ten identified a part of the city. None gave the apartment as their neighborhood.

I believe that this finding, while it is derived from a different residential setting, has relevance for the Baltimore study because it supports the multi-level definition of neighborhood suggested in Chapter 2. Neighborhood can be defined at several levels, and these levels are connected so that a Retreat-type *home setting* may be located within a Small-town-type *neighborhood setting*, which in turn may be part of a Center-type *compound neighborhood*. The residential experience may be affected, then, by the quality of the neighborhood at all three levels. Different interpretations of "place" in the Baltimore study would not, however, invalidate the qualities associated with each of the types, because the assignments were made to the place descriptions and not to their geographical references; that is, the qualities of Type 1 belong to a place that matches the place description of Type 1, whether that place is envisioned as the complex, or as part of the city.

The typology was tested again in a separate study. Thirteen of the 30 qualities (ones with high ratings) were selected and included in a larger study of Baltimore neighborhoods.[7] This study included a random selection of three blocks in each of 30 neighborhoods and up to 24 telephone interviews with household heads in each block. Residents living in apartments were excluded from the study. In all, 704 interviews were completed.

Respondents were asked to rate their present neighborhoods on each of the 13 qualities. In some cases the wording of the statements was changed from that of the original study in order to suit the telephone format. (The changes are noted below.) Respondents were told:

I am going to read some descriptions that may or may not apply to your neighborhood. After I have read each one, please tell me if that description is true or untrue of your neighborhood as it is now.

In each case, respondents were first asked if the statement was true or untrue, and then if it was very or somewhat true, or very or somewhat untrue. The 13 qualities were:

A place that is entirely residential (Quality 3)
A place that has a definite center, where a lot of neighborhood activity happens

and you are likely to run into people from the neighborhood (an elaboration of the original Quality 13 for greater clarity)

A wide diversity of people live here (Quality 15)

A place with high quality stores (Quality 16)

A place with high quality restaurants (the original Quality 16 was separated into two questions)

A place where people know one another (Quality 17)

A place where neighbors are outgoing and friendly (Quality 18)

A place where people take care of one another (Quality 22)

A place where there is some pressure to join local groups and socialize (the original Quality 25 was inverted)

A place where residents are private and go their own ways (Quality 26)

A place where residents have a similar life-style (Quality 28)

A place to raise children (Quality 30)

A place with a wide selection of goods and services close to home (Quality 31)

I expected that the sample would pick up residents in Center, Small-town and Residential Partnership neighborhoods. Based on the previous findings and the fact that the sample did not include apartment dwellers, I did not expect to find respondents who said they lived in Retreat neighborhoods. Based, then, on the earlier findings, I expected the 13 qualities to reveal three underlying dimensions. As shown in Table 9.6, a principal-compo-

Table 9.6

Residents Rate Qualities of Their Neighborhoods
(Principal Components Analysis. Results after Varimax Rotation)

Qualities	Factor 1	Factor 2	Factor 3
High-quality stores	.28149	.72734	-.05270
High-quality restaurants	-.06007	.71841	.01120
Selection of goods	.39661	.54864	.03948
Residents are diverse	-.17624	.43430	.01140
Has a center	.00765	.38666	.37265
Residents private	.09994	.08534	-.68449
Know one another	.33082	-.06460	.65926
Neighbors friendly	.45086	.01503	.59927
Pressure to join	-.10099	.29723	.39261
Place for children	.71227	.16458	.08600
Entirely residential	.61482	-.18861	-.16451
Residents similar	.58657	-.01645	.11809
Neighbors care	.56872	.13500	.45911

nents analysis of the responses does, in fact, reveal three factors or clusters of qualities that are very close to what was expected. Factor 2 is the Center, Factor 3 the Small-town, and Factor 1 the Residential Partnership. These correlations support the distinctiveness of the types and, as they are based on an assessment of real places, not ideal types, they also show that real places are reasonably true to type.

Another finding of this study reflects on popular images of good neighborhoods. Residents were asked a second round of questions. They were told:

I am going to read a list of changes that can happen in some neighborhoods. We are not saying that anyone is planning any changes in your neighborhood. We are not involved with people who do make changes in neighborhoods. But for each change, if it were to happen in your neighborhood, do you think it would make your neighborhood better, worse or neither?

Residents were then asked twelve of the same questions (question 3, about residential land use, was omitted here because it was expanded into a series of questions later in the interview), but the questions were rephrased to indicate a direction of change. For example: If neighbors were more friendly, if residents in the neighborhood were more diverse, if more residents in the neighborhood knew one another, if residents were more active in community affairs. In each case, respondents were first asked if the change would make the neighborhood better or worse, and then if it would make it a little or a lot better, or a little or a lot worse.

This time, a principal-components analysis showed only two dimensions (Table 9.7). Three of the five items associated with the Center still hang together, but the items associated with the Small-town and the Residential Partnership now go together to make a single factor. It seems that when thinking about existing neighborhoods respondents recognized three different types of places, but when thinking about possible improvements they identified only two. A reasonable explanation is that a Center is the most singular of the types—Residential Partnerships (which many associate with "the suburbs") are often thought of as small towns—so that people evaluate possible improvements according to whether they will make their neighborhood more like a Center, or less.

Additional studies are needed to test the relevance of the four types in other places and in other cultural contexts. In the meantime there is, I suggest, enough support for the typology to warrant further elaboration of the types and an exploration of their practical applications.

Table 9.7

Residents Rate Changes in Their Neighborhoods
(Principal Components Analysis. Results after Varimax Rotation)

Qualities	Factor 1	Factor 2	Factor 3
High-quality stores	.09461	.81242	.09318
High-quality restaurants	.05842	.79545	-.17540
Selection of goods	.20806	.76310	-.04425
Neighbors care	.73094	.15906	-.06447
Neighbors friendly	.68346	.12424	-.12699
Know one another	.67612	.12442	-.15620
Active in community	.65683	.11805	.07904
Has a center	.54197	.33470	.00005
Place for children	.42340	.39099	.05152
Residents private	.39545	-.01986	.00936
Residents similar	.05763	.06097	.93073
Residents are diverse	.28672	.21445	-.35443

The Baltimore study hints at some of these applications. For example, the finding that most people want to live in Small-town settings and that more people want to than actually do live there suggests the need for more settings of this type. Today, there is widespread interest in the principles that influenced the design of small towns in the past, but there is a question as to how one can generate the complex, interwoven relationships and attitudes that are essential for good Small-town settings. Residential Partnerships, which require only weak and simple social relationships, are easier to plan; and, in fact, we have had so much success with them that, in the United States, we have built little else during most of the twentieth century. If, however, the study findings are generally true, then this is not the type of setting in which most people prefer to live. More people would like to live in Centers, but although we build many new concentrations of activity, some exceedingly large, they lack the qualities of good Center-type settings. In fact, there are so few good examples of Center-type settings outside the old center city that respondents in the study identified the type with that one geographic location. Concerns such as these have important design implications.

NOTES

1. Actually, 33 qualities were identified in Chapter 7, but as three of these qualities applied equally to all neighborhoods, they would not serve to distinguish one type from another and so they were omitted. These three qualities were (1) *a place that is clean and well maintained*, (10) *a place where residents feel safe and secure*, and (27) *a place that has a reputation as a desirable place to live.*

2. Respondents were asked questions about the "place" or "part of the city" in which they live in order to avoid using the word "neighborhood" and the possible question "What do you mean by neighborhood?" But the phrase that was used instead of "neighborhood" is equally ambiguous. Each respondent is free to choose his or her own definition of "place," and differences in responses may reflect different units of reference. This possible problem is discussed later.

3. Compare Marsh's (1990) comment that in the early days of the suburbs the move from the center-city appealed to men, but women felt the lack of opportunities for social interaction. Compare, also, findings by Shlay and Digregorio (1985) that women prefer a more "citified" living environment than men.

4. In a separate study, 76 residents of Roland Park were given an abbreviated version of the questionnaire. Here too, all four descriptors triggered images of real places. Fifty-three percent identified Roland Park as a Residential Partnership. The majority of residents, therefore, agree with the assessment of the general Baltimore study. I have more to say about the Roland Park study in Chapter 11.

5. Here are the major differences between the two sub-sets, that is, between the ratings given by those who lived in the type of place they were rating and those who did not. Respondents who said they lived in Centers rated Type 1 more highly on: *a place to put down roots and settle* (p=<.001), *a place that is entirely residential* (p=<.001), and *a place where relationships are long-lasting and personal* (p=<.010). Respondents who said they lived in Small-town places rated Type 2 more highly on: *a place that suits the needs of newcomers to the city* (p=<.010). Respondents who said they lived in Residential Partnerships rated Type 3 more highly on: *living here, one can manage without a car* (p=<.010). Respondents who said they lived in Retreats did not rate Type 4 significantly differently on any qualities.

6. "Good places to live: The Americana Finnmark study" by Sarah Kane, a student in the Urban Studies and Planning program at the University of Maryland, College Park, 1994.

7. The study, titled *Longitudinal Effects of Crime and Signs of Disorder on Communities*, was funded in 1994 by the National Institute of Justice, a division of the U.S. Department of Justice. Grant #93-IJ-CX-0022, with Ralph B. Taylor as Co-Principal Investigator.

CHAPTER TEN

Elaboration

H aving proposed a four-part typology and tested its validity, I will now elaborate on each type by matching it with relevant concepts in the neighborhood literature.[1] The literature does not, of course, make reference to Center, Small-town, Residential Partnership, or Retreat by name, and so I have taken considerable liberty in aligning the types with the concepts. For example, the description of the Center draws on studies by Milgram and Proshansky of people in central cities; that of the Small-town draws on Furay's analysis of life in a small town; and that of the Residential Partnership draws on Baumgartner's analysis of residential attitudes in a suburb. This does not mean, for example, that every suburb is necessarily a Residential Partnership, but rather that suburbs that fit Baumgartner's description also fit the Residential Partnership type.

Because each type is characterized by the nature and intensity of social relationships among neighbors rather than members of a household, the types are least relevant at the most immediate level of neighborhood, which I have called the home setting.[2] The types are more relevant at the other two levels of neighborhood: The neighborhood setting (a group of home settings) and the composite neighborhood (a group of neighborhood settings). The area covered by a single type may range in size from one to many city blocks, and it may be located anywhere in the metropolitan region.

What follows are descriptions of good neighborhoods of each type. They represent, in a very general way, an urban design program.

CENTER NEIGHBORHOODS

Center neighborhoods are more facility-dependent than other neighborhood types, and they have more connecting facilities within the neighborhood area. They are the most cosmopolitan and open of all the types. People who like living in a Center neighborhood look for a setting that is bustling, varied and changing, where they can constantly go to new and different places and meet new and different people.

A good Center neighborhood includes what is best about in-town living: It is a crowded, bustling, varied, and ever-changing environment, stimulating and exciting rather than quiet and restful. Main streets are pleasant pedestrian environments, where people are not physically insulated from one another and where there are many opportunities for chance meetings and interactions. Plazas and parks bring different uses together rather than keep them apart. All public spaces are active, inviting, hospitable, and brightly lit at night. Uses that abut these spaces are designed to generate pedestrian activity; they are varied, small in scale, visible and recognizable from the street, uninterrupted for long stretches, accessible to the general public, and they have closely spaced points of entry. In addition, they remain open well into the night.

Bal du Moulin de Galette, by Pierre-Auguste Renoir (1876), Musée d'Orsay, Paris. Photo courtesy of Réunion des Musées Nationaux.

Figure 10.1

A good Center neighborhood caters to residents' needs during off-work hours, and so it emphasizes non-work activities—it is playful. Old buildings present opportunities for imaginative and playful adaptations—the creation of housing units with unusual volumes and shapes, interesting details, and historical significance. Diversity, which is necessary for liveliness, is not so extreme as to spoil the spirit of fun. (A downtown resident told me that she resented constantly being made to feel guilty by the sight of homeless people sleeping on the doorstep.)

With all of its activity, a Center neighborhood is inevitably noisy, and so the housing units are designed with more than usual attention to sound insulation. To relieve the feeling of crowding, the neighborhood offers intimate views into quiet squares, parks, and courtyards and distant views over rooftops, perhaps toward mountains or the sea.

A good Center often features impressive buildings, extravagant amenities, important monuments, notable public spaces, and the latest architectural innovations.

People who live in a good Center neighborhood can find what they need for an active life within easy distance of home. This generally requires a fine-grain mix of activities, a dense pattern of development, and an efficient public transportation system.

Many facilities address people's desires rather than their basic needs; they include fine restaurants, unusual stores, and major sporting and entertainment facilities. A good Center neighborhood enjoys considerable duplication and redundancy, with special places that serve highly specialized user groups. There are no places where all residents come together; Instead, there are choices among many competing, ever-changing facilities that serve diverse interests and tastes. Residents are not loyal to any of them; they sample them all, switching from one to another in a constant search for novelty and variety.

A good Center neighborhood caters to nonresidents and new arrivals. Clear structure of space, good directions, and visible, legible functions make it easy to find one's way around. There are hotels, inns and hostels. There are places to meet new people, and there are places to rest, and to find refreshment and information.

Because Center residents see and meet a great many different people every day and they do not have personal knowledge of most of them, they are highly selective and superficial in many of their engagements and are often suspicious and cautious in their initial dealings (Lofland 1973). Because they rely heavily on appearances, first impressions are important.

A good Center neighborhood has buildings in a range of architectural styles, and it houses people of different ages, classes, and cultures. The various social regions are fine-grained, their borders are permeable and paths cross, there are places where different groups come together and meet, and places where they coexist and learn something about one another without necessarily making contact. This makes it possible for residents to experience great diversity in the course of their daily lives (Sennett 1990). They are not necessarily less prejudiced than people in other settings, but they have learned to deal with their prejudices (Anderson 1985).

A good Center neighborhood is sensitive to the moods, forces and fashions of the moment. It is constantly changing and full of surprises, a work-in-progress rather than a completed set piece. It reflects many independent decisions by many different people, and as a result it is somewhat chaotic, with elements that are conflicting and inharmonious.

The very factors that make a Center tolerant of dissimilar social values and behaviors also weaken the informal mechanisms that define and regulate social order; as a result, a Center neighborhood, even a good one, is especially vulnerable to crimes and acts of incivility. People who look for a Center life-style will accept noise, crowds, competition, and unpredictability, but they are less tolerant of insecurity, poor maintenance, and a bad reputation. These three qualities, undesirable in any neighborhood, are more likely to be found in a Center than in any other type.

There is nothing new in this. Problems of this kind have long been associated with living in a Center, and residents quickly learn the value (and the stressfulness) of defensive behaviors and a defensible physical environment (Newman 1973). What is new (at least in American cities) is that successful Centers in the past could depend on the presence of many reluctant participants—residents who, given a choice, would rather have lived somewhere else but who were tied to the Center because they needed to be close to work. Today, these residents can live elsewhere. Those who prefer a green and tranquil residential environment will find it outside the Center. The Center attracts people who look for the special residential experience that it offers, and a sense of security is a prime requisite.

Good Centers include policing and surveillance to increase residents' safety. Design features include clear demarcation and differentiation of public and private spaces; placing uses, activities, and entrances where they will ensure the continuous presence of people who can provide surveillance; providing formal space managers and encouraging informal ones; tailoring shared facilities to the number of people who are able to effectively police themselves. (These and other techniques are discussed in Jacobs 1961, Newman 1973, and Whyte 1980.)

There is another approach to safety in a Center, which is to reconstitute it as a Small-town or Residential Partnership, types with greater built-in resistance to incivilities. There are many examples of this form of protective coloration. The principal of a company developing a $600 million, 42-acre project of condos and townhouses in downtown Baltimore described it as a "village with all the features and amenities and conveniences of being down-town" (Mirabella 1993). The 1994–2014 comprehensive plan for Seattle identifies four types of neighborhoods and refers to them as "villages," which places them in the curious position of having to call downtown an "Urban Center Village" (Seattle Planning Department 1993). This approach, if it amounts to more than semantics and if done properly, may increase safety; but at the same time it diminishes the essential character of a Center that is its main attraction. The patient may recover from the disease and die of the cure.

While a country setting attracts residents who look for relaxation in a natural environment, a good Center neighborhood attracts residents who look for relaxation in theaters, concert halls, galleries, restaurants, promenades, and places where people meet and watch one another. It is attractive to single people, young people who are starting out, older people who are starting again, newcomers, upwardly mobile professionals, people who are relatively free of family obligations, and those who enjoy social life outside of home and family. It is also attractive to people with nontraditional life-styles and people who are not yet ready to settle down. As there is a high rate of turnover among residents, a good Center neighborhood offers rental accommodations at various price levels and institutions to assist with home finding and financing.

A Center neighborhood can be hard on parents with young children. While some are convinced that children can benefit from growing up in a Center—they learn to be sophisticated, how to deal with the "real" world— there is no doubt that crowding, the presence of so many strangers, the scarcity of open space, and the intensity of street traffic create a need for constant supervision. A parent cannot simply send a child out to play. In addition, some parents do not like children to be exposed to behaviors that challenge their (the parents') values and teachings. For many parents, a Center neighborhood, even a good one, will never compete successfully with other neighborhood types as a good place in which to raise children.

In summary, a good Center is active and lively, has a full range of facilities, offers a wide range of choice, serves visitors and newcomers, has a diversity of people and places, is constantly changing and evolving, provides special protection against incivilities, and represents a wide range of needs, tastes and values.

Existing Centers, typically, are inherited from the past and located in the heart of the city. Recent large-scale developments prove that we are capable of creating new Centers if we want to and that we can build them anywhere in the urban area. But to be successful, a Center must be true to type, very different from the "fantasy urbanism" of the shopping mall with its highly coordinated, carefully controlled environment (Crawford 1992).

SMALL-TOWN NEIGHBORHOODS

Small-town neighborhoods are less facility-dependent than Centers, and they have fewer connecting facilities within the neighborhood area; they are also less cosmopolitan and less open. People who like living in a Small-town neighborhood look for a setting with a strong sense of community and continuity, where people are friendly, and stores, institutions, and public places cater to local residents.

Sidewalk Superintendents by Stevan Dohanos, 1948.
© The Curtis Publishing Company.

Figure 10.2

A good Small-town neighborhood is a familiar, manageable, more-or-less self-contained world, centered around its local businesses and institutions. These tend to be small. They offer (within the compound neighborhood) a full complement of retail, employment, religious, educational and entertainment services. Residents always see people they know there, and there are some facilities where most people know one another. Residents gather there to socialize and to affirm their common interests and group identity, as well as to transact business. Local facilities allow a blending of home and public life. They make it possible for circles of business, family, and friendship to intersect. A good Small-town neighborhood is visually distinct, bounded, and with a generally-agreed-upon name. It is small enough so that each resident knows many others by face or name and reputation. Typically, it has a concentration of stores, institutions, and public places (perhaps "Main Street," "The Avenue," or "The Center"), which serves as the focus of common identity.

Residents go outside the neighborhood for special and big-ticket items, but in general they shop locally even though cheaper and more varied goods and services may be available outside the neighborhood. They are willing to pay the extra cost involved either because they feel that the services are unique (providing, for example, one-of-a-kind goods, opportunities for companionship, personal service, ready credit), or because travelling outside the neighborhood is difficult (as in the case of some elderly people, some children), or because residents are simply unwilling to spend time or effort to shop around. Local stores depend on this localistic attitude for their survival.

A good Small-town neighborhood develops and perpetuates a system of local social networks. This requires a population that remains in place over a long period of time. Newcomers take time to assimilate into the social fabric of local communities, and high residential mobility prevents the development of extensive friendship bonds and local associational ties (Kasarda and Janowitz 1974).

A stable population, typically, means that residents have steady employment and a high rate of home ownership. Residents know one another—who they are, what they are like, and what they do—and they have frequent contact with the same people over a long period of time. This makes it next to impossible for residents to present an edited version of themselves to their neighbors (Halpern 1992, p. 5). They tend to gossip and repeat over and over again anecdotes that reaffirm group values and mores, and they keep informal accounts of favors owed to others and due from them. Their actions and attitudes are colored more by personal experiences and relationships than by outside ideas or examples. They focus on local issues and have strong feelings about familiar things. They build a long-lasting network of relationships that has a strong identification with the place.

This kind of community is more characteristic of working-class than middle-class residents. Even then, it needs time to develop, which means that a good Small-town environment cannot be created all of a piece; it has to evolve.

In a good Small-town neighborhood, the stores and institutions maintain a local flavor; they cater mainly to "regulars." Residents outrank outsiders and are treated as privileged users while outsiders are treated as guests. Places and procedures are often not sign-posted—they rely on people being in the know. Typically, outsiders can find facilities that are more convenient, cheaper, and more efficient elsewhere in the region. Those who patronize Small-town facilities are attracted by the local flavor and the feeling of authenticity.

New residents who move into the neighborhood are slow to win acceptance, and the community's "inner life," with its shared confidences, appreciation of idiosyncracies, and easy allusions, remains impenetrable to them for a long time (Furay 1983).

A good Small-town neighborhood is located out of the direct path of growth, and its edges are defined and protected by the adjacent land uses. The neighborhood has informal social mechanisms that discourage or slow down the rate of change within the area and formal associations that negotiate with the city and with potential developers to stop, revise, or adapt proposed developments so that residents can accommodate to them and so that they minimize disruption to ongoing community life.

A Small-town neighborhood is attractive to retired people and people who are married with young children. It attracts people who are conservative, settled, homebodies, who look for a sense of belonging and continuity over time, and who feel nostalgic about the days when life was a lot less complicated. It attracts those who have grown up in small towns. It also attracts immigrants and other minority groups, who like to or must live among people who understand them and who can be counted upon for assistance in times of need.

In summary, a good Small-town neighborhood has a clear center and well defined boundaries, a full complement of local facilities and institutions, a stable residential population and a network of friendships. It favors residents over outsiders, is protected from change, and represents a range of needs, tastes, and values.

A Small-town environment is what most people say they look for in a place to live, and so it is not surprising to see it invoked by designers of new residential areas and redesigners of old ones.[3] Their plans typically incorporate design features that facilitate interaction among neighbors. Higher residential densities increase the likelihood of chance meetings, the presence of yards and porches increases the likelihood of socializing, mixed uses draw people with different roles and purposes together, a pleasant walking environment encourages people to interact in an informal way, and, of course, local parks, stores, community centers, and institutions create places for people to come together.

These provisions create opportunities for interaction, but they do not in themselves ensure that interaction will take place or that it will be the right kind; this depends ultimately on having the right kind of people and the right kind of institutions. The distinctiveness of their built forms makes Small-town neighborhoods very attractive to planners, but it often leads them to think of the settings as a physical rather than social entity (Southworth 1993), and there are many instances of neighborhood facilities, centers, and plazas that stand unused (see, for example, Guterson 1992). It is far easier to create the look of a small town than the experience of one.

Attempts to create new Small-town settings have to buck three strong, prevalent trends. First, the Small-town experience requires a localistic attitude on the part of residents. Most city people in the United States today, with access to an automobile and a complete network of urban highways, have become accustomed to shopping throughout the region for goods and services; instead of simply going to the nearest grocery store, they search out the one that has the best french bread, organic vegetables, or homemade pasta. There is a serious question as to which residents are willing to give up this freedom of choice in return for the comfort of shopping in their own neighborhood.

Second, small stores have traditionally been an important feature of Small-town neighborhoods; they serve as information centers, hangouts, and sponsors of local events; they generate pedestrian traffic and reflect and reinforce the sense of community. But in recent years, retail establishments, building on their ability to draw automobile customers from ever-larger distances, have taken advantage of economies of scale to become bigger and more widely spaced, offering a more extensive selection of goods and services at lower prices. Neighborhood-based establishments have struggled to compete. With a footloose local population, many small merchants have had to lower standards and cater to the low end of the market, or raise prices and switch from basic to specialty items. Many stores that sell staples have gone out of business and not been replaced, or have been replaced by chains that offer less personal service and have a weaker commitment to the local area. Survival of neighborhood stores and institutions may depend on a radical restructuring of the current patterns of retailing and service delivery. The demise of neighborhood-based stores has a parallel in neighborhood-based public facilities. Concern for increased overall efficiency, economy, and equity has led to the consolidation of public service facilities, which has meant the end of the neighborhood school, firehouse, library, and post office. Each facility that leaves the neighborhood or that expands its market area beyond the neighborhood weakens the ties that bind neighborhood residents together.

Third, ease of travel combined with improvements in electronic communications, allows residents to develop interests and pursue social activities outside the neighborhood. This makes them less dependent on their neighbors for companionship and for a sense of belonging. Increasingly, people are coming to regard the neighborhood as a place where one can get away from social ties, not find them.

Because of these changes in social patterns, many people who think they want a Small-town setting are really looking for a different kind of community, one with a looser form of engagement, that has more limited rules of association and requires less commitment.

The critical question is not whether the small town can be rehabilitated in the image of its earlier strength and growth—for clearly it cannot—but whether American life will be able to evolve any other integral community to replace it. (Lerner 1957, p. 3)

For a great many people the Residential Partnership, not the Small-town, is that integral community.

RESIDENTIAL PARTNERSHIP NEIGHBORHOODS

Residential Partnerships are more unit-dependent than Small-towns, and they have fewer connecting facilities within the neighborhood area; they are also more parochial and more closed. People who like living in a Residential Partnership neighborhood look for an exclusive, trouble-free, all-residential setting, one that has its own private facilities.

A good Residential Partnership creates a cocoon of tranquility around the housing units of its members. It emphasizes the recreational functions of home, offering its residents special amenities such as expansive views, attractive landscapes and, sometimes, recreational facilities such as walking paths, swimming pools, and health centers.

In the interest of maintaining tranquility, a good Residential Partnership typically has its own system of governance and formal and informal proce-

Illustration by W. Heath Robinson, from *How to Live in a Flat*, 1937. #12315pp27. © The British Library.

Figure 10.3

dures to screen out potential neighbors who may be unpredictable or disagreeable. Residents tend to avoid intimate relationships with one another in order to avoid occasions for disagreements. When problems arise, they are inclined to avoid the offender, learn to live with him, or approach him in a conciliatory fashion. They depend on neighborhood officials, such as police and inspectors, to deal with direct confrontations.

A good Residential Partnership is essentially a bedroom community. It has good connections to public transportation and highway systems, and these provide residents with easy access to home-related services in other neighborhoods and nonresidential parts of the city. Residents use a variety of external facilities, and they are not likely to meet fellow residents at any of them.

In a good Residential Partnership, all amenities within the neighborhood area are for the benefit of residents. Frequently, these amenities are privately owned, included in the sale or rental price of the units, run by a formal organization of residents, and maintained by fees that are backed by covenants. To establish that the neighborhood area is for residents only, it is sometimes fenced and gated.

Exceptions to the residents-only rule are made in the case of facilities that are both needed by residents and meet certain conditions: They are located so as not to draw outsiders through the neighborhood (which generally means on a boundary), are adequately screened from adjoining residents, and are subject to legally enforceable restrictions on their size, conditions of use, and hours of operation. Typically, they are not open in the evenings or at night.

A good Residential Partnership is a community. Typically, however, this is a community in which the ties are fragile and easily ruptured. If the tranquility of the neighborhood is threatened, residents are as likely to withdraw as to resist.

A Residential Partnership is attractive to those who want an environment that provides minimal distractions outside the home, that reflects their own needs, tastes and values, and over which they can exercise a great deal of control. It is attractive to people who are fearful of conditions in the larger society, to those for whom home rather than community is the center of domestic life, and to those who grew up in the suburbs and think of themselves as "not city people."

In summary, a good Residential Partnership is a tranquil setting for domestic life, a community of limited liability[4] representing a single set of needs, tastes, and values. It provides amenities for residents only, but is not self-sufficient—residents are dependent on outside facilities and services.

Today, the Residential Partnership is the most common type of neighborhood being built in the United States. It is found in the suburbs and in condominium developments throughout the urban area, in clusters of single-family and row houses, and in apartment buildings. The control that it affords is especially important to middle- and upper-middle income residents, and especially in places where public environments are seen as threatening or the level of public services as inadequate. Residential Partnerships are also popular with developers because they have some of the social features of Small-town neighborhoods, but these do not depend on relationships that are substantial, hard to conjure up, and in need of a long maturation time. The simple provision of amenities and the immediate response of the market are the only signs of success that a developer needs.

Residential Partnerships are not without problems. When they are large, residents complain about not being able to get anywhere without a car. Mothers complain about the time they must spend as chauffeurs to their children, and children complain about being dependent on their mothers to get around. A prospective graduate student, in his application to the University of Maryland, referred to this lack of access as one of his reasons for wanting to pursue a career in urban planning.

Growing up in a "planned community," I learned at a young age the harsh reality that greets so many unsuspecting suburban youths: You can't get anywhere without a car. Whether I wanted to see a friend, participate in an extracurricular activity, or simply seek out spontaneous human contact, I had to get good old Mom to drive me in the trusty station wagon. Unfortunately, there was a catch—Mom worked. I was screwed. So in those days before I received my driver's license (I never did get the car to go along with the license), I made a promise to myself that I would someday design a city that was accessible for people of all ages.

People who are obliged to remain at home all day—women with young children, men and women who work out of their homes, and the elderly—criticize Residential Partnerships for being dull; tourists complain that there is nothing interesting to see or do there; and designers decry their lack of urbanity. Social commentators blame the Residential Partnership for contributing to residential segregation, because it allows the separation of age and social groups (Figure 10.4); it allows the elite to create separate residential enclaves, with their own services and schools. This "secession of the successful" leads them in the name of community, to forsake their stake in the public good (Reich 1991).

Some Residential Partnerships have restrictive covenants that effectively dictate what residents may and may not do there—for example, where and

There is concern that residents of private residential enclaves will not want to contribute to the cost of public services. Artist Bill Holbrook. Reprinted with special permission of King Features Syndicate.

Figure 10.4

what they may plant, what building materials and colors they may select, how much their house has to cost, and what constitutes offensive conduct. In extreme cases they fix the color of the curtains, set a maximum weight for residents' pets, and establish a minimum age for occupancy. Typically, these restrictions are rigidly administered by residents' associations, and while most residents accept them as a condition of ownership, some see them as unreasonable limitations on their personal freedom (McKenzie 1994; Louv 1983).

Some of these criticisms draw strength from the fact that many Residential Partnerships being built today are poor examples of their type. In addition, I suspect that some critics fail to recognize Residential Partnerships as a distinct type, but see them either as inadequate Small-town neighborhoods (too restrictive, social ties too weak), or failed Retreat neighborhoods (too much community, too little privacy). In addition, Residential Partnerships dominate the contemporary housing market. Stacked one next to the other, unrelieved by other types of neighborhoods, they create a monotonous landscape. People who would prefer something else but cannot find anything suitable, blame Residential Partnerships for not being that something else.

RETREAT NEIGHBORHOODS

Retreats are the most unit-dependent of all the neighborhood types, and they have no connecting facilities within the neighborhood area. People who like living in a Retreat neighborhood look for a setting with pleasant surroundings, where they can be physically and socially detached from their neighbors.

A good Retreat neighborhood is a place that reinforces one's identity as a unique individual rather than a member of a community. It is what is best about country living in the minds of city people—a private place where one can be alone, quiet, rested, and contemplative, a place for creation, comfort, reflection, and healing. It is a place where enjoyment of one's physical surroundings is not disturbed by people.

A good Retreat minimizes occasions that bring together those who would rather stay apart. There are few, if any, shared facilities. Public spaces separate people. Outdoor spaces provide a backdrop, a prospect, and a buffer between neighbors.[5]

In a good Retreat neighborhood the housing units are largely self-sufficient. Residents know who their neighbors are, but they do not bump into them in the course of everyday life and are only dimly aware of their presence. Neighbors are amiable but not forward, discreet rather than intimate,

Artist Thomas Fogarty (1873–1938). Picture courtesy of the Library of Congress.

Figure 10.5

considerate, helpful only if called upon. They do not intrude on one's sense of being alone in the landscape.

Units are designed and equipped to satisfy a full range of residential functions and to contain them so as to minimize interference or chance encounters. Special attention is given to the placement of door- and window-openings and the separation of potentially intrusive uses. A resident is able to look out and not see anybody, and people outside are unable to see in.

Privacy is enhanced by spacing the units far apart and screening views into and out of them (as in the case of detached houses, large estates and lots on the edge of the city, and urban mansions with walled gardens), or by locating units in buildings with visual and acoustic privacy built into the design of the structure (as in the case of apartments), or by locating units in inaccessible spots such as on cliffsides or rooftops. Individual residents maintain a certain social distance between themselves and their neighbors.

In a good Retreat neighborhood, the appearance of the surroundings as seen from the unit reinforces the feeling of remoteness and separation. Valued views include natural features and spacious gardens, as well as buildings seen from a distance so that their formal qualities are more apparent than their social implications. These views are protected from being destroyed or blocked.

Views from the unit create a strong symbolic relationship between the unit and the landscape in which it is placed. Frank Lloyd Wright's own house in rural Wisconsin offers an excellent example of such a relationship.

From within the cavernous loggia, there is a preliminary view of the valley and river directly ahead, just over the parapet of the shallow terrace. Before coming out into the open, however, you turn ninety degrees to the right. Through the Dutch door of the corner entrance into the living room, there is another vista, this time across the room and over the dining terrace. The view is up the valley toward the family chapel to the southeast. Once you come around the bookshelf and opposite the fireplace, the view opens out in an arc of 270 degrees. It cuts across the room and over the hills in a single, effortless, arching movement which seems to follow the curve of the earth itself, as the stone fireplace to the rear, diagonally opposite the corner window, anchors the vista back in the hill behind. (Levine 1992)

This kind of relationship is also possible in the heart of the city, when the urban landscape is revealed as an abstract composition of forms and shapes, with the qualities of a natural phenomenon.

See it at nightfall when the moon sheds its silver light on its rectilinear masses, when thousands of lights scintillate in numberless windowpanes and the waters of the bay, in restless waves, lap against its shores voluptuously, while boats carry messages of the hopes of men. At such moments, the soul of Manhattan seems to emerge from the very depths of this fantastic conglomeration of enormous masses and, exhorting the city with a caress, cry: Forwards! (Francisco Mujica 1929, quoted in Mansfield 1990, p. 3)

A good Retreat neighborhood is not readily accessible to outsiders. It may be off the beaten track, or difficult to find, or visitors may be excluded or screened by gatekeepers. Good Retreats are found on the upper floors of buildings, mountainsides, and waterfronts, sites that dramatize the isolation of the unit. While a good Retreat is inconvenient for outsiders to reach, it does, however, offer its residents ready access to outside goods and services.

A Retreat neighborhood is good for people who do not feel the need to live in a residential community. It attracts people who are inwardly directed and those who value originality. It attracts creative people who look to the physical environment for inspiration, people who like to be alone, people with alternative life-styles, and people who seek refuge from public life. It is least attractive to people who grew up in a large city. Because Retreat-type people are individuals who want to be away from rather than with others, they are not easy to characterize as a group; they include people from different classes, income levels, and stages in the life cycle.

In summary, a good Retreat neighborhood focuses on the individual rather than the community. It is private and secluded, represents the individual householder's needs, tastes, and values, and is not easily accessible to strangers. Views are of unusual importance.

Retreat neighborhoods, as other types, have their detractors. There are those who feel that as modern technology continues to reduce the need for face-to-face contact, more people will choose the physical isolation of a Retreat neighborhood and the quality of interpersonal interaction will be diminished even as its frequency is increased. E. M. Forster parodied this concern more than eighty years ago. He describes a time in the future when people will have done away with physical contact altogether; they never need to leave home.

Then she generated the light, and the sight of her room, flooded with radiance and studded with electric buttons, revived her. There were buttons and switches every-where—buttons to call for food, for music, for clothing. There was the hot-bath button, by pressure of which a basin of (imitation) marble rose out of the floor, filled to the brim with warm deodorized liquid. There was the cold-bath button. There was the button that produced literature. And there were of course the buttons by which she communicated with her friends. The room, though it contained nothing, was in touch with all that she cared for in the world. (Forster 1964)

Detractors of the Retreat feel that the experience of sharing a neighborhood is important because it helps to create a sense of community, helps to knit individuals into a society; people who abdicate their membership in the collective are shirking their democratic responsibilities. People who live in Retreat neighborhoods are encouraged to be selfish and to disregard the interests of others; ultimately, they lose the skills that are needed to work out differences through discussion and negotiation (Perin 1977). While this argument has merit, it is not necessarily true. Preference for a Retreat neighborhood does not necessarily mean abdication from community; residents may be active members of city-wide civic, religious, social, sports, or professional associations, and the boundaries of these associations may be expanded as the internet replaces over-the-fence conversation.

There are others who are concerned about the effect of low-density Retreat-type neighborhoods on the environment. One type of Retreat—large-lot exurban housing, commonly associated with "sprawl"—demands extensive roads and utilities, is wasteful of energy, and results in the rapid expansion of the urban area and the loss of farmland and countryside.

SUMMARY

Each of the four neighborhood types—Center, Small-town, Residential Partnership, and Retreat—has its own peculiar qualities of form and appearance and has a different way of dealing with the basic issues of privacy, security, community, and self-identity. Each serves different life-style needs: A Center is a place for new beginnings—diverting, changing, and open; a Small-town is a place of belonging—friendly, familiar, and enduring; a Residential Partnership is a place that is quiet, safe, and predictable; and a Retreat is a place of escape—solitary and unspoiled.

All of these types are, of course, metaphors rather than descriptions of particular places; they are more clear-cut, single-minded, and extreme and have greater internal consistency than the places they represent. They are primary colors at maximum saturation levels, which seldom appear in that form in the real world, but which provide a standard against which real-world variations in saturation, hue, and brightness may be measured and compared. Or we can think of them as "good figures," pure circles, triangles, and squares that we use to organize our perceptions of the tangled shapes we see around us. I would argue that a neighborhood gets better as it move closer to a desired type; and when it reaches the type, it is as good as it can be. If, for example, residents prefer a Center neighborhood, then, for them, the neighborhood will become better as it moves closer to type. With the types as fixed points, we can also identify the relative positions of intermediate points. If residents prefer a type that lies midway between a Center and a Small-town, then, for them, the neighborhood will become better as it moves closer to that position.

The neighborhood settings that make up a compound neighborhood are not necessarily all of the same type, and so a compound neighborhood may be characterized as a particular combination of types. Here are some common examples:

Center/Center combination. Two Center settings, each with its own distinctive identity and character, and with shared facilities distributed through both settings, and with good transportation connections linking them. Examples are Uptown and

Midtown, or the Theater District and the Waterfront as components of downtown.

Small-town/Center combination. A stable residential area with its own "main street" and local institutions, located next to a dominant downtown setting. The small-town setting is not quite as self-sufficient in combination as when it is alone, and it attracts more visitors. Examples are Little Italy and Chinatown next to the downtown neighborhood.

Residential Partnership/Center combination. A closed, self-contained residential enclave attached to a dominant Center. Residents have their own health club and social rooms and small variety store. Beyond that, they depend on the Center for home-related facilities. Examples are a full-service apartment building and an exclusive housing development within the downtown neighborhood.

Retreat/Center combination. A quiet oasis of housing that excludes outsiders but does not provide residents with any shared facilities or services. Residents do not get together. They depend on the Center for all of their home-related needs. Examples are an apartment building and a closed housing complex within the downtown neighborhood.

Residential Partnership combination. An example is a housing development with two sectors, where residents of each sector have their own private playground and parking lot, and they share a private community and sports center. Residents of both sectors go outside the neighborhood for most home-related needs.

The relationship between the two components may differ. The facilities that are shared by the combined neighborhoods may be evenly distributed through all of the component settings (coequal settings), or most of these facilities may be located in one of the settings (hierarchical settings), or all of the facilities for one setting may be located in another (nested settings). And, of course, compound neighborhoods may consist of more than two types of settings. One could, for example, think of a Retreat (no-service apartment house) in a Residential Partnership (exclusive, serviced community), in a Small-town (distinctive area with its own main street), in a Center (downtown).

I have shown how the typology can be used to describe functional connections between settings. It may also be used to describe the way settings change over time. For example, a neighborhood in a seaside resort may be a Center type in the season and revert to a Small-town type during the rest of the year. Or a country Retreat may grow, over time, into an exclusive Residential Partnership, then develop as a Small-town, and finally grow into a Center. The first is an example of sudden and reversible change; the second of gradual, one-directional change.

The four types of neighborhoods are essentially different, and no one combines the good points of all. Each has good and bad features, one the complement of the other. Tranquility can be restful but dull; change can be stimulating but unsettling; community ties can be comforting but restraining, just as the absence of community can be liberating but lonely. Choosing one neighborhood over another means choosing certain qualities over others. Each setting satisfies some people, or people at some stage of their lives.

An important characteristic of a good city is that it offers its residents a choice of all four types of neighborhoods.

NOTES

1. Especially relevant writings include those by Baumgartner 1988; Bell 1968; Dobriner 1958; Furay 1983; Girouard 1985; Greer 1966; Milgram 1970; Oldenburg 1989; Park 1971; Perin 1977; Proshansky 1978; Sennett 1990; and Webber 1963.

2. Earlier, I referred to a study that showed all four types used by residents to describe their home setting. However, a neighborhood defined at this level is a very particular place and hard to generalize, being both active and quiet, private and open, used by residents and visitors; as a result it can be interpreted to fit quite different types and still not be characterized by any one of them.

3. See, for example, the arguments for Traditional Neighborhood Developments, Pedestrian Pockets, Urban Villages, and Transit-Oriented Developments (van der Ryn and Calthorpe 1986; Duany and Plater-Zyberk 1991; Calthorpe 1993). Allen comments: "A cherished myth of suburban communities is that they are self-contained islands in a disagreeable metropolitan sea" (Allen 1977). The new town of Columbia, Maryland, was planned as a series of small villages, each around its own center; the idea, according to a personal account by Robert Tennenbaum, planner for Columbia, was to capture the feeling of the small town where developer James Rouse grew up. A suburban mall on Cape Cod was redesigned as a three-block center and called "downtown" (Flanagan 1991).

4. This is Janowitz's term for residents whose commitment to their community is impermanent. When the community fails to meet their needs, they withdraw (Janowitz 1967).

5. Szczygiel (1996) interviewed 22 people who worked in a central Pennsylvanian town, but lived in an outlying farming area. They wanted to live "in the country" rather than in "a development" in the country. They enjoyed the view of adjacent agricultural land but not of their neighbors' houses. A suggestion for having commonly owned land was not popular because it would mean having to be involved in a homeowners association. They expressed a strong desire for privacy.

CHAPTER ELEVEN
Application

I have described four distinctively different types of neighborhoods. Assuming that the findings of the Baltimore studies are generally valid (they need, of course, to be tested in other places), my argument, the central thesis of this book, is that all cities, in order to satisfy significant groups in the population, must offer all four types of neighborhoods. The absence of any of the types would deny housing choices and so diminish the overall quality of life. Not only must cities offer all four types of neighborhoods, but they must offer good examples of each, which means that each type must possess, to the highest degree possible, the qualities that I have identified.

Some of these qualities refer to physical attributes of the setting, while others refer to the social relationship between neighbors. A plan for good neighborhoods must address both sets of qualities.

Physical qualities are concerned with the form, appearance, and sanctioned use of neighborhood structures and spaces (for example, a quiet, all-residential environment, a dense pattern of development, and organization around a strong center), and are addressed through familiar planning devices such as land use regulations, street design standards, site planning guidelines, density limits, height restrictions, and locational criteria for public buildings. But while concern for the physical qualities of a neighborhood is generally accepted as the basis for public policy, concern for the social behavior of its residents (for example, their friendliness, sophistication, and civic involvement) is not. The prevalent belief in the United States is that it is not appropriate for a public agency to establish behavioral standards for prospective residents—which is to say, to plan who will live in a particular neighborhood and who will not.

This was not always so. At one time, it was generally held that norms of civil behavior are properly shared only by people of the same class or race and that it is necessary to screen residents—admit the right kind of people and exclude the wrong—in order to create good neighborhoods. With this reasoning as justification, lending practices and zoning ordinances were deliberately designed to favor certain races (Power 1983), and restrictive covenants were designed to exclude people of different ethnic background and "foreigners." The Federal Housing Administration's standard restrictions (cited in Bauer 1945) provide an example of these practices:

No race or nationality other than those for whom the premises are intended, shall use or occupy any building on any lot, except that this covenant shall not prevent occupancy by domestic servants of a different race or nationality employed by an owner or tenant.

Today, we believe that people should be free to live wherever they choose as long as they can afford the price. And while it is true that public policies affect housing price and so shape the field of choice, we do not lay down standards for being good neighbors. We only prohibit behaviors that are clear nuisances, are unsafe or unhealthy (such as rowdiness, poor maintenance, and overcrowding).

These limitations do not, however, apply to the private sector. Residents who pass through the income mesh may find that the lease or title deed to their property, written and administered by a housing developer or residents' association, includes standards and rules of behavior. It may prescribe, for example, the choice of landscape elements, pets, exterior paint, and curtain colors. Residents' associations have gone so far as to impose a minimum age requirement for residents. They have invented neighborhood histories and traditions to support their design standards (Dorst 1989). Private policies such as these clearly have an effect on the overall residential experience, and so they are important elements of a neighborhood plan. A neighborhood plan must include the policies formulated not only by planners who represent local government (policies that affect, for example, land use and development regulations), but also by developers, realtors, marketing agents, entrepreneurs, building managers, advertisers, and residents' associations whose policies affect, for example, the selection of residents, the promotion of the neighborhood, the provision and operation of shared spaces and facilities, the creation of community organizations, and the programming of social activities. I believe that a good neighborhood plan will ensure that all of these policies, public and private, converge to reinforce the qualities of a particular type of neighborhood. In order to create different types of good neighborhoods,[1] we need type-specific policies, a different set of policies for each type.

Here, by way of illustration, are some concerns that have significantly different policy implications for different types of neighborhoods.

CENTER NEIGHBORHOODS

Center neighborhoods are the most cosmopolitan and open of all the types. Plans should provide for the greatest mix of residential and non-residential uses of all neighborhood types and should encourage the development of many and diverse local facilities that connect residents with one another and with outsiders.

The Baltimore study suggests that more people would like to live in Center-type neighborhoods, but that good Centers are hard to find because the old ones, which are mainly downtown, have many problems, and new ones are not being built. The old Centers need to be improved; in particular they must be made safer, and the housing stock be modernized to suit present-day tastes. These improvements must be made by retaining the characteristics that are peculiar to a Center and not by changing them into Small-towns or Residential Partnerships. In addition to improving the old Centers, we need to create new Centers in the metropolitan region.

Location. In order to support regional facilities, a Center neighborhood must be located at a major transportation hub. ➤

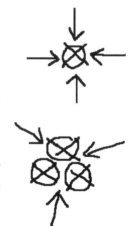

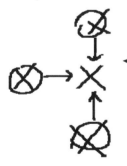

Several Center neighborhoods may cluster around a ◄ nonresidential complex;

or they may create a multi-nuclear complex of their own, with several Centers in close proximity, or connected by rapid transit. ➤

Land use. Permit mixed use and high density development. Encourage regional employment, retail and tourist uses. Locate regional public facilities that bring residents, and residents and outsiders together. Provide local-serving residential services and protect them against economic pressures that might squeeze them out. Encourage uses that remain open at night.

Housing. Encourage a wide range of housing sizes and prices so as to accommodate a diversity of residents. Encourage the provision of a wide range of rental units and anticipate a high rate of turnover. Monitor housing so as to retain a balance of social and economic groups. Create programs to promote Center living, targeting households without children and people who are socially active rather than homebodies.

Economic Development. Attract workplaces, specialty stores, and cultural institutions that serve a regional market, including uses that are not part of any residential setting (they may be part of work or entertainment settings) and that serve residents who live outside the Center.

Transportation. Create good pedestrian environments within the Center. Provide public transportation within the Center and to neighborhoods and major nonresidential concentrations and open spaces outside the Center. Make a commitment to transit by discouraging auto use and limiting parking.

Urban Design. Encourage many small uses, each in separate ownership. Aim for liveliness and variety. Design and program public spaces for active use; make them open to public view and provide on-site management. Encourage experimentation and change, but also institute measures to preserve places of visual and historical interest. Build privacy into the design of the unit rather than the neighborhood; use devices that will enhance privacy at close quarters.

SMALL-TOWN NEIGHBORHOODS

Small-town neighborhoods are the most community-oriented of the four types. They have fewer nonresidential uses than Centers and are more parochial and less open. Their most important characteristic is a friendly, caring, and familiar relationship among residents, something that takes time to evolve. Plans should encourage the creation of stable communities, with many internal points of connection for local residents and a clear sense of identity.

The Baltimore study suggests that Small-towns are the kind of neighborhood most people aspire to, but they are perhaps the hardest to sustain. This is because residents today are more mobile, less dependent on their neighborhood for friendships and services, and so less likely to construct the interlocking layers of friendships and dependencies that are the essence of the Small-town character. Many older neighborhoods were once of this type, and those that survive tend to be working class. I suspect that many people who say they want to live in Small-town neighborhoods would really prefer the more limited and protective community of a Residential Partnership.

Location. Small-town neighborhoods include facilities that cannot survive if they depend on residents alone, and so they must be readily accessible from a major road.

In order to increase their locational advantage, several Small-town neighborhoods may form a cluster;

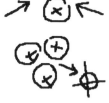

or they may be attached to a nonresidential complex;

or to a Center neighborhood.

Land Use. Plan for a concentration of nonresidential uses in a central location within the neighborhood. Encourage and support local institutions such as schools, churches, fire houses, and libraries. Ensure that the neighborhood remains of a manageable size and, if possible, that it retains clearly defined boundaries.

Housing. Promote home ownership and a mix of housing suitable for all stages of the life cycle. Attract stable households with families. Provide a full complement of housing-related facilities within walking distance of home. Introduce special monitoring to ensure a continuing balance of social classes. Encourage policies that favor decentralization of schools, police stations, fire stations, post offices, and movie houses.

Economic Development. Encourage local-serving institutions and facilities, preferably under local ownership or management. Provide a full range of residential services and create conditions under which they are able to survive in competition with large, regional facilities. This may require experiments aimed at changing the present pattern of retailing through, for example, public subsidies, resident ownership of local facilities with a profit-sharing arrangement to encourage local use, mobile units in specially designed locations with a variety of regularly scheduled services, and neighborhood sample outlets for large retail stores that will deliver orders to customers' homes.

Transportation. Provide easy access for residents to goods and services outside the neighborhood. Provide convenient, but less easy, access for nonresidents to the commercial center. Create a walking environment. Provide public transportation to increase the size of the area that is convenient to home, to discourage the use of the private car and reduce the need for parking.

Urban Design. Policies should be designed to strengthen the role of local organizations; measures might include having them manage public open spaces, supporting the development of a local newspaper, promoting recognition of the neighborhood name, assisting with running local parades, festivals and other community events. All planning actions should be subject to review and approval by the community.

RESIDENTIAL PARTNERSHIPS

Residential Partnerships are the most closed of all the neighborhood types. Plans should be designed to protect the residential character of the neighborhood and to exclude nonresidential uses that are not extensions of the residents' home settings and that depend on use by nonresidents. Internal planning decisions should be approved by a residents' association.

Residential Partnerships tend to promote large-scale residential segregation. To avoid this, encourage Residential Partnerships that are small and that include renters and people of different income levels.

Location. Residents of Residential Partnerships are heavily dependent on facilities outside the neighborhood area. Consequently, they must have easy access to a major road. They are best located just off the road, so that nonresidents are not drawn through the neighborhood.

A Residential Partnership may use the outside facilities of a nonresidential complex; ➤

or it may be attached to a
◄ Center neighborhood;

or to a Small-town neighborhood. ➤

Land Use. A Residential Partnership is essentially a restricted residential area, with only those nonresidential uses and services that directly improve the residential environment. The future should be predictable, which means that all development should conform to an approved plan; changes to the plan should not be encouraged, but, if adopted, they should be subject to review and approval by the community. Regulations should be protective of the visual environment.

Housing. Establish a mechanism for screening prospective residents; this may include formal qualifying requirements, targeting applicants through advertising, and promoting an appropriate image. In order to fight discrimination, a population mix should be included in the plan.

Economic Development. Furthering economic development is secondary to meeting the residential needs of families. Any nonresidential functions should, if possible, be owned and operated by the residents' association and should not be open at night.

Transportation. Residential Partnerships should provide residents with good access to a range of facilities throughout the metropolitan area. Where most residents get around by car, the Partnership should have good access to the highway system, but the connection should be a dead-end, a street that is used solely by residents.

Urban Design. Provide meeting places for members and their guests. To avoid interfering with the residential character of the setting, nonresidential uses should not be highly visible to outsiders, and their design and operation should be subject to approval by a residents' association. Design features of a Residential Partnership include well defined boundaries and distinctive points of entry.

RETREAT NEIGHBORHOODS

Retreat neighborhoods are the most private of all the types, being essentially extensions of the individual home. They have the weakest sense of community and offer residents no connecting facilities within the neighborhood area. Plans should protect the privacy of the individual householder from all other users.

The Baltimore study suggests that the Retreat is the least popular type of neighborhood and that it can be found in conjunction with the other neighborhood types, on the outskirts of the city or in the heart of downtown. The study was, however, not conclusive in establishing the character of the Retreat neighborhood.

Location. Retreat neighborhoods are best located away from well-travelled routes, so that access to external facilities may be indirect.

These facilities may be located in a nonresidential complex;   ➤

or in a Center or Small-town ◄ neighborhood.

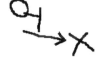

Land Use. Discourage all uses that intrude on the privacy of the individual householder. There need be no public or communally-owned facilities or open spaces.

Housing. There should be restrictions to prevent visual intrusion and noise that disrupts the privacy of individual householders. Beyond that, individuals should be free to express themselves as they like.

Economic Development. Any nonresidential uses should be regulated to prevent intrusion into the residents' privacy.

Transportation. Retreats are best located in such a way that strangers have to go out of their way to find them. They should provide residents with access to facilities outside the neighborhood, but the access need not be the most direct.

Urban Design. Planning agencies should not rely on a residents' association to take responsibility for the planning or management of local facilities. Regulations should be designed to control the design and operation of nonresidential uses, to protect interesting views and natural features and prevent them from being blocked. Landscape treatment is important. In high density areas, privacy can be achieved with courtyards and squares.

NEIGHBORHOOD PATTERNS

Neighborhood types are useful not only for planning the neighborhood but also for planning the pattern of neighborhoods that make up the city.

In our definition of neighborhood we recognized that residential functions extend beyond the neighborhood area into other neighborhoods and into nonresidential parts of the city. One cannot think about a good neighborhood without thinking about networks of connected places. Individual residents develop their own connections to suit their circumstances and life-style (see Bonnes et al. 1990 and 1992; Rapoport 1990; Lynch 1976, pp. 150–157; Ladd 1972), but the possibilities that are open to them are limited by the overall pattern and structure of neighborhoods in the city.

There are different concepts of what this pattern and structure should be.

For example, Howard's Garden City consists of a series of Small-town neighborhoods that share civic and employment centers.　　　　➤

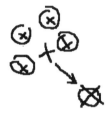

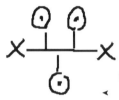

One might think of Le Corbusier's Radiant City as a series of Residential Partnerships connected to major cultural/commercial and industrial complexes.　◄

Perry's Neighborhood Unit consists of a series of Small-town neighborhoods connected to separate commercial complexes, and then to other parts of the city.　　　　➤

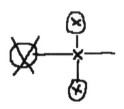

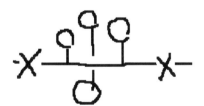

Wright's Broadacre City consists essentially of a series of Retreats connected to small-scale commercial, employment, and cultural centers.　◄

Each of these schemes provides for a single type of neighborhood.

The new town of Columbia, Maryland, has two types of neighborhood. A series of Residential Partnerships are clustered around "village" and "community" centers to create two levels of Small-town compound neighborhoods. The neighborhoods are connected to separate regional commercial and employment complexes. ➤

None of these planned cities offers a full range of neighborhood types. None of them includes Center neighborhoods.

What is needed is a pattern like this: ➤

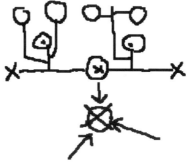

NEIGHBORHOOD PLANNING

The idea that the typology can help us to create a good pattern of neighborhoods begs the question as to whether a single good neighborhood, let alone a pattern, can indeed be achieved through planning. It raises questions as to just how the typology can be useful. These matters will now be addressed in the form of questions and responses.

Can Good Neighborhoods Be Planned?

Neighborhoods, as I have defined them, are creatures of residents' perceptions, and are essentially created by residents. If residents create neighborhoods, does it make any sense for people other than residents to attempt to plan them? What, in other words, is the role of the professional planner?

While planners cannot determine the way that residents perceive the environment, residents' perceptions are influenced by physical and social elements that are subject to planning. The local pattern of land uses and services, the availability of suitable meeting places, the design and management of open spaces, the selection of residents, and the susceptibility of the area to change—all of these can be planned, and all affect the quality of the residential environment as we perceive it.

Only residents can create good neighborhoods, but planners can create conditions that give rise to them.

Even If Neighborhoods Can Be Planned, Is There Any Need to Plan Them?

A 1979 study in Baltimore City[2] identified 249 resident-defined, named neighborhoods ranging in size from 100 to 16,000 people; very few of these areas had been laid out in accordance with a neighborhood plan. If neighborhoods will happen in the absence of a plan, is there need for a plan?

The fact that neighborhoods can happen in the absence of a plan does not mean that they cannot be planned, or that they cannot be improved through planning. Planning may not be necessary in simple societies where shared interests and concerns provide a common focus for individual decisions. But in societies with diverse populations, a plan can provide the common focus; it can shape uses, distribute populations, facilitate interactions, generate activities, and in this way increase the likelihood that a neighborhood will be created, that it will be of a certain type, and that it will be true to that type. A neighborhood that is true to type is more desirable than one that is not, not because a particular life-style can only happen in a congruent setting, but because when it does, the experience is more fulfilling and more delightful.

Neighborhoods Are Constantly Changing. Won't a Neighborhood Plan Soon Become Outdated?

A follow-up to the 1979 Baltimore study[3] showed that some of the neighborhoods had changed substantially by 1980; some had changed their boundaries, and some had changed their names. If neighborhoods adjust and adapt to changing social and economic conditions, does it make any sense to prepare long-range neighborhood plans?

While some neighborhoods change, many others persist over a long period of time, and it seems that the longer they persist the more resistant they become to change (Guest, Lee, and Staeheli 1982).

Careful planning can make it easier for a neighborhood to resist change, or to adapt to it.

Do All Residents See Themselves Living in a Neighborhood? If They Do Not, Why Plan Neighborhoods?

Some residents think of themselves as residents of the city as a whole. They position themselves in relation to the center (such as "in West Baltimore") or to a major landmark (such as "near the University") or a regional transportation facility (such as "near the Metro station"). Some analysts argue that with increased mobility the concept of neighborhood has become outmoded.

The presence of neighborhoods is recorded in a great many cities, and all residents—even those who do not accept that they live in a neighborhood—are more concerned about conditions closer to their home than further away. The neighborhood area has relevance even for them, though it may represent a less multilayered concept.

How Do Planners Establish a Neighborhood's Boundaries and Type?

Most neighborhoods, as I have defined the word, have no absolute boundaries in the sense of fixed, determining edges; residents have different interpretations of the boundaries. The problem is complicated by the fact that there are different boundaries for home setting, neighborhood setting, and compound neighborhood. If any two residents may come up with different definitions of their neighborhood boundaries, how do planners determine the actual *boundaries and type for planning purposes?*

To determine neighborhood boundaries, planners must first establish which definition of neighborhood is most appropriate for the purposes of the plan. Then they must find the boundaries that the largest number of residents agree upon.

There are several ways planners can approach the task of classification. They can ask a sample of residents to rate the neighborhood in relation to the thirty qualities of good neighborhoods that were used in the Baltimore study and are presented in Chapter 9. High-scoring qualities will, then, define the type. Use of the typology reduces the thirty qualities to four descriptions, which makes the task less time-consuming and tedious. We have then only to ask residents, which descriptor best represents the neighborhood? An even more convenient method is for planners who are familiar with the area to classify the neighborhood themselves (the Baltimore study shows a high level of agreement between these planners and local residents), but they need more than objective information on which to base their assessment. Objective information about the place—such as its density, land use, natural boundaries, and building arrangement—will tell planners what the place will support, but it will not necessarily tell them what the residents will support, because residents are capable of adapting virtually any place to fit a preferred life-style. Objective information about the people—such as their median age, family composition, income, and formal and informal organizations—will tell what their life-style is likely to be; but to know what it actually is, planners will need to know how residents use the built environment, what uses they consider appropriate and desirable, on what terms they engage with one another and with strangers, how far beyond the housing unit their feeling of home extends, whether their outlook is primarily localistic or metropolitan, and to what extent their activities and attitudes are shaped by a concern for homemaking, community, career, or simply having a good time.

This kind of information can be obtained by means of systematic interviews and observations, by talking to people who are knowledgeable about the area, and reading up on local history and tradition. Familiarity with the attitudes and behaviors of residents is particularly necessary for public planners to be able to identify a Retreat and to distinguish between Residential Partnership and Small-town types.

Whichever method is used, planners are unlikely to find that all residents agree about the qualities of a neighborhood. Any listing of qualities only holds for a particular reference group. The planners must set up a process to identify the group or groups whose interests will be represented by the plan. If this is the dominant group, then the plan has a single client and the area may be a single type; if there are several co-equal groups, then the plan has several clients and the area may be a combination of types.

Once the qualities of a neighborhood are identified, planners must find a match with one of the types. A perfect match is not likely—a real place is hardly ever altogether true to type. The planners may find that the neighborhood has some qualities of one type and some of another (for example, some qualities of a Center and some of a Small-town), or that it combines the physical qualities of one with the social qualities of another (for example, Partnership-type facilities with Center-type residents, or Center-type facilities and a Small-town mentality). If the planners cannot match all of the qualities of a neighborhood, they must decide which are the *predominant* qualities.

All neighborhood plans require two classifications: One to represent the neighborhood as it is at present and one to represent the neighborhood as it should be in the future. The difference between the two sets the direction for the plan.

I have discussed the problem of matching the qualities of a real neighborhood with those of an imaginary one. When it comes to the preferred neighborhood, however, a match should be easier because we are comparing two imaginary places. And because each type represents not only a final destination but also a direction—one that leads to a string of intermediate destinations—it also serves as a reference point for residents who do not choose to go all the way. The preferred types are not only for upper- and middle-class residents; they are also useful when planning for residents who set their sights somewhat lower.

Differences between the existing and preferred types will suggest a direction and a range of type-specific policies. For example, in a pilot study referred to in Chapter 9, 76 residents of a Baltimore neighborhood were given the four descriptions. They were asked to name the description that was closest to the present neighborhood, and the one that was closest to the place where they would most like to live.

Table 11.1

Percentage of Respondents Who Chose Each Type (n=76)

	Center	Small-town	Partnership	Retreat
Present type	7	37	53	4
Preferred type	16	65	16	4

The responses (see Table 11.1) show that the present neighborhood is mainly a Residential Partnership, but that residents would prefer more of a Small-town environment. A neighborhood plan should recommend changes that will move the neighborhood in the desired direction.

Is the Neighborhood Typology of General Relevance?

Do the four neighborhood types apply in all cities, in all cultures?

The four types need to be tested in other places. I include the interview form in the Appendix with the hope that other researchers will use it to test the Baltimore findings. My hypothesis is that types will hold, with some variations, wherever people are able to make choices.

Where there are no choices, however, the question of type itself becomes irrelevant. This was brought home to me on a visit to Beijing in 1995. In China, housing is provided by the individual's work unit at very little cost to the resident; the floor area of their unit is established according to their age and rank and it is generally located near the workplace. For most people private housing is not an option. Under these circumstances, asking residents what qualities they would prefer in a residential setting is comparable to asking Oliver Twist what seasonings he would prefer in the food at Dotheboys Hall. The reply is of no consequence. The housing preferences of Chinese residents will, however, be of consequence in the future and so the typology should be of interest to those who presently plan for the future.

In summary, I suggest that neighborhood types can be useful for planning. At the city-wide level, they raise questions about the continuing representation of a full range of neighborhood types and they point to the fact that it takes more than good neighborhoods to make a good city. In a sense, it takes a good city to make good neighborhoods.

NOTES

1. I have taken a view of good neighborhoods that represents the interests of neighborhood residents. On occasion, these interests may clash with those of non-residents and of larger public policy. For example, policies that strengthen the sense of community may strengthen exclusionary practices. Public planners may decide that this is too high a price to pay for a good neighborhood and settle for something less good (in my terms), but more equitable.

2. See Taylor, Ralph B., Sidney Brower, and Whit Drain. *Toward A Neighborhood-Based Data File: Baltimore.* Baltimore MD: Center for Metropolitan Planning and Research, The Johns Hopkins University, October 1979.

3. *Longitudinal Effects of Crime and Signs of Disorder on Communities.* U.S. Department of Justice, grant #93-IJ-CX-0022, Ralph B. Taylor and Sidney Brower, co-principal investigators.

Appendix

FORM USED IN THE BALTIMORE SURVEY DISCUSSED IN CHAPTER 9

Introduction

Hello. My name is _____ . I am a _____ at_____ and
I am studying ideas about different kinds of places to live in the city. I am interview-
ing people in a number of locations and your address came up in a random sam-
pling. I would appreciate it if you would answer a few questions.

I should explain that anything you say will be treated as confidential in the sense
that it will not be associated with you personally, but will be combined with responses of other residents. We will simply conclude that, for example, so-many
people said so-and-so. Your participation is, of course, purely voluntary, and you
may end the interview at any time.

I would be very grateful if you would agree to participate in this study. May I
proceed with the questions?

Thank you.

Area Type   _____
Respondent #   _____
Interviewer   _____
Date completed
      Part I   _____
      Part II   _____

Part I

Please understand that I am not here to test you, but to learn about places in the city. There are no right or wrong answers to any of the questions I will ask you. I am interested in your opinions.

1. I am going to give you short descriptions of four different types of places to live, in or around the city, and I will ask you to tell me which description, in your opinion, comes closest to describing this part of the city where you live now. I will call these types of places 1, 2, 3 and 4. Place 1 is described on this card.

    HAND OUT TYPE CARD 1

    A part of the city that is lively and busy, with lots to see and do. It has a mix of many different people and uses, and it attracts visitors from other parts of the city and beyond.

    This is Place 2.

    HAND OUT TYPE CARD 2

    A part of the city that has the feeling of a small town, with its own institutions and meeting places. People who live here know one another and are able to recognize those who do not live here.

    This is Place 3.

    HAND OUT TYPE CARD 3

    A separate residential part of the city, a place for family and home life. Residents go to other parts of the city for work, shopping, and entertainment.

    Finally, this is Place 4.

    HAND OUT TYPE CARD 4

    A part of the city where one feels removed from other people and their activities. People who live here tend to be self-sufficient and go their separate ways.

    Which of these four descriptions, in your opinion, comes closest to describing this part of the city where you live now?

2. What name do residents give to this part of the city?

3. Think of the places that you have lived in, including places you have lived in in the past.

    Have you lived in a place like *Place 1?*
    Have you lived in a place like *Place 2?*
    Have you lived in a place like *Place 3?*
    Have you lived in a place like *Place 4?*

4 . Imagine for a moment that you are moving from your present home and that you are able to choose among all four types of places to live. Which type of place would be your first choice as a place for you to live now? Which would be your

second, third and fourth choices?

RECORD CHOICES

Please rate these four places on a ten-point scale, where 10 means you think this is an *extremely desirable* place for you to live, 1 means this is an *extremely undesirable* place for you to live, and 5 means you are *undecided*.

TAKE BACK THE FOUR TYPE CARDS

Now, I have a few general questions.

5. Do you live with a husband/wife or partner?

6. Altogether how many adults live in your (house, apartment, room)?

How many children and how old is each child?

7. Do you rent the (house, apartment, room) or do you own it?

8. How long have you lived in this part of the city?

IF MORE THAN TWO YEARS, CIRCLE #8

9. What is your age; that is, are you in your teens, between twenty and thirty, between thirty and forty, etc.?

IF 18 YEARS OR OLDER, CIRCLE #9

10. How many years of schooling have you completed?

IF TEN YEARS OR MORE, CIRCLE # 10

IF #s 8, 9, AND 10 HAVE NOT ALL BEEN CIRCLED

That is the end of the interview. Thank you very much for your assistance.

* IF #s 8, 9, AND 10 HAVE ALL BEEN CIRCLED

The rest of the interview will take about thirty minutes. IF NOT CONVENIENT: When would be a convenient time for me to come back and complete the interview?

Part II

Time Interview began _____

In this part of the interview I want to find out what qualities you associate with different kinds of places. This is the way it works. I'll start off by handing you a card with a single quality written on it. I'll ask you to imagine the type of place that represents this particular quality. Then I'll give you thirty other cards, and I'll ask you to pick out qualities that go along with the first one. We will repeat this procedure four times. Each time I will give you a single quality (a different quality each time) and ask you to pick out other qualities that go along with it.

I repeat that this interview is not about facts; I want your ideas and opinions about places to live. There are no right or wrong answers to any of these questions. I am not here to test you, but to learn about places in the city.

Do you have any questions?

> SHUFFLE PLACE CARDS TO DETERMINE ORDER OF PRESENTATION
> OF THE FOUR PLACES, AND RECORD THIS ORDER ON SCHEDULE A

PLACE 1

The first (next) set of questions is about a place we will call *Place 1*. Here is a description of Place 1: *A place that is lively and busy, with lots to see and do.*

> PUT OUT PLACE CARD 1

Remember, this is a place that is in or near the city

Please think about the good qualities of a place like that; that is, think about an *ideal Place 1*. Now, go through these cards one by one. Keep the cards that describe qualities that you think belong in an ideal Place 1, and return the remaining cards to me.

> IF RESPONDENT CANNOT DECIDE WHETHER A CERTAIN QUALITY
> BELONGS OR NOT, SAY: If you think this may be a quality of an ideal
> Place 1, include it. You will have a chance later to say whether it is an
> important quality or not.

You have selected cards that represent qualities of an ideal Place 1. Please look through the cards and tell me if there are other qualities that belong in an ideal Place 1 that should be added.

> IF YES

What are these qualities?

> RECORD ADDITIONAL QUALITIES ON SCHEDULE B AND NUMBER
> CONSECUTIVELY
> CREATE ADDITIONAL QUALITY CARDS
> RETURN SELECTED AND ADDITIONAL QUALITY CARDS TO RESPON-
> DENT

These, then, are the qualities of an ideal Place 1. Obviously, some qualities are more important than others. Please go through the cards again, and arrange them in three piles. In the left-hand pile put qualities that are *very important* in an ideal Place 1. In the middle pile put qualities that are *somewhat important* in an ideal Place 1. In the right-hand pile put qualities that are *desirable but not important* in an ideal Place 1.

Remember, the description of Place 1 is *a place that is lively and busy, with lots to see and do.* Now, please arrange the cards in the three piles.

11. CHECK RATINGS ON SCHEDULES A AND B
    REMOVE ADDITIONAL QUALITY CARDS
    ASSEMBLE ALL ORIGINAL QUALITY CARDS (INCLUDING THOSE THAT
    WERE SET ASIDE) AND SHUFFLE
    REMOVE PLACE CARD 1

PLACE 2

The first (next) set of questions is about a place we will call *Place 2*. Here is a description of Place 2: *A place that has the feeling of a small town, with its own institutions and meeting places.*

    PUT OUT PLACE CARD 2

Remember, this is a place that is in or near the city

Please think about the good qualities of a place like that; that is, think about an *ideal Place 2*. Now, go through these cards one by one. Keep the cards that describe qualities that you think belong in an ideal Place 2, and return the remaining cards to me.

    IF RESPONDENT CANNOT DECIDE WHETHER A CERTAIN QUALITY
    BELONGS OR NOT, SAY: If you think this may be a quality of an ideal
    Place 2, include it. You will have a chance later to say whether it is an
    important quality or not.

You have selected cards that represent qualities of an ideal Place 2. Please look through the cards and tell me if there are other qualities that belong in an ideal Place 2 that should be added.

    IF YES

What are these qualities?

    RECORD ADDITIONAL QUALITIES ON SCHEDULE B AND NUMBER
    CONSECUTIVELY
    CREATE ADDITIONAL QUALITY CARDS
    RETURN SELECTED AND ADDITIONAL QUALITY CARDS TO RESPON-
    DENT

These, then, are the qualities of an ideal Place 2. Obviously, some qualities are more important than others. Please go through the cards again, and arrange them in three piles. In the left-hand pile put qualities that are *very important* in an ideal Place 2. In the middle pile put qualities that are *somewhat important* in an ideal Place 2. In the right-hand pile put qualities that are *desirable but not important* in an ideal Place 2.

Remember, the description of Place 2 is *a place that has the feeling of a small town, with its own institutions and meeting places*. Now, please arrange the cards in the three piles.

12. CHECK RATINGS ON SCHEDULES A AND B

REMOVE ADDITIONAL QUALITY CARDS
ASSEMBLE ALL ORIGINAL QUALITY CARDS (INCLUDING THOSE THAT
WERE SET ASIDE) AND SHUFFLE
REMOVE PLACE CARD 2

PLACE 3

The first (next) set of questions is about a place we will call *Place 3*. Here is a description of Place 3: *A separate residential part of the city, a place for family and home life. Residents go to other parts of the city for work, shopping, and entertainment.*

PUT OUT PLACE CARD 3

Remember, this is a place that is in or near the city. Please think about the good qualities of a place like that; that is, think about an *ideal Place 3*. Now, go through these cards one by one. Keep the cards that describe qualities that you think belong in an ideal Place 3, and return the remaining cards to me.

IF RESPONDENT CANNOT DECIDE WHETHER A CERTAIN QUALITY
BELONGS OR NOT, SAY: If you think this may be a quality of an ideal
Place 3, include it. You will have a chance later to say whether it is an
important quality or not.

You have selected cards that represent qualities of an ideal Place 3. Please look through the cards and tell me if there are other qualities that belong in an ideal Place 3 that should be added.

IF YES

What are these qualities?

RECORD ADDITIONAL QUALITIES ON SCHEDULE B AND NUMBER
CONSECUTIVELY
CREATE ADDITIONAL QUALITY CARDS
RETURN SELECTED AND ADDITIONAL QUALITY CARDS TO RESPON-
DENT

These, then, are the qualities of an ideal Place 3. Obviously, some qualities are more important than others. Please go through the cards again, and arrange them in three piles. In the left-hand pile put qualities that are *very important* in an ideal Place 3. In the middle pile put qualities that are *somewhat important* in an ideal Place 3. In the right-hand pile put qualities that are *desirable but not important* in an ideal Place 3.

Remember, the description of Place 3 is *a separate residential part of the city, a place for family and home life. Residents go to other parts of the city for work, shopping, and entertainment.*

Now, please arrange the cards in the three piles.

13. CHECK RATINGS ON SCHEDULES A AND B

REMOVE ADDITIONAL QUALITY CARDS
ASSEMBLE ALL ORIGINAL QUALITY CARDS (INCLUDING THOSE THAT
WERE SET ASIDE) AND SHUFFLE
REMOVE PLACE CARD 3

PLACE 4

The first (next) set of questions is about a place we will call *Place 4*. Here is a description of Place 4: *A place where one feels removed from other people and their activities.*

PUT OUT PLACE CARD 4

Remember, this is a place that is in or near the city Please think about the good qualities of a place like that; that is, think about an *ideal Place 4*. Now, go through these cards one by one. Keep the cards that describe qualities that you think belong in an ideal Place 4, and return the remaining cards to me.

IF RESPONDENT CANNOT DECIDE WHETHER A CERTAIN QUALITY
BELONGS OR NOT, SAY: If you think this may be a quality of an ideal
Place 4, include it. You will have a chance later to say whether it is an
important quality or not.

You have selected cards that represent qualities of an ideal Place 4. Please look through the cards and tell me if there are other qualities that belong in an ideal Place 4 that should be added.

IF YES

What are these qualities?

RECORD ADDITIONAL QUALITIES ON SCHEDULE B AND NUMBER
CONSECUTIVELY
CREATE ADDITIONAL QUALITY CARDS
RETURN SELECTED AND ADDITIONAL QUALITY CARDS TO RESPON-
DENT

These, then, are the qualities of an ideal Place 4. Obviously, some qualities are more important than others. Please go through the cards again, and arrange them in three piles. In the left-hand pile put qualities that are *very important* in an ideal Place 4. In the middle pile put qualities that are *somewhat important* in an ideal Place 4. In the right-hand pile put qualities that are *desirable but not important* in an ideal Place 4.

Remember, the description of Place 4 is *a place where one feels removed from other people and their activities*. Now, please arrange the cards in the three piles.

14. CHECK RATINGS ON SCHEDULES A AND B
REMOVE ADDITIONAL QUALITY CARDS
ASSEMBLE ALL ORIGINAL QUALITY CARDS (INCLUDING THOSE THAT
WERE SET ASIDE) AND SHUFFLE
REMOVE PLACE CARD 4

Now I am going to ask you some questions about the people who choose to live in Places 1, 2, 3 and 4. I will repeat the description of each place.

15. Place 1 is *a part of the city that is lively and busy, with lots to see and do.* What kind of people do you think would most want to live in such a place?

16. Why do you think *these people particularly* would find this an attractive place to live?

17. Place 2 is *a part of the city that has the feeling of a small town, with its own institutions and meeting places.* What kind of people do you think would most want to live in such a place?

18. Why do you think *these people particularly* would find this an attractive place to live?

19. Place 3 is *a separate residential part of the city, a place for family and home life. Residents go to other parts of the city for work, shopping, and entertainment.* What kind of people do you think would most want to live such a place?

20. Why do you think *these people particularly* would find this an attractive place to live?

21. Place 4 is *a part of the city where one feels removed from other people and their activities.* What kind of people do you think would most want to live in such a place?

22. Why do you think *these people particularly* would find this an attractive place to live?

23. At the beginning of the interview, I asked you which of these four cards comes closest to describing this part of the city where you live now. Please look at the cards again.

     HAND OUT THE FOUR TYPE CARDS

Now that you have had time to think about it I ask the question again: Which description comes closest to describing this part of the city?

24. Please tell me what kind of changes would make this part of the city even more like the place described here.

25. Please look at the other three cards. I would like you to name places in or around the city that, in your opinion, fit each of these descriptions. They may be real or fictional places such as Manhattan or Grover's Corners; or you may use terms like downtown, the suburbs, a high-rise apartment, or a development. Whatever you think best fits each description.

That completes the interview. Thank you for your help.

Time interview ended _____

Interviewer's Report

> AS SOON AS POSSIBLE AFTER COMPLETING THE INTERVIEW, THE IN-
> TERVIEWER SHOULD ANSWER THE FOLLOWING QUESTIONS.

Area name given by planners _____

Address of respondent: _____

Sex of respondent   _____

In your opinion, did the respondent have difficulty answering questions about:

    Place 1 _____

    Place 2 _____

    Place 3 _____

    Place 4 _____

Please comment, giving reasons for your observations.

In your opinion, did the respondent have problems understanding any of the questions? Please comment.

In your opinion, did the respondent give truthful and thoughtful answers to all of the questions. Please comment.

QUALITY CARDS (EACH QUALITY ON A SEPARATE CARD)

1. Living here, one can manage without a car
2. A place one can find sophisticated neighbors
3. A place with world-class restaurants, stores and cultural facilities
4. A wide selection of goods and services close to home
5. One can have an active social life close to home
6. A place that is right in the center of activity
7. A wide diversity of people live here
8. A place where there are many tourists
9. A place that is always full of surprises
10. Living here you do not have to spend as much time caring for the house
11. A place to meet new people
12. A place that has a definite center
13. A place with convenient public transportation
14. A place where there is no pressure to socialize or join anything
15. A place that is protected from the larger problems of society
16. A place to put down roots and settle
17. A place where most people know one another
18. A place to raise children
19. A place where residents are involved in community affairs
20. A place where one will always meet people one knows
21. A place where neighboring homes are close to one another

22. A place where neighbors are genuine and down-to-earth
23. A place where neighbors are outgoing and friendly
24. A place where people take care of one another
25. A place where residents are private and go their own ways
26. A place that is entirely residential
27. A place that is quiet and relaxing
28. A place that suits the needs of newcomers to the city
29. A place where all residents have a similar life-style
30. A place where relationships are long-lasting and personal

Bibliography

Agee, James. *A Death in the Family*. New York: Grosset and Dunlap, 1967.

Ahrentzen, Sherry Boland. Managing conflict by managing boundaries: How professional homemakers cope with multiple roles at home. *Environment and Behavior, 22*, 6, November 1990, pp. 723–752.

——. Home as a workplace in the lives of women. In Irwin Altman and Setha M. Low (eds.), *Place Attachment*. New York: Plenum, 1992, pp. 113–137.

Allen, Irving Lewis. New towns and the suburban dream. In I. L. Allen (ed.), *New Towns and the Suburban Dream*. Port Washington, NY: Kennikat Press, 1977, pp. 3–20.

Alpern, Andrew. *Apartments for the Affluent: A Historical Survey of Buildings in New York*. New York: McGraw-Hill, 1975.

Amato, Paul R. City size, sidewalk density, and friendliness toward strangers. *Journal of Social Psychology, 111*, 1980, pp. 151–152.

Anderson, Elijah. Race and neighborhood transition. In Paul E. Peterson (ed.), *The New Urban Reality*. Washington, DC: Brookings Institution, 1985, pp. 99–127.

Applebaum, Richard P. City size and urban life: A preliminary inquiry into some consequences of growth in American cities. In *Urban Affairs Quarterly, 12*, 2, December 1976, pp. 139–170.

Appleyard, Donald. *Livable Streets*. Berkeley, CA: University of California Press, 1981.

Archer, Dane, Rosemary Gartner, Robin Akert, and Tim Lockwood. Cities and homicide: A new look at an old paradox. *Comparative Studies in Sociology, 1*, 1978, pp. 73–95.

Aries, Philippe. *Centuries of Childhood: A Social History of Family Life*. New York: Random House, 1962.

Arnold, Joseph L. The neighborhood and city hall: the origin of neighborhood associations in Baltimore, 1880-1911. *Journal of Urban History, 6*, 1, November 1979, pp. 3–30.

Audirac, Ivonne, Anne H. Shermyn, and Marc T. Smith. Ideal urban form and visions of the good life: Florida's growth management dilemma. *Journal of the American Planning Association, 56*, 4, Autumn 1990, pp. 470–482.

Baldwin, James. *Go Tell It on the Mountain*. New York: Dell, 1970.

Baltimore City Department of Planning. *Downtown Employees' Attitudes about Downtown Living, 1987*. Baltimore, MD: Department of Planning, February 1988.

Barker, Roger G. Behavior settings: Human habitats and behavior machines. In Roger G. Barker and associates, *Habitats, Environments and Human Behavior*. San Francisco: Jossey-Bass, 1978.

Barth, Gunther. *City People: The Rise of Modern City Culture In Nineteenth-Century America*. New York: Oxford University Press, 1980.

Bauer, Catherine. Good neighborhoods. *Annals of the American Academy of Political and Social Science, 242*, November 1945, pp. 104–115.

Baumgartner, M. P. *The Moral Order of a Suburb*. New York: Oxford University Press, 1988.

Bedarida, Francois, and Anthony Sutcliffe. The street in the life and structure of the city: Reflections on nineteenth-century London and Paris. *Journal of Urban History, 6*, 4, August 1980, pp. 379–396.

Bell, Wendell. Social choice, life styles, and suburban residence. In W. M. Dobriner (ed.), *The Suburban Community*. New York: G. P. Putnam's Sons, 1958, pp. 225–247.

———. The city, the suburb, and a theory of social choice. In Scott Greer et al. (eds.), *The New Urbanization*. New York: St. Martin's Press, 1968, pp. 132–168.

Bellamy, Edward. *Looking Backward*. New York: Lancer Books, 1968 (original publication 1888).

Benchley, Robert. *My Ten Years in a Quandary, and How They Grew*. New York: Blue Ribbon Books, 1939.

Berger, Bennett M. The myth of suburbia. In Roland L. Warren (ed.), *Perspectives on the American Community: A Book of Readings*. Chicago: Rand McNally, 1966, pp.167–178.

Berreby, David. Arrogance, order, amity and other national traits. *New York Times*, Week in Review, May 26, 1996, pp. 1,6.

Berry, Brian J. L. Islands of renewal in seas of decay. In Paul E. Peterson (ed.), *The New Urban Reality*. Washington, DC: Brookings Institution, 1985, pp. 69–96.

Binford, Henry C. *The First Suburbs: Residential Communities on the Boston Periphery, 1815-1860*. Chicago: University of Chicago Press, 1985.

Birch, David L., et al. *America's Housing Needs: 1970 to 1980*. Cambridge, MA: Joint Center for Urban Studies of the Massachusetts Institute of Technology and Harvard University, 1973.

———. *The Behavioral Foundations of Neighborhood Change*. Washington, DC: U.S. Department of Housing and Urban Development, 1979.

Birch, Eugenie Ladner. Radburn and the American planning movement: The persistence of an idea. *Journal of the American Planning Association, 46*, 4, October 1980, pp. 424–439.

Black, J. Thomas. Private-market housing renovation in central cities: An Urban Land Institute survey. In Shirley Bradway Lask and Daphne Spain (eds.),

Back to the City: Issues in Neighborhood Renovation. New York: Pergamon, 1980, pp. 3–12.

Blake, Brian F., Karl Weigl, and Robert Perloff. Perception of the ideal community. *Journal of Applied Psychology, 60,* 5, 1975, pp. 612–615.

Blake, William. London. In Alfred Kazin (ed.), *The Portable Blake.* New York: Viking, 1946, p.112 (first published 1794).

Blaser, Werner. *Courtyard Houses in China.* Basel, Switzerland: Birkhauser Verlag, 1979.

Block, Davida. *A Guide to Effective Real Estate Advertising.* New York: McGraw-Hill, 1981.

Blumenfeld, Hans. The urban pattern. In Paul D. Spreiregen (ed.), *The Modern Metropolis: Its Origins, Growth, Characteristics, and Planning.* Cambridge, MA: MIT Press, 1967, pp. 50–60.

———. Metropolis extended: Secular changes in settlement patterns. *Journal of the American Planning Association, 52,* 3, Summer 1986, pp. 346–348.

Bombeck, Erma. *The Grass Is Always Greener over the Septic Tank.* New York: McGraw-Hill, 1972.

Bonnes, Mirilia, Gianfranco Secchiaroli, and Anna Rita Mazzotta. The home as an urban place: The inter-place perspective on the person/home relationship. In M. V. Giuliani (ed.), *Home: Social, Temporal and Spatial Aspects.* San Giuliano Milanese: Progetto Finalizzato Edilizia, 1992, pp. 199–214.

Bonnes, Mirilia, Lucia Mannetti, Gianfranco Secchiaroli, and Giancarlo Tanucci. The city as a multi-place system: An analysis of people-urban environment transactions. *Journal of Environmental Psychology, 10,* 1990, pp. 37–65.

Boulton, Jeremy. *Neighbourhood and Society: A London Suburb in the Seventeenth Century.* London: Cambridge University, 1987.

Brail, Richard K., and F. Stuart Chapin. Activity patterns of urban residents. *Environment and Behavior, 5,* 2, June 1973, pp. 163–190.

Brower, Sidney. *Design in Familiar Places: What Makes Home Environments Look Good.* New York: Praeger, 1988.

Calthorpe, Peter. *The Next American Metropolis: Ecology, Community, and the American Dream.* Princeton, NJ: Princeton University Press, 1993.

Campbell, Angus, Philip E. Converse, and Willard L. Rogers. *The Quality of American Life.* New York: Russell Sage Foundation, 1976.

Carlos, Serge. Religious participation and the urban-suburban continuum. *American Journal of Sociology, 75,* 5, March 1970, pp. 742–759.

Carp, Frances M., Rick T. Zawadski, and Hossein Shokrkon. Dimensions of urban environmental quality. *Environment and Behavior, 8,* 2, June 1976, pp. 239–264.

Cavalcanti, Maria de Betania. Totalitarian states and their influence on city form: The case of Bucharest. *Journal of Architectural and Planning Research, 9,* 4, Winter 1992, pp. 275–286.

Chapin, F. Stuart, Jr. *Human Activity Patterns in the City: Things People Do in Time and in Space.* New York: John Wiley and Sons, 1974.

Chapin, F. Stuart, Jr., and Edward J. Kaiser. *Urban Land Use Planning* (third edition). Urbana, IL: University of Illinois Press, 1974.

Cheever, John. *The Stories of John Cheever*. New York: Alfred A. Knopf, 1978.

Church, George J. The boom towns—no longer suburbs, not quite cities: Welcome to megacounties. *Time Magazine*, June 15, 1987, pp. 14–17.

Clay, Phillip L. The rediscovery of city neighborhoods: Reinvestment by long-time residents and newcomers. In Shirley Bradway Laska and Daphne Spain (eds.), *Back to the City: Issues in Neighborhood Renovation*. New York: Pergamon, 1980, pp. 13–26.

Coleman, Richard P. *Attitudes towards Neighborhoods: How Americans Choose to Live*. Cambridge, MA: Joint Center for Urban Studies of MIT and Harvard University, working paper no. 49, 1978.

Conzen, M.R.G. The use of town plans in the study of urban history. In H. J. Dyos (ed.), *The Study of Urban History*. New York: St. Martin's Press, 1968, pp. 113–130

Cook, Christine C. Components of neighborhood satisfaction: Responses from urban and suburban single-parent women. *Environment and Behavior, 20, 2*, March 1988, pp. 115–149.

Cowan, Ruth Schwartz. *More Work for Mother: The Ironies of Household Technology from the Open Hearth to the Microwave*. New York: Basic Books, 1983.

Crawford, Margaret. The world in a shopping center. In Michael Sorkin (ed.), *Variations on a Theme Park: The New American City and the End of Public Space*. New York: Hill and Wang, 1992, pp. 3–30.

Cullen, Gordon. *The Concise Townscape*. New York: Van Nostrand Reinhold, 1961.

Dahir, James. *The Neighborhood Unit Plan: Its Spread and Acceptance*. New York: Russell Sage Foundation, 1947.

Dahmann, Donald C. Subjective assessments of neighborhood quality by size of place. *Urban Studies, 20*, 1983, pp. 31–45.

Davis, Judy S., Arthur C. Nelson, and Kenneth J. Dueker. The new 'burbs: The exurbs and their implications for planning policy. *Journal of the American Planning Association, 60, 1*, Winter 1994, pp. 45–59.

de Wolfe, I. *The Italian Townscape*. New York: George Braziller, 1966.

Dennis, Michael. *Court and Garden: From the French Hotel to the City of Modern Architecture*. Cambridge, MA: MIT Press, 1988.

Dillard, Annie. *An American Childhood*. New York: Harper and Row, 1987.

Dobriner, William M. Local and cosmopolitan as contemporary suburban character types. In W. M. Dobriner (ed.), *The Suburban Community*. New York: G. P. Putnam's Sons, 1958, pp. 132–142.

―――. *Class in Suburbia*. Englewood Cliffs, NJ: Prentice-Hall, 1963.

Dorst, John D. *The Written Suburb: An American Site, An Ethnographic Dilemma*. Philadelphia, PA: University of Pennsylvania Press, 1989.

Douglas, Harlan P. *The Suburban Trend*. New York: The Century Co., 1925.

Downs, Roger M., and David Stea. *Maps in Minds: Reflections on Cognitive Mapping*. New York: Harper and Row, 1977.

Duany, Andres, and Elizabeth Plater-Zyberk. In Alex Krieger and William Lennertz (eds.), *Towns and Town-Making Principles*. New York: Rizzoli, 1991.

Durrell, Lawrence. Landscape and character. In Alan G. Thomas (ed.), *Spirit of Place: Letters and Essays on Travel*. New York: E. P. Dutton, 1969, pp. 156–163.

Ebner, Michael H. *Creating Chicago's North Shore: A Suburban History.* Chicago: University of Chicago, 1988.

Elazar, Daniel J. Suburbanization: Reviving the town on the metropolitan frontier. *Publius ,* Winter 1975, pp. 53–79.

Fava, Sylvia Fleis. Contrasts in neighboring: New York City and a suburban community. In Roland L. Warren (ed.), *Perspectives on the American Community: A Book of Readings.* Chicago: Rand McNally, 1966, pp. 167–178.

Fein, Albert. *Frederick Law Olmsted and the American Environmental Tradition.* New York: George Braziller, 1972.

Feldman, Roberta M. Settlement-identity: psychological bonds with home places in a mobile society. *Environment and Behavior, 22,* 2, March 1990, pp. 183–229.

———. Society's salvation or demise: The meaning of the city/suburb distinction in contemporary U.S. metropolitan society. *Research in Community Sociology, 4,* 1994, pp. 229–251.

Finifter, Ada W., and Paul R. Abramson. City size and feelings of political competence. *Public Opinion Quarterly, 39,* 2, 1975, pp. 189–198.

Fischer, Claude S. Urbanism as a way of life: A review and an agenda. *Sociological Methods and Research, 1,* 2, November 1972, pp. 187–242.

———. The metropolitan experience. In Amos H. Hawley and Vincent P. Rock (eds.), *Metropolitan America in Contemporary Perspective.* New York: Halsted Press, 1975, pp. 201–234.

———. *To Dwell among Friends: Personal Networks in Town and City.* Chicago: University of Chicago Press, 1982.

———.*The Urban Experience* (second edition). New York: Harcourt Brace Jovanovich, 1984.

Fishman, Robert. *Urban Utopias in the Twentieth Century: Ebenezer Howard, Frank Lloyd Wright, and le Corbusier.* Cambridge, MA: MIT Press, 1982.

———. *Bourgeois Utopias: The Rise and Fall of Suburbia.* New York: Basic Books, 1987.

FitzGerald, Frances. *Cities on a Hill: A Journey through Contemporary American Cultures.* New York: Simon and Schuster, 1981.

Flanagan, Barbara. A Cape Cod mall is disappeared. *New York Times,* Home section, March 14, 1991, pp. C1, C3.

Forster, E. M. The machine stops. In *The Eternal Moment and Other Stories.* New York: Grosset and Dunlap, 1964, pp. 13–85.

Forsyth, George H., and Kurt Weitzmann. *The Monastery of Saint Catherine at Mount Sinai, Plates.* Ann Arbor, MI: University of Michigan Press, no date.

Franck, Karen A. Friends and strangers: The social experience of living in urban and non-urban settings. *Journal of Social Issues, 36,* 3, 1980, pp. 52–71.

Franklin, Julia. *Selections from the Works of Fourier* (with an introduction by Charles Gide). London: Swan Sonneschein and Co., 1901.

Freedman, Jonathan L. *Crowding and Behavior.* New York: Viking, 1975.

French, Jere Stuart. *Urban Space: A Brief History of the City Square.* Dubuque, IA: Kendall/Hunt, 1978.

Fried, Marc. Residential attachment: Sources of residential and community satisfaction. *Journal of Social Issues, 38,* 3, 1982, pp. 107–119.

———. The neighborhood in metropolitan life: Its psychosocial significance. In Ralph B. Taylor (ed.), *Urban Neighborhoods: Research and Policy.* New York: Praeger, 1986.

Friedmann, John, and John Miller, Jr. The urban field. *Journal of the American Institute of Planners, 31,* November 1965, pp. 312–320.

Fromm, Dorit. *Collaborative Communities: Cohousing, Central Living, and Other New Forms of Housing with Shared Facilities.* New York: Van Nostrand Reinhold, 1991.

Furay, Conrad. The small town mind. In C. D. Geist and Jack Nachbar (eds.), *The Popular Culture Reader* (third edition). Bowling Green, OH: Bowling Green University Popular Press, 1983, pp. 41–54.

Gale, Dennis E. Middle class resettlement in older urban neighborhoods: The evidence and the implications. *Journal of the American Planning Association, 45,* 3, July 1979, pp. 293–304.

———. Neighborhood resettlement: Washington, DC. In Shirley Bradway Laska and Daphne Spain (eds.), *Back to the City: Issues in Neighborhood Renovation.* New York: Pergamon, 1980, pp. 95–115.

———. *Neighborhood Revitalization and the Postindustrial City: A Multinational Perspective.* Lexington, MA: D. C. Heath, 1984.

Galster, George C., and Garry W. Hesser. Residential satisfaction: Compositional and contextual correlates. *Environment and Behavior, 13,* 6, November 1981, pp. 735–758.

Gans, Herbert J. Planning and social life: Friendship and neighbor relations in suburban communities. *Journal of the American Institute of Planners, 27,* 2, May 1961, pp. 134–140.

———. The balanced community: Homogeneity or heterogeneity in residential areas? *Journal of the American Institute of Planners, 27,* 3, August 1961, pp. 176–184.

———. Urbanism and suburbanism as ways of life: A reevaluation of definitions. In Arnold M. Rose (ed.), *Human Behavior and Social Processes: An Interactionist Approach.* Boston, MA: Houghton Mifflin, 1962, pp. 625–648.

Garreau, Joel. *Edge City: Life on the New Frontier.* New York: Doubleday, 1991.

Geller, Daniel M. Responses to urban stimuli: A balanced approach. *Journal of Social Issues, 36,* 3, 1960, pp. 86–100.

Giedion, Sigfried. *Space, Time and Architecture: The Growth of a New Tradition.* Cambridge, MA: Harvard University Press, 1946.

Girouard, Mark. *Cities and People: A Social and Architectural History.* New Haven, CT: Yale University, 1985.

Goffman, Erving. *Interaction Ritual.* Garden City, NY: Doubleday, 1967.

Goldsmith, Oliver. *The Deserted Village.* Boston, MA: J. E. Tilton and Co., 1866 (original publication 1770).

Goldston, Robert. *Suburbia: Civic Denial.* New York: Macmillan Company, 1970.

Grahame, Kenneth. *The Wind in the Willows.* New York: Charles Scribner's Sons, 1933.

Greenberg, Stephanie W. The relationship between work and residence in an industrializing city: Philadelphia, 1880. In William W. Cutler III and Howard Gillette, Jr. (eds.), *The Divided Metropolis: Social and Spatial Dimensions of Philadelphia, 1800-1975*. Westport, CT: Greenwood Press, 1980, pp. 141–168.

Greer, Scott. The social structure and political process of suburbia. In Roland L. Warren (ed.), *Perspectives on the American Community: A Book of Readings*. Chicago: Rand McNally, 1966, pp. 167–178.

————. Urbanism reconsidered: A comparative study of local areas in a metropolis. In Robert Gutman and David Popenoe (eds.), *Neighborhood, City and Metropolis: An Integrated Reader in Urban Sociology*. New York: Random House, 1970, pp. 276–285.

Guest, Avery M., and Barrett A. Lee. Consensus on locality names within the metropolis. *Sociology of Social Research, 67*, 4, 1983, pp. 374–391.

Guest, Avery M., Barrett A. Lee, and Lynn Staeheli. Changing locality identification in the Metropolis: Seattle, 1920-1978. *American Sociological Review, 47*, August 1982, pp. 543–549.

Guterson, David. No place like home on the manicured streets of a masterplanned community. *Harper's Magazine, 285*, 1710, November 1992, pp. 55–64.

Hadden, Jeffrey K., and Josef J. Barton. An image that will not die: Thoughts on the history of anti-urban ideology. In I. L. Allen (ed.), *New Towns and the Suburban Dream*. Port Washington, NY: Kennikat Press, 1977, pp. 23–60.

Halpern, Sue. *Migrations to Solitude*. New York: Pantheon Books, 1992.

Hamerton, Philip Gilbert. *Landscape*. Boston, MA: Roberts Brothers, 1885.

Hancock, John. The apartment house in urban America. In Anthony D. King (ed.), *Buildings and Society: Essays on the Social Development of the Built Environment*. London: Routledge and Kegan Paul, 1980, pp. 151–189.

Handy, Susan L., and Patricia L. Mokhtarian. Planning for telecommuting: Measurement and policy issues. *Journal of the American Planning Association, 61*, 1, Winter 1995, pp. 99–111.

Haney, Wava G., and Eric S. Knowles. Perception of neighborhoods by city and suburban residents. *Human Ecology, 6*, 1978, pp. 201–214.

Hanson, J., and B. Hillier. Domestic space organization: Two contemporary space codes compared. *Architecture and Behavior, 2*, 1982, pp. 5–25.

Harrison, Molly. *The Kitchen in History*. New York: Charles Scribner's Sons, 1972.

Hawkins, Brett W., and Stephen L. Percy. On anti-suburban orthodoxy. *Social Science Quarterly, 72*, 3, September 1991, pp. 478–490. (See also the responses by Max Neiman and John R. Logan, and the rejoinder by Hawkins and Percy, all in the same issue.)

Hayden, Dolores. *Seven American Utopias: The Architecture of Communitarian Socialism, 1790-1975*. Cambridge, MA: MIT Press, 1976.

————. *The Grand Domestic Revolution: A History of Feminist Designs for American Homes, Neighborhoods and Cities*. Cambridge, MA: MIT Press, 1981.

————. *Redesigning the American Dream: the Future of Housing, Work and Family Life*. New York: W. W. Norton, 1984.

Hays, Samuel P. From the history of the city to the history of the urbanized society. *Journal of Urban History, 19*, 4, August 1993, pp. 3–25.

Hillier, Bill, and Julienne Hanson. *The Social Logic of Space*. New York: Cambridge

University Press, 1984.

Hinshaw, Mark, and Kathryn Allott. Environmental preferences of future housing consumers. *Journal of the American Institute of Planners, 38*, 2, March 1972, pp. 102–107.

Hodgins, Eric. *Mr. Blandings Builds His Dream House*. New York: White Lion, 1947.

Home, Robert. The evolution of the use classes order. *Town Planning Review, 63*, 2, April 1992, pp. 187–201.

Howard, Ebenezer. *Garden Cities of Tomorrow*. London: Faber and Faber, 1945 (original publication 1898).

Howells, William Dean. *Suburban Sketches*. Boston, MA: Houghton, Osgood and Co., 1880.

Hugo, Victor. *Les Miserables* (translated by Charles E. Wilbour). London: J. M. Dent and Sons Ltd., Everymans Library 363, 1909.

Huizinga, Johan. *The Waning of the Middle Ages*. London: Penguin, 1955 (first published 1924).

Hummon, David M. Urban views: Popular perspectives on city life. *Urban Life, 15*, 1, April 1986, pp. 3–36.

————. *Commonplaces: Community Ideology and Identity in American Culture*. Albany, NY: State University of New York Press, 1990.

Hunter, Albert. *Symbolic Communities: The Persistence and Change of Chicago's Local Communities*. Chicago: University of Chicago Press, 1974.

————. The loss of community: An empirical test through replication. *American Sociological Review, 40*, 5, October 1975, pp. 537–552.

————. Symbols of incivility: Social disorder and fear of crime in urban neighborhoods. Paper presented at the annual meeting of the American Society of Criminology, Dallas, TX, 1978.

————. The urban neighborhood: Its analytical and social contexts. *Urban Affairs Quarterly, 14*, 3, March 1979, pp. 267–288.

Jackson, Alan A. *Semi-Detached London: Suburban Development, Life and Transport, 1900-39*. London: Allen and Unwin, 1973.

Jackson, J. B. *The Necessity for Ruins and Other Topics*. Amherst, MA.: University of Massachusetts Press, 1980.

Jackson, Kenneth T. *Crabgrass Frontier: The Suburbanization of the United States*. New York: Oxford University Press, 1985.

Jacobs, Jane. *The Death and Life of Great American Cities*. New York: Random House, 1961.

Janowitz, Morris. *The Community Press in an Urban Setting* (second edition). Chicago: University of Chicago, 1967.

Jones, Tanya. "Like one big family" in the middle of the city. *The Sun*, December 25, 1994, p. 1K.

Kallus, Rachel, and Hubert Law-Yone. Neighborhood: Metamorphosis of an idea. Paper presented at the Twelfth International Conference of the International Association for People-Environment Studies, Marmaras, Greece, July 1992a.

————. What is a neighborhood: The structure and function of an idea. International Research Conference on European Cities: Growth and Decline, The Hague, Netherlands, April 1992b.

Kasarda, John D., and Morris Janowitz. Community attachment in mass society. *American Sociological Review, 39,* 1974, pp. 328–339.

Kaufman, Michael T. Nineteen blocks up Broadway: It seems a world away. *New York Times,* Metro section, March 26,1994, p. 23.

Keats, John. *The Crack in the Picture Window.* Boston: Houghton Mifflin, 1952.

Keller, Suzanne. *The Urban Neighborhood: A Sociological Perspective.* New York: Random House, 1968.

Korte, Charles. Helpfulness in the urban environment. In Andrew Baum, Jerome E. Singer, and Stuart Valins (eds.), *Advances in Environmental Psychology,* Volume 1: *The Urban Environment.* Hillsdale, NJ: Lawrence Erlbaum Associates, 1978, pp. 131–144.

————. Urban-nonurban differences in social behavior and social psychological models of urban impact. *Journal of Social Issues, 36,* 3, 1980, pp. 29–51.

Korte, Charles, Ido Ypma, and Anneke Toppen. Helpfulness in Dutch society as a function of urbanization and environmental input level. *Journal of Personality and Social Psychology, 32,* 6, 1975, pp. 996–1003.

Kostof, Spiro. *The City Shaped: Urban Patterns and Meanings through History.* Boston: Little, Brown and Unwin, 1991.

Kranz, Birgit, and Karin Palm Lindén. Forms of collective housing, forms of living alternatives. Paper presented at XIIIth World Congress of Sociology, Bielefeld, Germany, July 1994.

Krupat, Edward, and William Guild. The measurement of community social climate. *Environment and Behavior, 12,* 2, June 1980, pp. 195–206.

Ktsanes, Thomas, and Leonard Reissman. Suburbia: New homes for old values. *Social Problems, 7,* 3, Winter 1959-60, pp. 187–195.

Ladd, Florence C. Black youths view their environment: Some views of housing. *Journal of the American Institute of Planners,* March 1972, pp. 108–116.

Lamanna, Richard A. Value consensus among urban residents. *Journal of the American Institute of Planners, 30,* 4, November 1964, pp. 317–322.

Lang, Marvel. Redefining urban and rural for the U.S. Census of Population: Assessing the need and alternative approaches. *Urban Geography, 7,* 2, 1986, pp. 118–134.

Langdon, Philip. *A Better Place to Live: Reshaping the American Suburb.* New York: HarperPerennial, 1995.

Lansing, John B., and Eva Mueller. *Residential Location and Urban Mobility.* Ann Arbor, MI: Survey Research Center, University of Michigan, 1964.

Lansing, John B., and Robert W. Marans. Evaluation of neighborhood quality. *Journal of the American Institute of Planners, 35,* 3, May 1969, pp. 195–199.

Lapham, Lewis H. City lights: A defense of New York. *Harper's Magazine, 252,* 1513, June 1976, pp. 8–14.

Lawrence, Roderick J. *Housing, Dwellings and Homes: Design Theory, Research and Practice.* New York: John Wiley & Sons, 1987.

Lax, Eric. *Woody Allen: A Biography.* New York: Alfred Knopf, 1991.

Le Corbusier. *The Radiant City: Elements of a Doctrine of Urbanism to be Used as the Basis for Our Machine-Age Civilization.* New York: Orion, 1967.

————. *The City of Tomorrow and Its Planning.* Cambridge, MA: MIT Press, 1971 (first English edition published 1929).

Lee, Terence. Urban neighborhood as a socio-spatial schema. In H. Proshansky, W. Ittelson, and L. Rivlin (eds.), *Environmental Psychology: Man and His Physical Setting*. New York: Holt, Rinehart and Winston, 1970, pp. 349–370.

Lees, Andrew. *Cities Perceived: Urban Society in European and American Thought, 1820-1940*. New York: Columbia University Press, 1985.

Lerner, Max. *America as a Civilization*. New York: Simon and Schuster, 1957.

Levine, Neil. The story of Taliesin: Wright's first natural house. In Narciso G. Menocal (ed.), *Taliesin 1911-1914 (Wright Studies No 1)*. Carbondale, IL: Southern Illinois University Press, 1992, pp. 2–27.

Levitas, Ruth. *The Concept of Utopia*. Syracuse, NY: Syracuse University Press, 1990.

Lipton, S. Gregory. Evidence of central city revival. *Journal of the American Planning Association, 43*, 2, April 1977, pp. 136–147.

Livability Committee. Author's notes taken at meetings of a special subcommittee of the Mayor's Task Force, 1991. (This Committee was part of Baltimore's Downtown Strategy and was charged with developing recommendations for improving living conditions in the downtown area.)

Lofland, Lynn H. *A World of Strangers: Order and Action in Urban Public Space*. New York: Basic Books, 1973.

Long, Larry H. Back to the countryside and back to the city in the same decade, in Shirley Bradway Laska and Daphne Spain (eds.), *Back to the City: Issues in Neighborhood Renovation*. New York: Pergamon, 1980, pp. 61–76.

Louv, Richard. *America II*. Los Angeles: Jeremy P. Tarcher, 1983.

Lowenthal, David. *The Past Is a Foreign Country*. London: Cambridge University Press, 1985.

Lynch, Kevin. *Managing the Sense of a Region*. Cambridge, MA: MIT Press, 1976.

———. *A Theory of Good Urban Form*. Cambridge, MA: MIT Press, 1981.

Macintosh, Duncan. *The Modern Courtyard House: A History* (Architectural Association paper number 9). London: Lund Humphries, 1973.

Mansfield, Howard. *Cosmopolis: Yesterdays' Cities of the Future*. New Brunswick, NJ: Center for Urban Policy Research, Rutgers University, 1990.

Marans, Robert W. *Basic Human Needs and the Housing Environment*. Ann Arbor, MI: Institute of Social Research, University of Michigan, 1975.

Marbella, Jean. Mickey house. *The Sun*, May 20, 1996, p. 1D.

Marsh, Margaret. *Suburban Lives*. New Brunswick, NJ: Rutgers University Press, 1990.

Mazie, Sara Mills, and Steve Rawlings. Public attitude towards population distribution issues. In Sara Mills Mazie (ed.), *Population Distribution and Policy* (U.S. Commission on Population Growth and the American Future, Research Reports, Volume 5). Washington, DC: U.S. Government Printing Office, 1972, pp. 603–615.

McCamant, Kathryn, and Charles Durrett, with Ellen Hertzman. *Cohousing: A Contemporary Approach to Housing Ourselves* (second edition). Berkeley, CA: Ten Speed Press, 1994.

McCauley, Clark, and James Taylor. Is there overload of acquaintances in the city? *Environmental Psychology and Nonverbal Behavior, 1*, 1, Fall 1976, pp. 41–55.

McKenzie, Evan. *Privatopia: Homeowner Associations and the Rise of Residential Private Government.* New Haven, CT: Yale University Press, 1994.

Meinig, D. W. Symbolic landscapes: some idealizations of American communities, in D.W. Meinig (ed.), *The Interpretation of Ordinary Landscapes.* New York: Oxford University Press, 1979, pp. 164–192.

Mencken, H. L. Interview with Donald Howe Kirkley, Sr., recorded at the Library of Congress on June 30, 1948, and released by Caedmon Records, PC1082, 1957.

Meyrowitz, Joshua. *No Sense of Place: The Impact of Electronic Media on Social Behavior.* New York: Oxford University Press, 1985.

Michelson, William. Potential candidates for the designers' paradise: A social analysis from a nationwide survey. *Social Forces, 46,* 1967, pp. 190-196.

————. Long and short range criteria for housing choice and environmental behavior. *Journal of Social Issues, 36,* 3, 1980, pp. 135–149.

Milgram, Stanley. The experience of living in cities. *Science, 167,* 3924, March 1970, pp. 1461–1468.

Miller, Frederick D., Sam Tsemberis, Gregory P. Malia, and Dennis Grega. Neighborhood satisfaction among urban dwellers. *Journal of Social Issues, 36,* 3, 1980, pp. 101–117.

Miller, Michael K., and A. E. Luloff. Who is rural? A typlogical approach to the examination of rurality. *Rural Sociology, 46,* 4, 1981, pp. 608–623.

Mirabella, Lorraine. First Singapore, now Baltimore. *The Sun,* October 25, 1993, p. 12C.

Moore, E. G. A typology of neighborhood change (resource paper no. 13). Washington, DC: Association of American Geographers, Commission on College Geography, 1972.

More, Thomas. *Utopia* (translated by Paul Turner). New York: Penguin Books, 1986 (original publication 1516).

Morris, William. News from Nowhere. In *Three Works by William Morris.* New York: International Publishers, 1969, pp. 179–401 (original publication 1890).

Moudry, Roberta M. Frederick Law Olmsted Sr.'s Roland Park: The idea of a suburb. Paper presented to the Friends of Maryland's Olmsted Parks and Landscapes, Baltimore, MD, May 1990.

Mouritzen, Poul Erik. City size and citizens' satisfaction: Two competing theories revisited. *European Journal of Political Research, 17,* 1989, pp. 661–688.

Mumford, Lewis. *The Story of Utopias: Ideal Commonwealths and Social Myths.* London: Harrap, 1923.

————. *Sketches from Life: The Autobiography of Lewis Mumford: The Early Years.* New York: Dial, 1982.

Munson, Byron E. Attitudes toward urban and suburban residence in Indianapolis. *Social Forces, 35,* 1956, pp. 76–80.

Munthe, Axel. *The Story of San Michele.* London: John Murray, 1950.

Nasar, Jack L. Adult viewers' preferences in residential scenes: A study of the relationship of environmental attributes to preference. *Environment and Behavior, 15,* 5, September 1983, pp. 589–614.

Nasaw, David. *Schooled to Order: A Social History of Public Schooling in the United*

States. New York: Oxford University Press, 1979.

Nelessen, Anton Clarence. *Visions for a New American Dream: Process, Principles, and an Ordinance to Plan and Design Small Communities*. Chicago: Planners Press, 1994.

Nelson, Arthur C. The planning of exurban America: Lessons from Frank Lloyd Wright's Broadacre City. *Journal of Architectural and Planning Research, 12*, 4, Winter 1995. pp. 337–356.

Newman, Joseph, and Clark McCauley. Eye contact with strangers in city, suburb, and small town. *Environment and Behavior, 9*, 4, December 1977, pp. 547–558.

Newman, Oscar. *Defensible Space: Crime Prevention through Urban Design*. New York: Macmillan, 1973.

Oldenburg, Ray. *The Great Good Place: Cafes, Coffee Shops, Community Centers, Beauty Parlors, General Stores, Bars, Hangouts and How They Get You Through The Day*. New York: Paragon House, 1989.

Olmsted, Frederick Law. Preliminary report upon the proposed suburban village at Riverside, near Chicago, by Olmsted Vaux and Co., Landscape Architects, Sept. 1, 1868. In *The Papers of Frederick Law Olmsted*, Volume 6, *The Years of Olmsted, Vaux and Company, 1865-1874*. David Schuyler and Jane Turner Censer (eds.), Baltimore, MD: Johns Hopkins University Press, 1992, pp. 273–290.

———. Public parks and the enlargement of towns (paper read before the American Social Science Association, Boston, 1870). *Journal of Social Science*, number 111, 1871.

Olsen, Donald J. *The City as a Work of Art: London, Paris, Vienna*. New Haven, CT: Yale University Press, 1986.

Pardailhe-Galabrun, Annik. *The Birth of Intimacy: Privacy and Domestic Life in Early Modern Paris*. Philadelphia: University of Pennsylvania Press, 1991.

Park, Robert E. The city: Suggestions for the investigation of human behavior in the urban environment. In Alan Trachtenberg, Peter Neill, and Peter C. Bunnell (eds.), *The City: American Experience*. New York: Oxford University Press, 1971, pp. 223–236 (reprinting of paper published in 1925).

Park, Robert E., Ernest W. Burgess, and Roderick D. McKenzie. *The City*. Chicago: University of Chicago Press, 1967.

Patel, Dinker I. *Exurbs: Urban Residential Developments in the Countryside*. Washington, DC: University Press of America, 1980.

Peek, Charles W., and George D. Lowe. Wirth, whiskey, and WASP's: Some consequences of community size for alcoholic use. *Sociological Quarterly, 18*, Spring 1977, pp. 209–222.

Perin, Constance. *Everything in Its Place: Social Order and Land Use in America*. Princeton, NJ: Princeton University Press, 1977.

Perks, Sydney. *Residential Flats of All Classes, Including Artisans' Dwellings*. London: B. T. Batsford, 1905.

Perry, Clarence A. The neighborhood unit. In *Regional Survey of New York and Its Environs, vii* (Neighborhood and Community Planning, monograph 1). New York: Committee on the Regional Plan of New York and Its Environs, 1929.

Pervin, Lawrence A. Performance and satisfaction as a function of individual-environment fit. *Psychological Bulletin, 69,* 1, pp. 56–68.

Peterson, George L. A model of preference: Qualitative analysis of the perception of the visual appearance of residential neighborhoods. *Journal of Regional Science, 7,* 1, 1967, pp. 19–31.

Piel, Gerard, and Osborn Segerberg, Jr. (eds.), *The World of Rene Dubos: A Collection from His Writings.* New York: Henry Holt and Co., 1990.

Plato. *The Republic* (translated with an introduction by H. D. Lee). Baltimore, MD: Penguin Books, 1955.

Posokhin, M. V. *Cities to Live In.* Moscow: Novosti Press Agency, 1974.

Power, Garrett. High society: The building height limitation on Baltimore's Mount Vernon Place. Manuscript, copyright 1982.

———. Apartheid Baltimore style: The residential segregation ordinances of 1910–1913. *Maryland Law Review, 42,* 2, 1983, pp. 289–328.

Powledge, Fred. Going home to Raleigh. In Alan Trachtenberg, Peter Neill, and Peter C. Bunnell (eds.), *The City: American Experience.* New York: Oxford University Press, 1971, pp. 276–293 (reprinted from *Harper's Magazine,* March 19, 1970).

Proshansky, Harold M. The city and self-identity. *Environment and Behavior, 10,* 2, June 1978, pp. 147–169.

Prose, Francine. Outer city blues. *New York Times Magazine,* April 21, 1996, p. 68.

Prost, Antoine. Public and private spheres in France. In A. Prost and G.Vincent (eds.), *A History of Private Life,* Volume 5, *Riddles of Identity in Modern Times.* Cambridge, MA: Harvard University Press, 1991, pp. 1–144.

Purdom. C. B. *The Garden City: A Study in the Development of a Modern Town.* New York: Garland Publishing Inc., 1985 (originally published London: J. M. Dent, 1913.)

Rainwater, Lee. Fear and the house-as-haven in the lower class. *Journal of the American Institute of Planners, 32,* 1, November, 1966, pp. 23–37. (Also, following comment by Roger Montgomery).

Rapoport, Amos. *House Form and Culture.* Englewood Cliffs, NJ: PrenticeHall, 1969.

———. *Human Aspects of Urban Form: Towards a Man-Environment Approach to Urban Form and Design.* New York: Pergamon, 1977.

———. Environmental preference, habitat selection and urban housing. *Journal of Social Issues, 36,* 3, 1980, pp. 118–134.

———. Some thoughts on units of settlement. *Ekistics, 48,* 291, November/December, 1981, pp. 447–453.

———. Urban design and human systems: On ways of relating buildings to urban fabric. In P. Laconte, J. Gibson, and A. Rapoport (eds.), *Human and Energy Factors in Urban Planning: A Systems Approach.* The Hague: Nijhoff, 1982, pp. 161–182.

———. *History and Precedent in Urban Design.* New York: Plenum Press, 1990.

Rapoport, Amos, and Ron Hawkes. The perception of urban complexity. *Journal of the American Institute of Planners, 36,* 2, March 1970, pp. 106–111.

Rasmussen, Steen Eiler. *Towns and Buildings.* Cambridge, MA: MIT Press, 1973.

Reich, Robert B. Secession of the successful. *New York Times Magazine,* January 29,

1991, pp. 17–45.

Reiss, Albert J. Rural-urban status differences in interpersonal contacts. In Robert Gutman and David Popenoe (eds.), *Neighborhood, City and Metropolis: An Integrated Reader in Urban Sociology*. New York: Random House, 1970, pp. 539–556.

Richman, Alan. Planning residential environments: The social performance standard. *Journal of the American Planning Association, 45*, 4, October 1979, pp. 448–457.

Richman, Alan, and F. Stuart Chapin, Jr. *A Review of the Social and Physical Concepts of the Neighborhood as a Basis for Planning Residential Environments*. Chapel Hill, NC: Department of City and Regional Planning, University of North Carolina at Chapel Hill (occasional paper series #50), 1977.

Riley, Katherine Louise. *The Use of Suburbia in the Fiction of John O'Hara, John Cheever, and John Updike*. Ph.D. dissertation, Department of English, University of Maryland, 1981.

Ross, H. Laurence. Uptown and downtown: A study of middle-class residential areas. *American Sociological Review, 30*, 2, April 1965, pp. 255–259.

Rothblatt, D. N., D. J. Garr, and J. Sprague. *The Suburban Environment and Women*. New York: Praeger, 1979.

Rubenstein, Harvey M. *Pedestrian Malls, Streetscapes and Urban Spaces*. New York: Wiley and Sons, 1992.

Rushton, J. Philippe. Urban density and altruism: Helping strangers in a Canadian city, suburb, and small town. *Psychological Reports, 43*, 1978, pp. 987–990.

Russell, James A., and Lawrence M. Ward. Environmental psychology. *Annual Review of Psychology, 33*, 1982, pp. 651–688.

Saalman, Howard. *Haussman: Paris Transformed*. New York: George Brasiller, 1971.

Sampson, Robert J. Local friendship ties and community attachment in mass society: A multilevel systemic model. *American Sociological Review, 53*, October 1988, pp. 766–779.

———. Linking the micro- and macrolevel dimensions of community social organization. *Social Forces, 70*, 1, September 1991, pp. 43–64.

Schorske, Carl E. The idea of the city in European thought: Voltaire to Spengler. In Oscar Handlin and John Burchard, *The Historian and the City*. Cambridge, MA: MIT Press, 1966, pp. 95–114.

Schuyler, David. *The New Urban Landscape: The Redefinition of City Form in Nineteenth-Century America*. Baltimore, MD: Johns Hopkins University Press, 1986.

Schwerdtfeger, Friedrich W. *Traditional Housing in African Cities: A Comparative Study of Houses in Zaria, Ibadan and Marrakech*. New York: J. Wiley, 1982.

Scott, Mel. *American City Planning since 1890*. Berkeley, CA: University of California Press, 1969.

Seattle Planning Department. *Toward a Sustainable Seattle: A Citizen's Guide to the Comprehensive Plan, 1994-2014*. Spring 1993.

Sennett, Richard. *The Uses of Disorder: Personal Identity and City Life*. New York: 1970.

———. *The Conscience of the Eye: The Design and Social Life of Cities*. New York: Alfred A. Knopf, 1990.

Sharpe, William, and Leonard Wallock. From "Great Town" to "Nonplace Urban Realm": Reading the modern city. In William Sharpe and Leonard Wallock (eds.), *Visions of the Modern City*. Baltimore, MD: Johns Hopkins University Press, 1987, pp. 1–50.

Shlay, Anne B. Castles in the sky: Measuring housing and neighborhood ideology. *Environment and Behavior, 17,* 5, September 1985, pp. 593–626.

Shlay, Anne B., and Denise A. Digregorio. Same city, different worlds: Examining gender- and work-based differences in perceptions of neighborhood desirability. *Urban Affairs Quarterly, 21,* 1, September 1985, pp. 66–86.

Simmel, Georg. The metropolis and mental life. Reprinted in R. Sennett (ed.), *Classic Essays in the Culture of Cities*. New York: Appleton-Century Crofts, 1968, pp. 47–60.

Sitte, Camillo. *The Art of Building Cities: City Building according to its Artistic Foundations*. New York: Reinhold, 1945 (originally published 1889).

Sjoberg, Gideon. *The Preindustrial City: Past and Present*. New York: Free Press, 1960.

Solow, Anatole A., Clifford C. Ham, and E. Owen Donnelly. The concept of the neighborhood unit: Its emergence and influence on residential environmental planning and development. Pittsburgh, PA: Graduate School of Public and International Affairs, University of Pittsburgh, 1969.

Sorkin, Michael (ed.). *Variations on a Theme Park: The New American City and the End of Public Space*. New York: Hill and Wang, 1992.

Southworth, Michael. An evaluation of neo-traditional communities at the urban edge. Paper presented at the Annual Conference of the Associated Collegiate Schools of Planning, Philadelphia, PA, 1993.

Spain, Daphne. Why higher income households move to central cities. *Journal of Urban Affairs, 11,* 3, 1989, pp. 283–299.

St. John, Craig, and Frieda Clark. Race and social class differences in the characteristics desired in residential neighborhoods. *Social Science Quarterly, 65,* 3, September 1984, pp. 803–813.

Stanton, Barbara Hadley. The incidence of home grounds and experiential networks: Some implications. *Environment and Behavior, 18,* 3, May 1986, pp. 299–329.

Steele, F. B. *The Sense of Place*. Boston, MA: CBI Publishing Co., 1981.

Stein, Clarence S. *Toward New Towns for America*. Cambridge, MA: MIT Press, 1966 (original publication date, 1951).

Stilgoe, John R. *Common Landscape of America, 1580–1845*. New Haven, CT: Yale University Press, 1982.

————. *Borderland: Origins of the American Suburb, 1820–1939*. New Haven, CT: Yale University Press, 1988.

Strasser, Susan. *Never Done: A History of American Housework*. New York: Pantheon, 1982.

Strauss, Anselm. Spatial representation and the orbits of city life. *The Sociological Quarterly, 1,* 3, July 1960a, pp. 167–180.

————. The changing imagery of American city and suburb. *Sociological Quarterly, 1,* 1, January 1960b, pp. 15–124.

Szczygiel, Bonj. The new exurbanites: Seeking answers to dissatisfaction with exurban life. In Nasar, Jack L. and Barbara Brown (eds.), *Public and Private Places.* Proceedings of the Twenty-seventh Annual Conference of the Environmental Design Research Association. Edmond, OK: EDRA, 1996, pp. 124–129.

Tallman, Irving, and Ramona Morgner. Life-style differences among urban and suburban blue-collar families. *Social Forces, 48,* 3, March 1970, pp. 334–348.

Taylor, Nicholas. *The Village in the City.* London: Temple-Smith, 1973.

Thoreau, Henry David. *Walden and the Essay on Civil Disobedience.* New York: Lancer Books, 1968 (first published in 1854).

Tod, Ian, and Michael Wheeler. *Utopia.* New York: Harmony Books, 1978.

Tomeh, Aida K. Informal group participation and residential patterns. *American Journal of Sociology, 70,* 1, July 1964, pp. 28–35.

Troy, P. N. Residents and their preferences: Property prices and residential quality. *Regional Studies, 7,* 1973, pp. 183–192.

Tyler, Anne. *The Accidental Tourist.* New York: Berkley Books, 1985.

Uzzell, Douglas. Conceptual fallacies in the rural-urban dichotomy. *Urban Anthropology, 8,* 3/4, 1979, pp. 333–350.

Vance, James E., Jr. *This Scene of Man: The Role and Structure of the City in the Geography of Western Civilization.* New York: Harper, 1977.

Van der Ryn, Sim, and Peter Calthorpe. *Sustainable Communities: A New Design Synthesis for Cities, Suburbs and Towns.* San Francisco: Sierra Club Books, 1986.

Varady, David P. Neighborhood confidence: A critical factor in neighborhood revitalization? *Environment and Behavior, 18,* 4, July 1986, pp. 480–501.

von Hoffman, Alexander. *Local Attachments: The Making of an American Urban Neighborhood, 1850-1920.* Baltimore, MD: Johns Hopkins University Press, 1994.

Waesche, James F. *Crowning the Gravelly Hill: A History of the Roland Park-Guilford-Homeland District.* Baltimore, MD: Maclay and Associates, 1987.

Wagenaar, Michael. Conquest of the center or flight to the suburbs: Divergent metropolitan strategies in Europe, 1850–1914. *Journal of Urban History, 19,* 1, November 1992, pp. 60–83.

Walmsley, D. Jim, and Gareth J. Lewis. The pace of pedestrian flows in cities. *Environment and Behavior, 21,* 2, March 1989, pp. 123–150.

Walton, James. *African Village.* Pretoria, South Africa: J. L. van Schaik, 1956.

Warner, Sam Bass, Jr. *The Private City: Philadelphia in Three Periods of Its Growth.* Philadelphia: University of Pennsylvania Press, 1968.

Warren, Donald I. Explorations in neighborhood differentiation. *Sociological Quarterly, 19,* Spring 1978, pp. 310–331.

Warren, Rachelle B., and Donald I. Warren. *The Neighborhood Organizer's Handbook.* Notre Dame, IN: University of Notre Dame Press, 1977.

Watman, W. S. *A Guide to the Language of Neighborhoods.* Washington, DC: National Center for Urban Ethnic Affairs, 1980.

Webb, Michael. *The City Square: A Historical Evolution.* New York: Whitney Library of Design, 1990.

Webber, Melvin M. Order in diversity: Community without propinquity. In Lowdon

Wingo, Jr. (ed.), *Cities and Space: The Future Use of Urban Land.* Baltimore, MD: Johns Hopkins University Press, 1963, pp. 23–54.

Weidemann, Sue, and James R. Anderson. Residents' perceptions of satisfaction and safety: A basis for change in multifamily housing. *Environment and Behavior, 14,* 6, November 1982, pp. 695–724.

Weiss, Michael J. *The Clustering of America.* New York: Harper and Row, 1988.

Wekerle, Gerda R. *A Woman's Place Is in the City.* Cambridge, MA: Lincoln Institute of Land Policy, 1979.

Wharton, Edith. *The Age of Innocence.* New York: Book-of-the-Month Club, 1993 (first published 1920).

Whyte, William. *The Social Life of Small Urban Places.* Washington, DC: Conservation Foundation, 1980.

Wilson, Robert L. Livability of the city: Attitudes and urban development. In F. Stuart Chapin, Jr. and Shirley F. Weiss (eds.), *Urban Growth Dynamics In a Regional Cluster of Cities.* New York: Wiley, 1962, pp. 359–399.

Wirth, Louis. Urbanism as a way of life. *American Journal of Sociology, 44,* 1, July 1938, pp. 1–24.

Wodehouse, P. G. *Blandings Castle and Elsewhere.* London: Hutchinson, 1980.

———. Jeeves and the Unbidden Guest. In *Selected Stories by P. G. Wodehouse.* New York: Random House, 1958, pp. 50–73.

Wolschke-Bulmahn, Joachim. The fear of the new landscape: Aspects of the perception of landscape in the German Youth Movement between 1900 and 1933 and its influence on landscape planning. *Journal of Architectural and Planning Research, 9,* 1, Spring 1992, pp. 33–47.

Wolschke-Bulmahn, Joachim, and Gert Groening. The ideology of the nature garden: Nationalistic trends in garden design in Germany during the early twentieth century. *Journal of Garden History, 12,* 1, 1992, pp. 73–80.

Wood, Robert C. *Suburbia: Its People and Their Politics.* Boston: Houghton Mifflin, 1958.

Wright, Frank Lloyd. *The Disappearing City.* New York: Payson, 1932.

———. *The Living City.* New York: Meridian, 1958.

Wright, Gwendolyn. *Building the Dream: A Social History of Housing in America.* Cambridge, MA: MIT Press, 1981.

Wright, Lawrence. *Clean and Decent: The Fascinating History of the Bathroom and the Water Closet.* Toronto, Canada: University of Toronto Press, 1960.

Zelan, Joseph. Does suburbia make a difference: An exercise in secondary analysis. In Sylvia F. Fava (ed.), *Urbanism in World Perspective: A Reader.* New York: Thomas Y. Crowell Co., 1968, pp. 401–408.

Zucker, Paul. *Town and Square: From the Agora to the Village Green.* Cambridge, MA: MIT Press, 1959.

Zuiches, James J., and Glenn V. Fuguitt. Residential preferences: Implications for population redistribution in nonmetropolitan areas. In Sara Mills Mazie (ed.), U.S. Commission on Population Growth and the American Future, Research Reports, Volume 5, *Population Distribution and Policy.* Washington, DC: U.S. Government Printing Office, 1972, pp. 621–630.

Index

Page numbers for illustrations are in italics.

ISBN 0-275-95181-2

90000>

EAN

9 780275 951818

HARDCOVER BAR CODE